Portia George
PG Enterprises Ministry
www.be-the-dream.org/

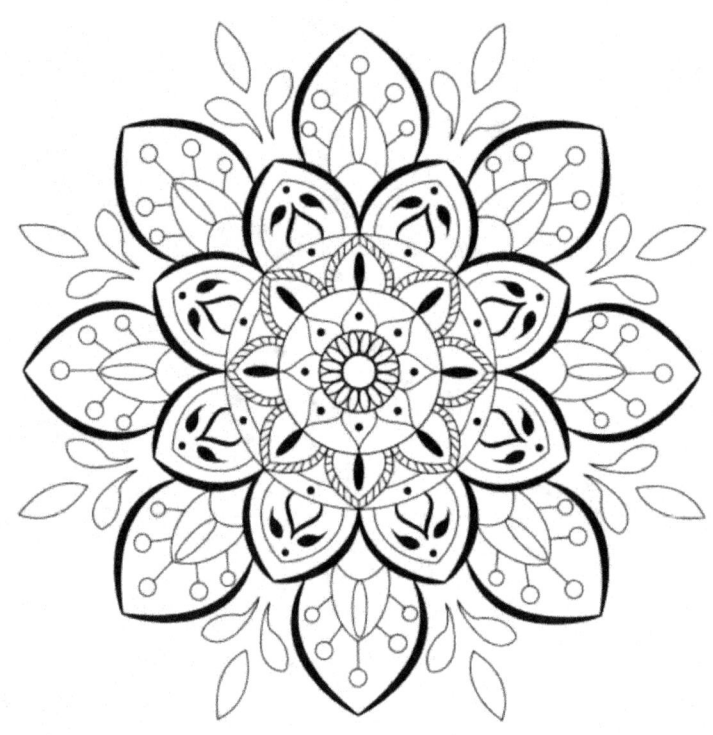

"Your word is a lamp to my feet
and a light to my path"
Psalm 119:105

This book belongs to

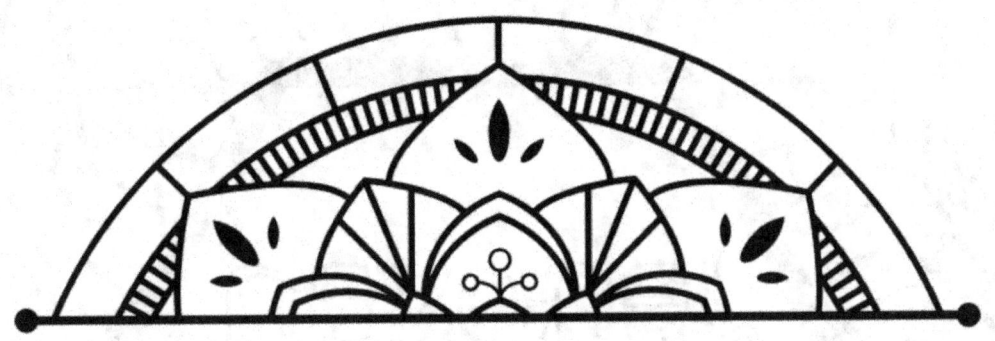

....

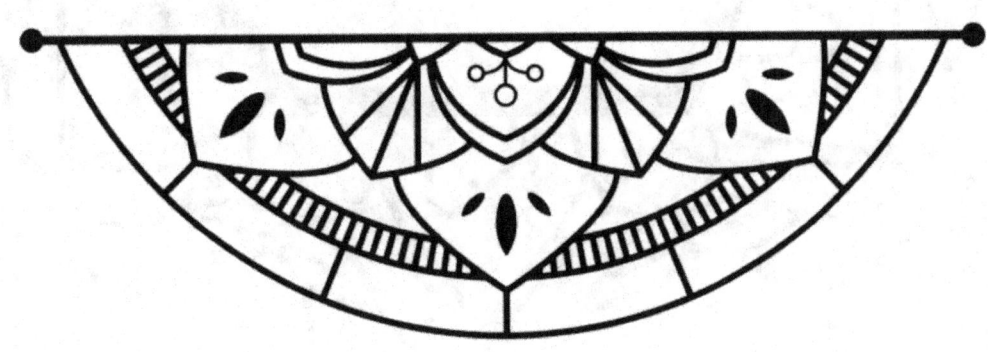

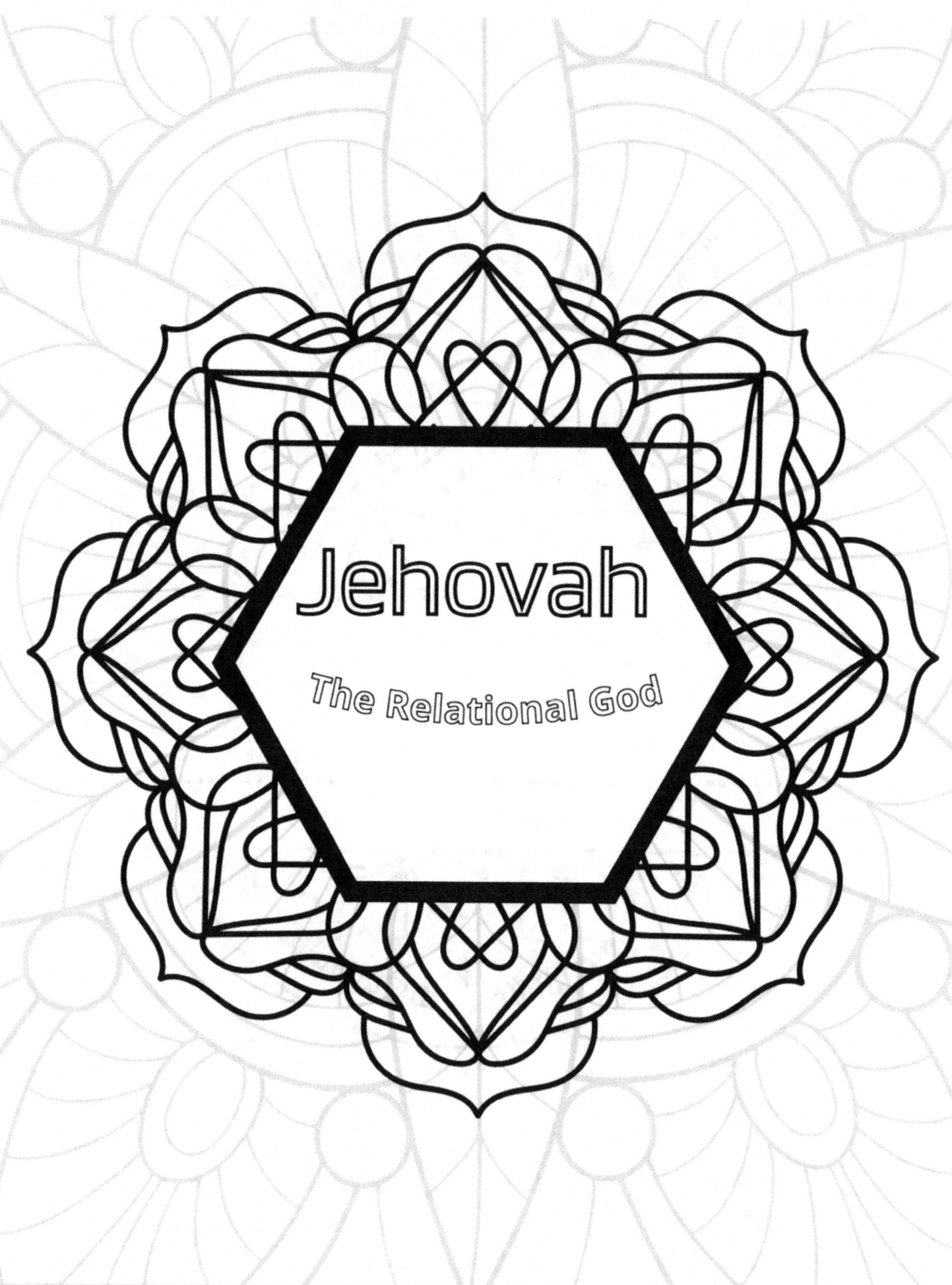

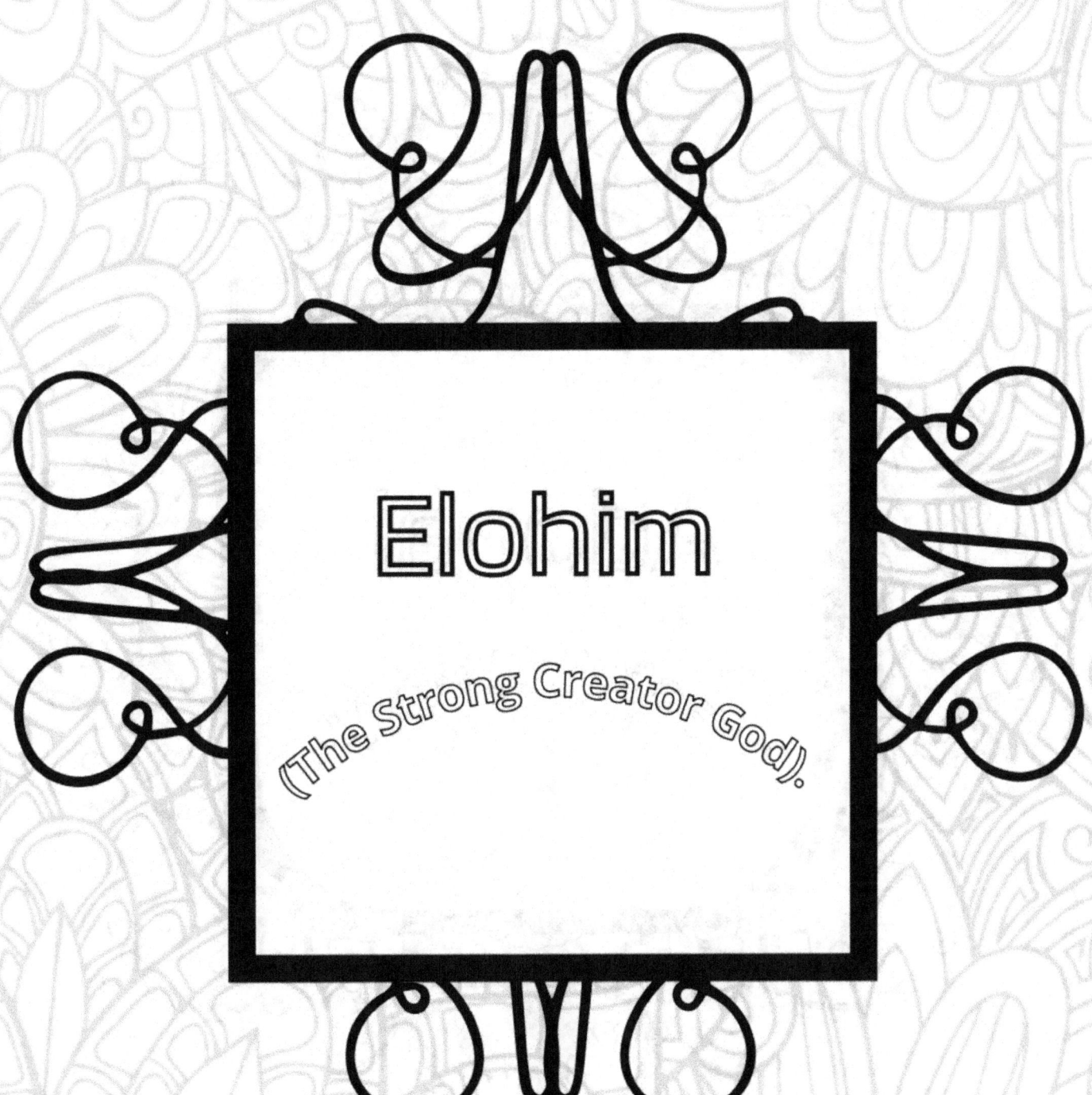

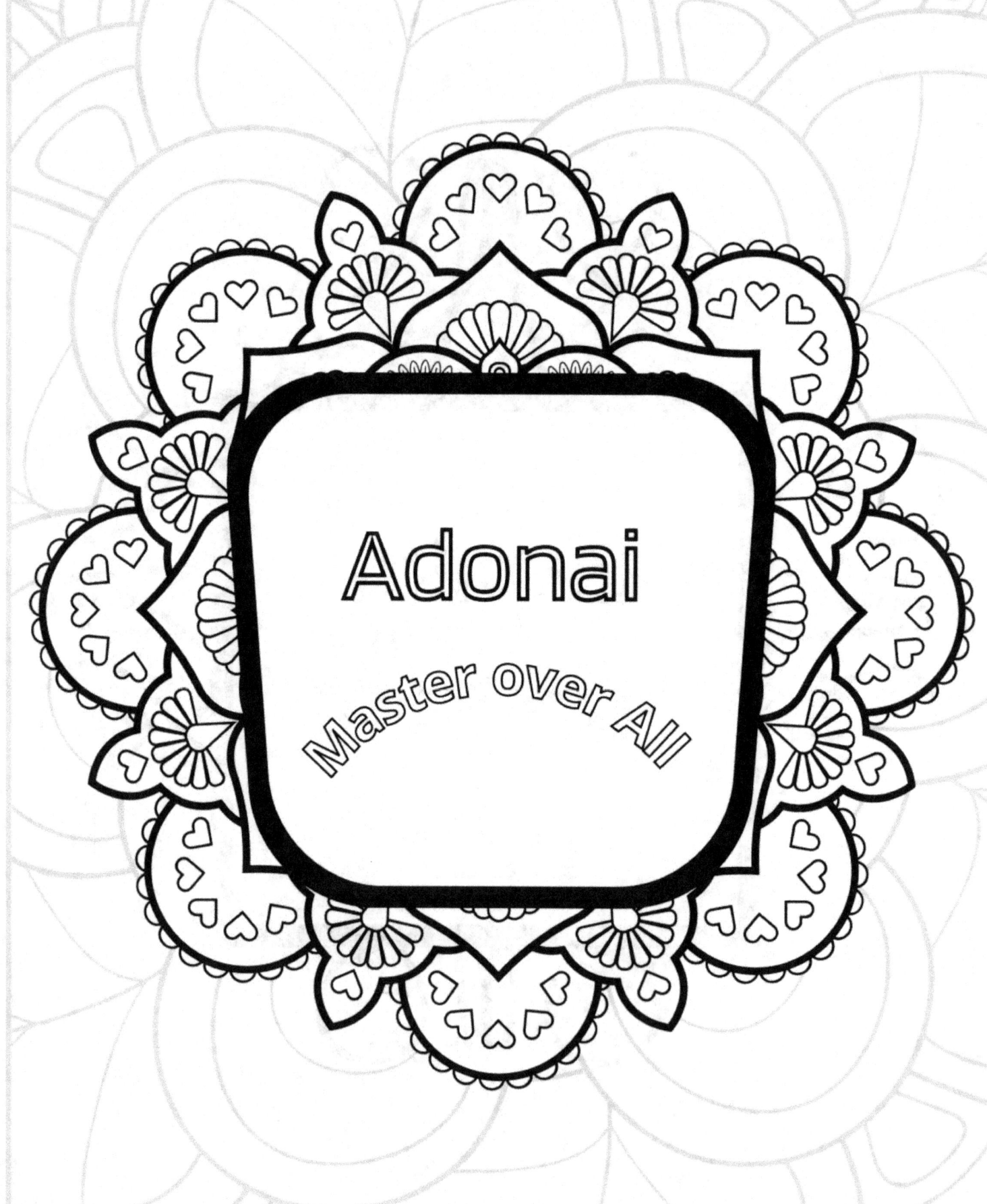

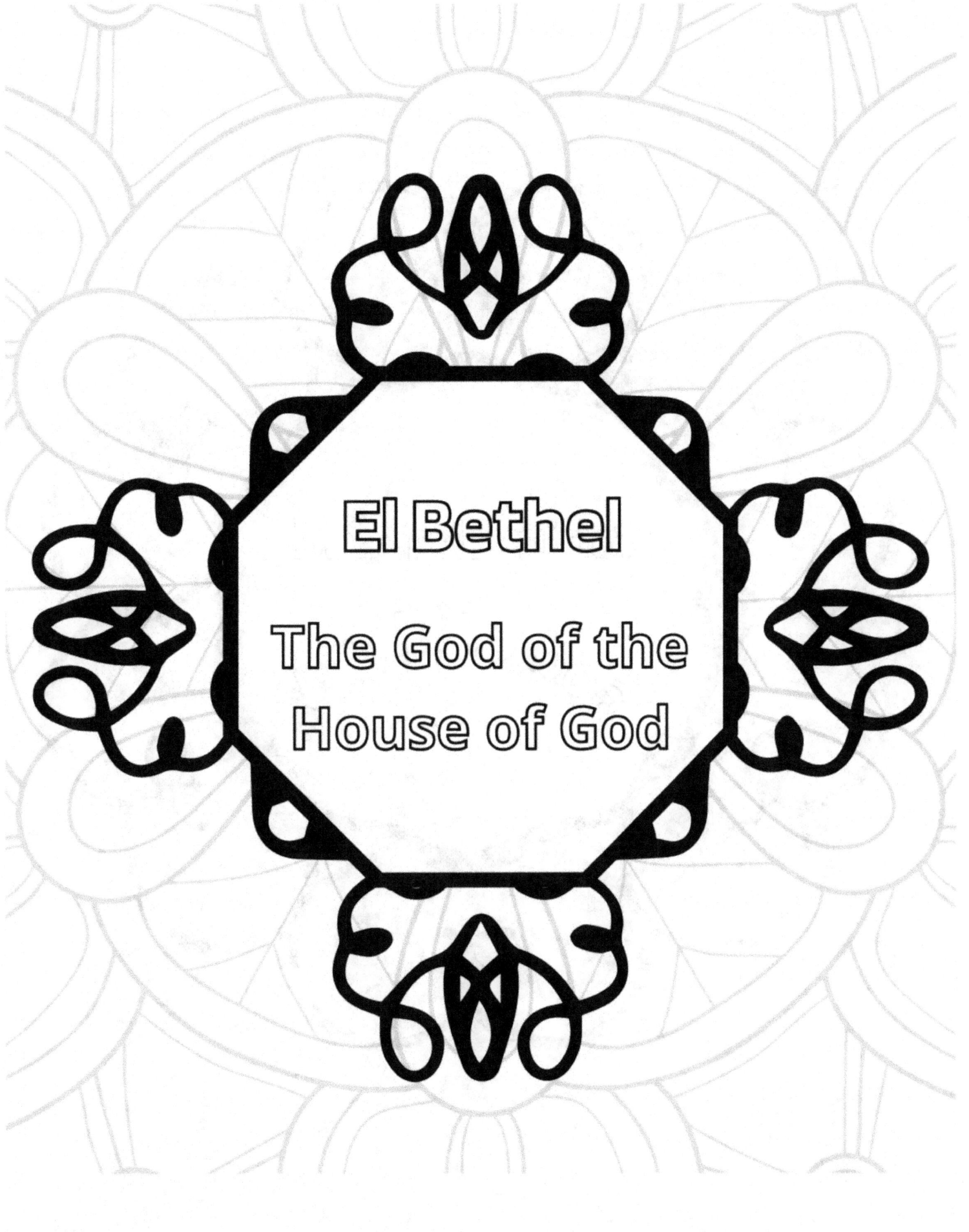

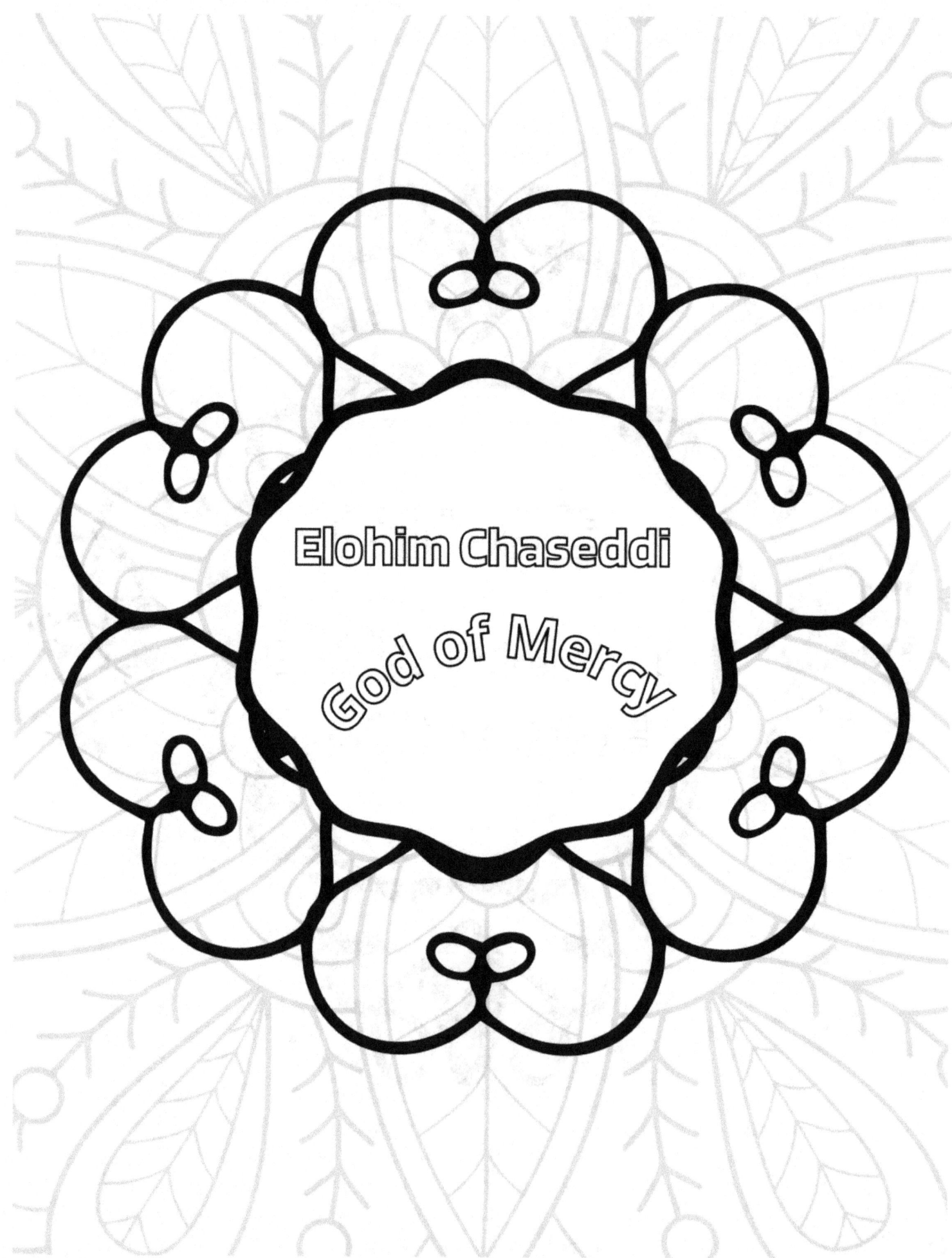

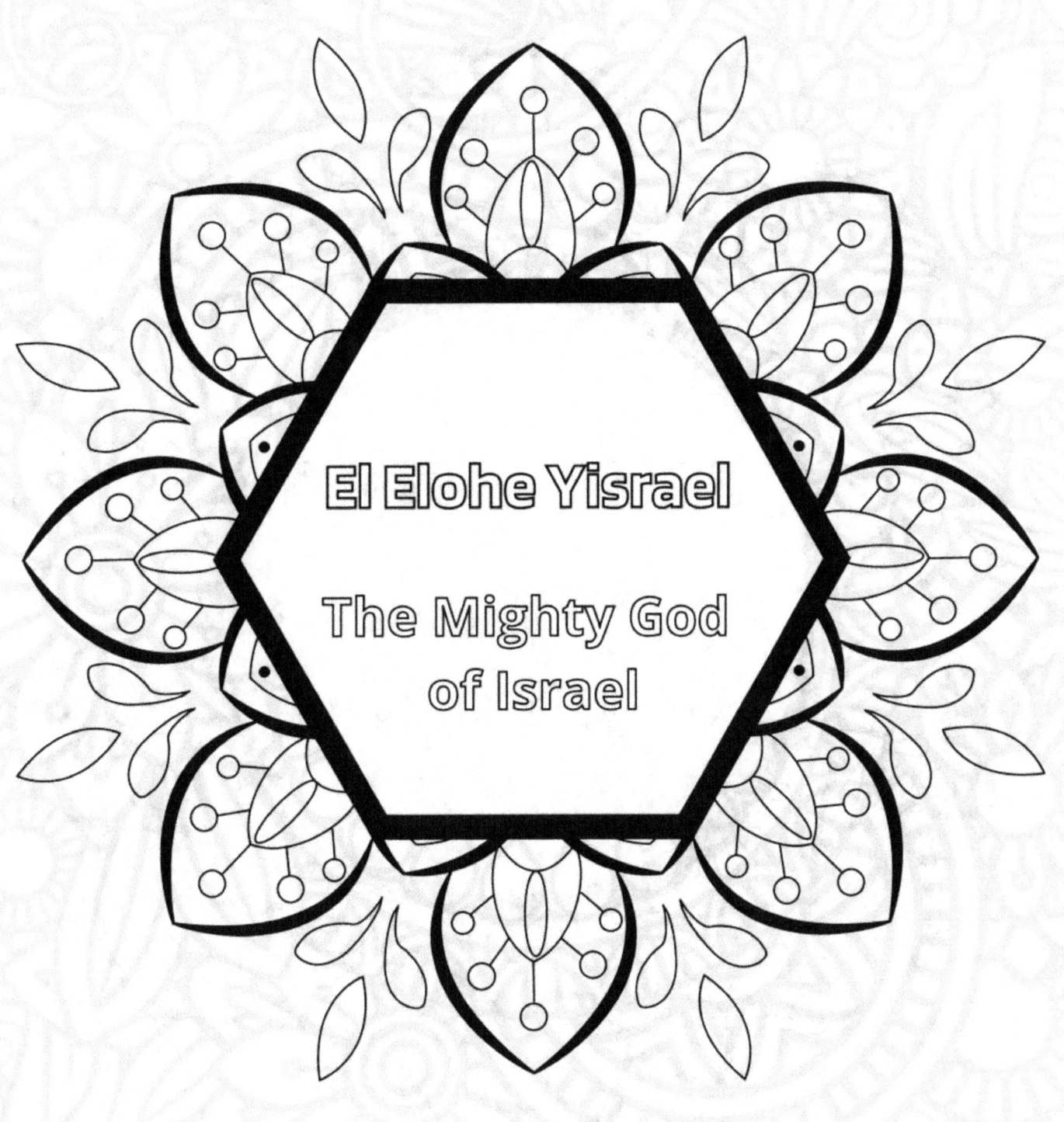

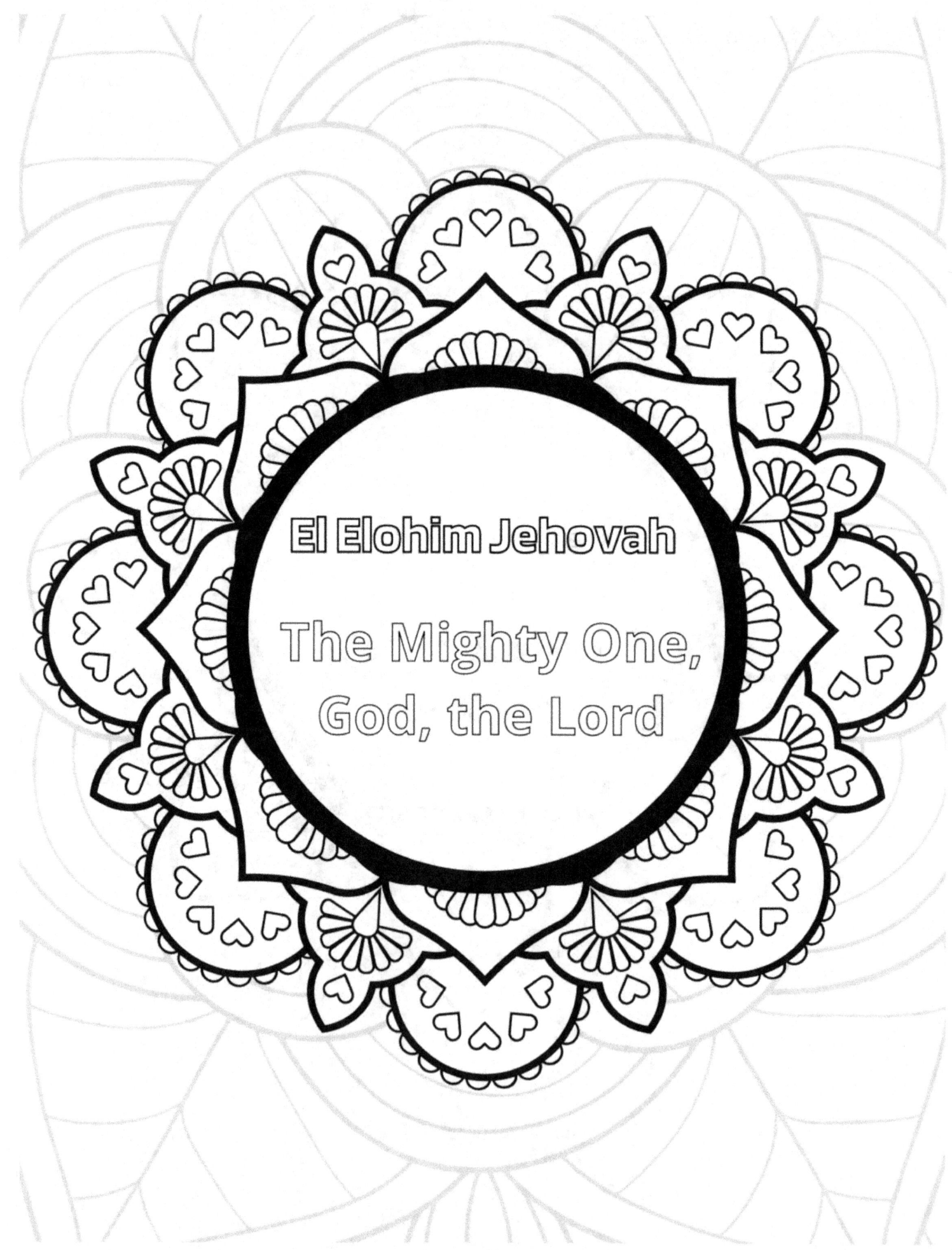

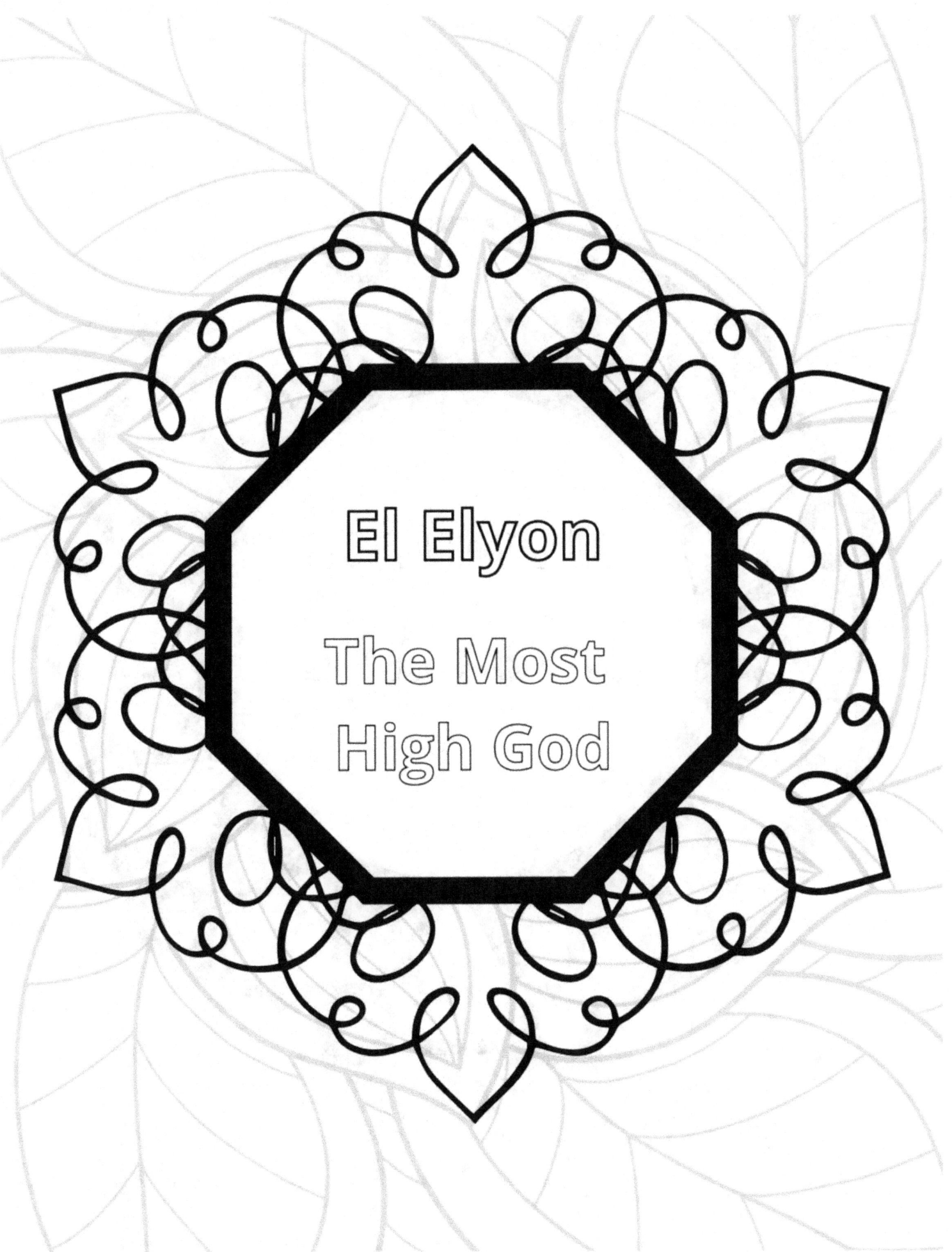

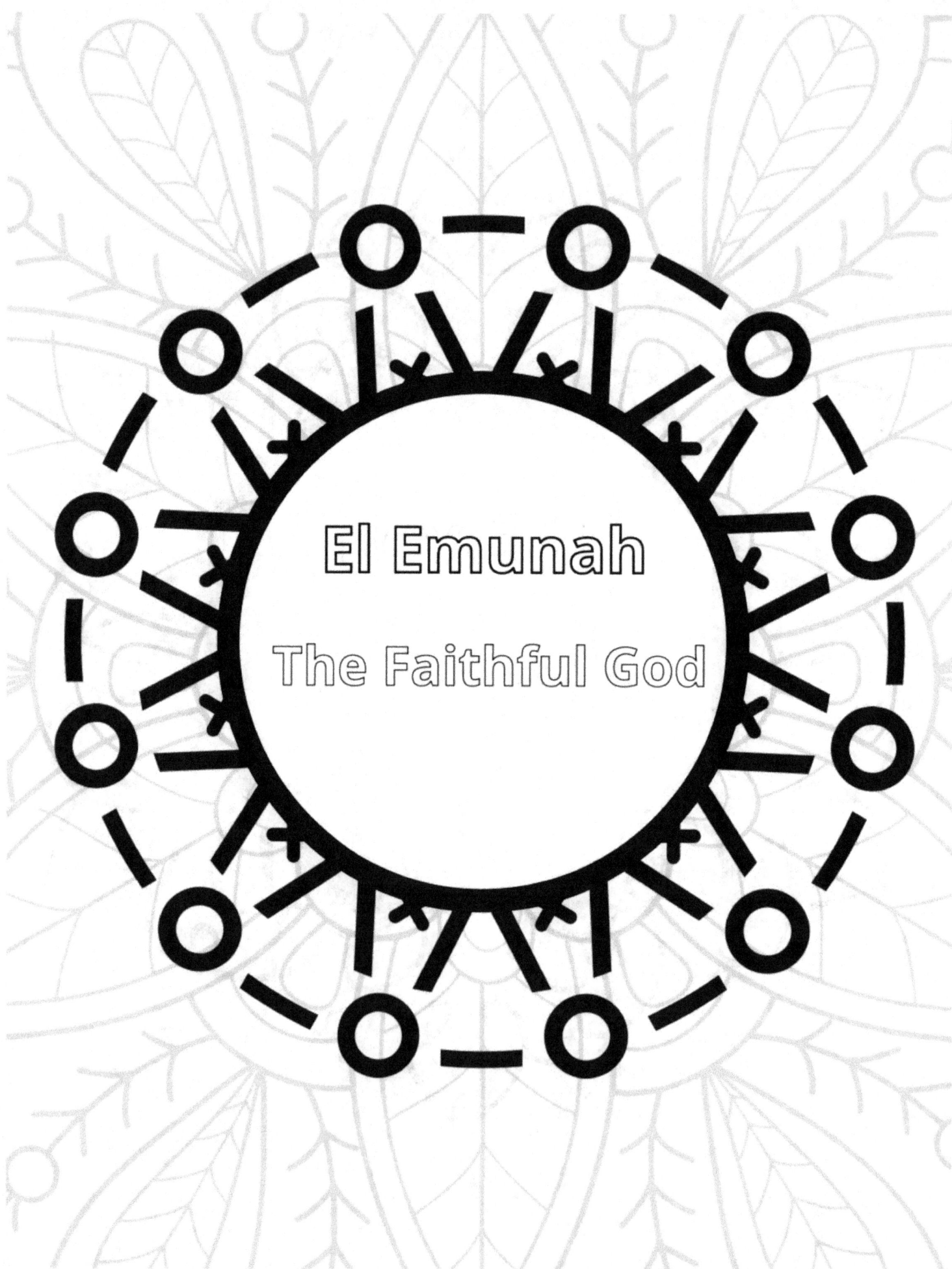

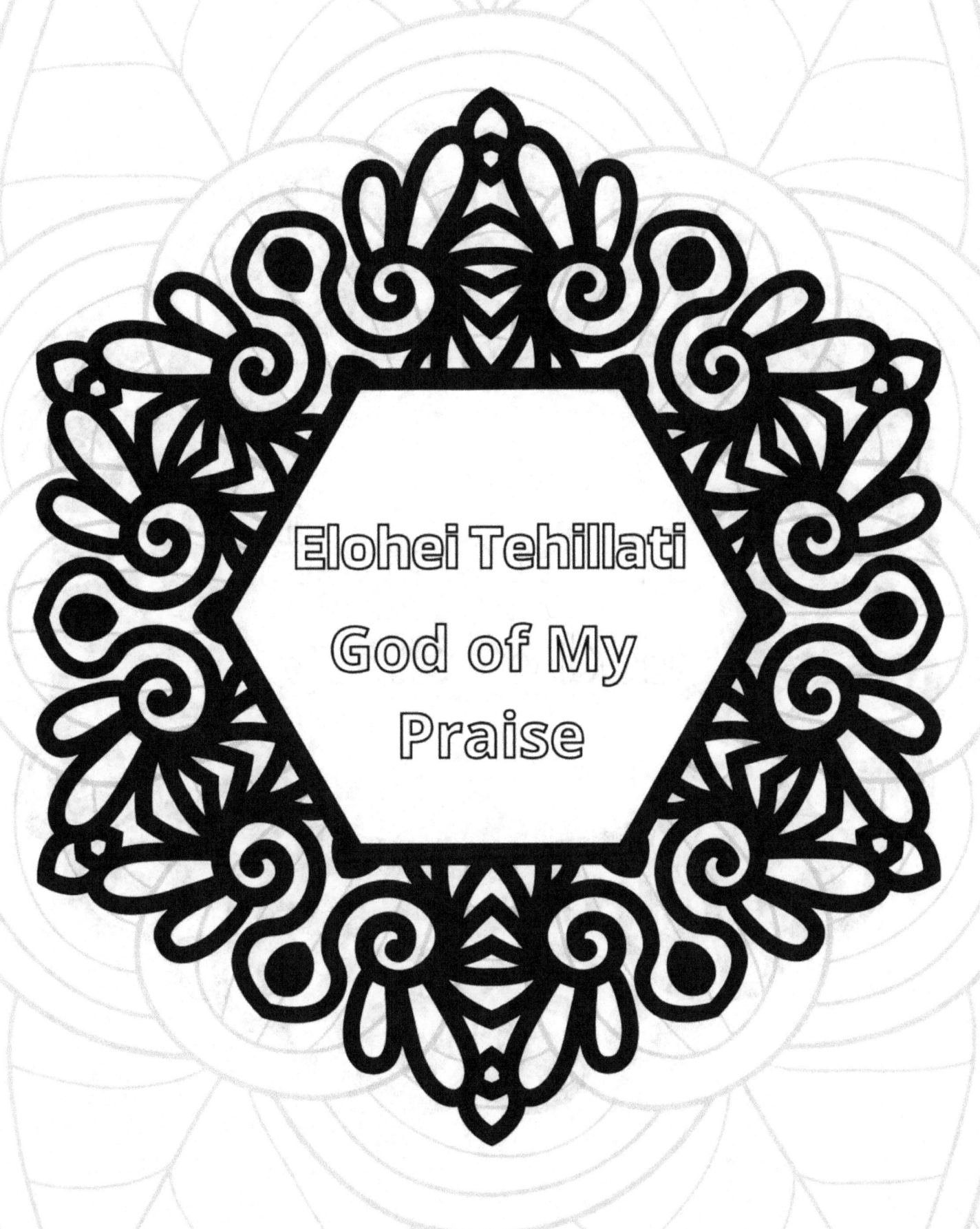

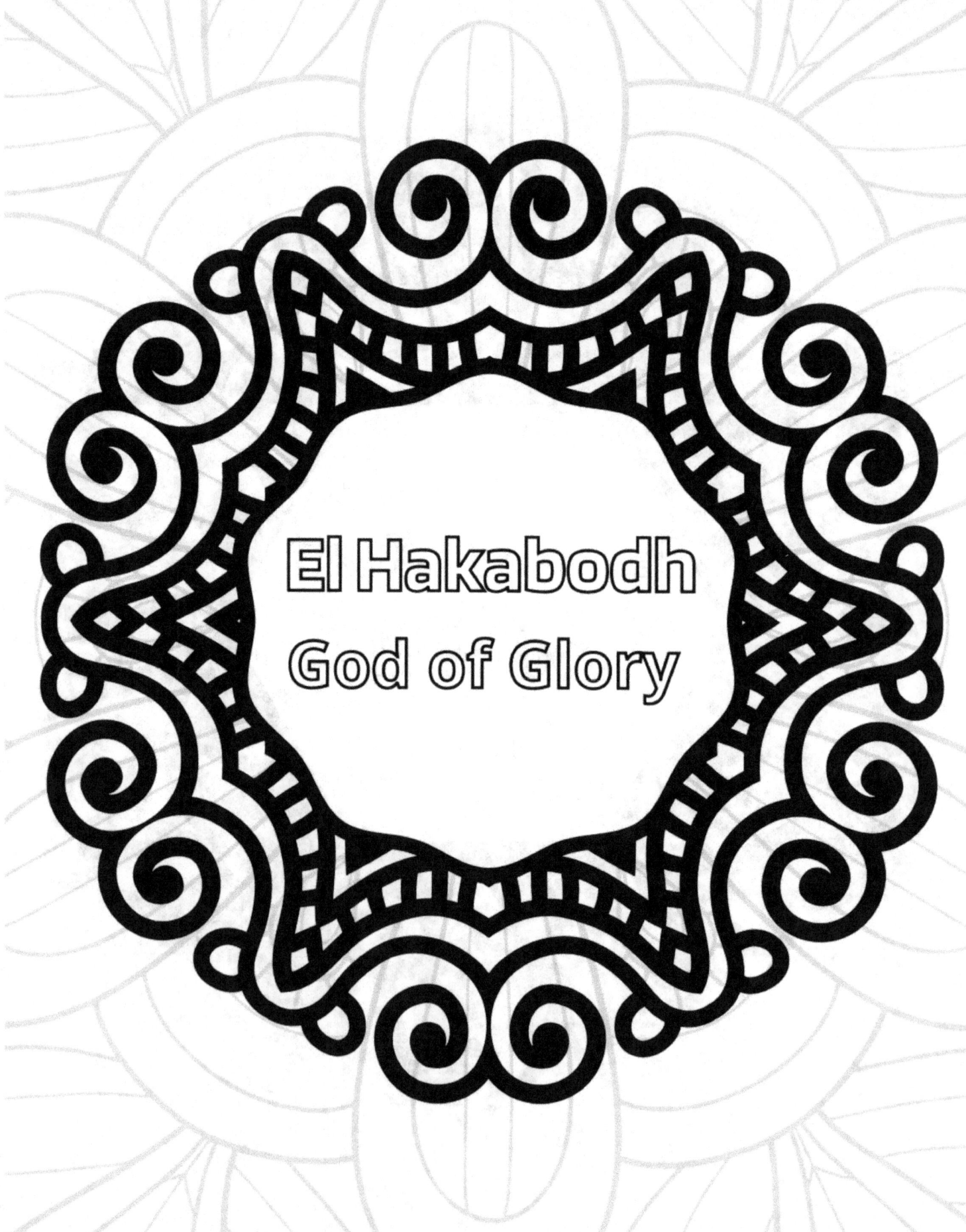

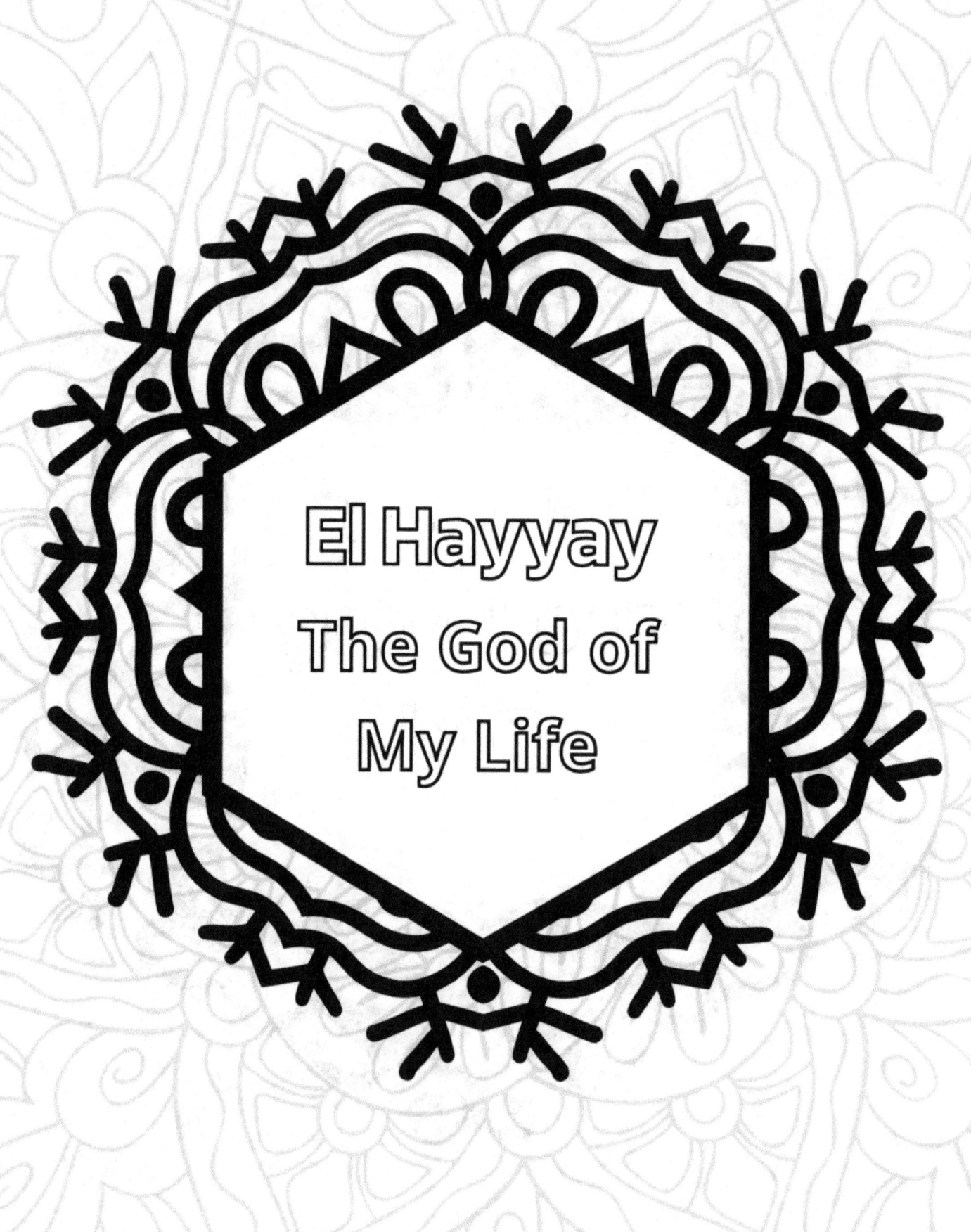

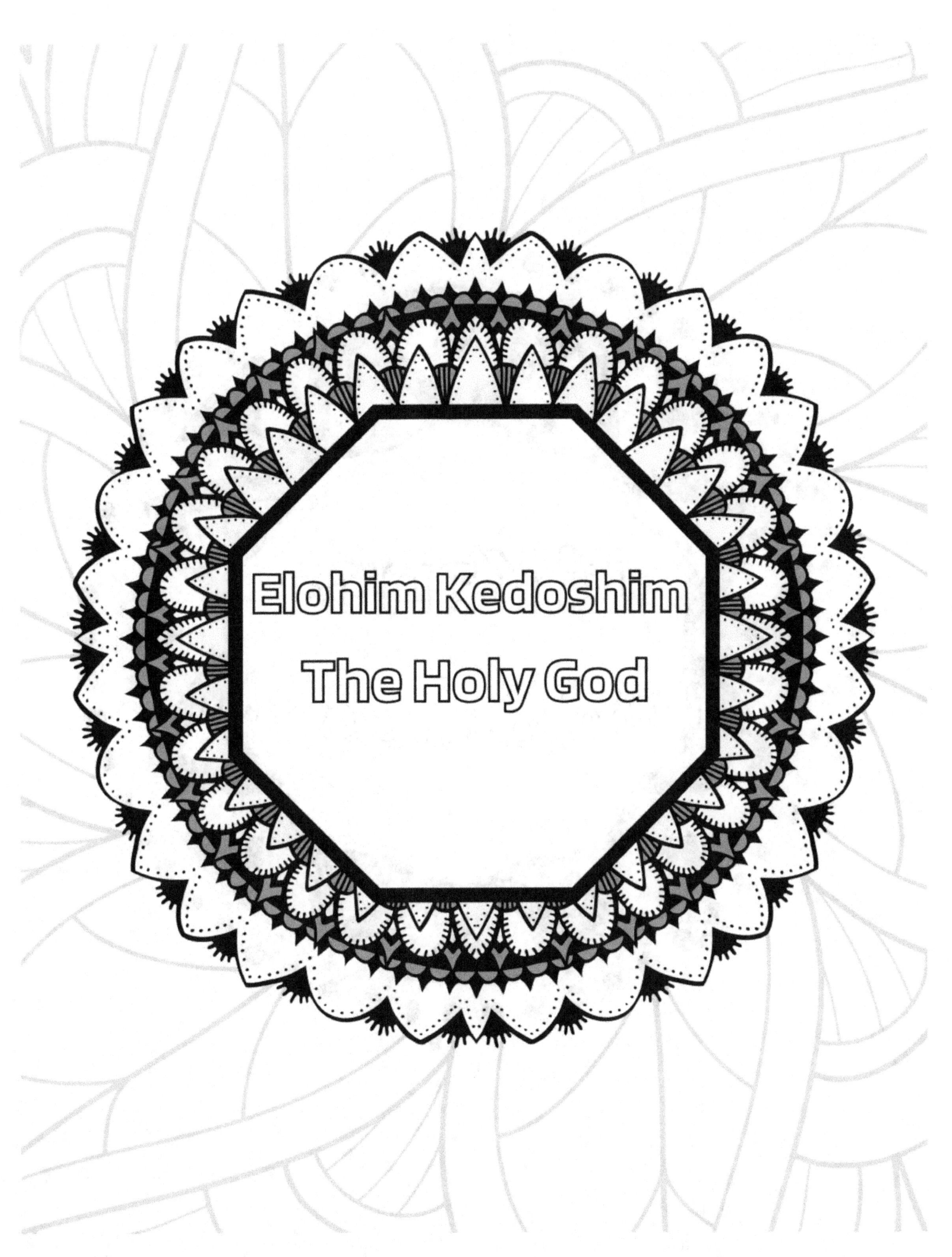

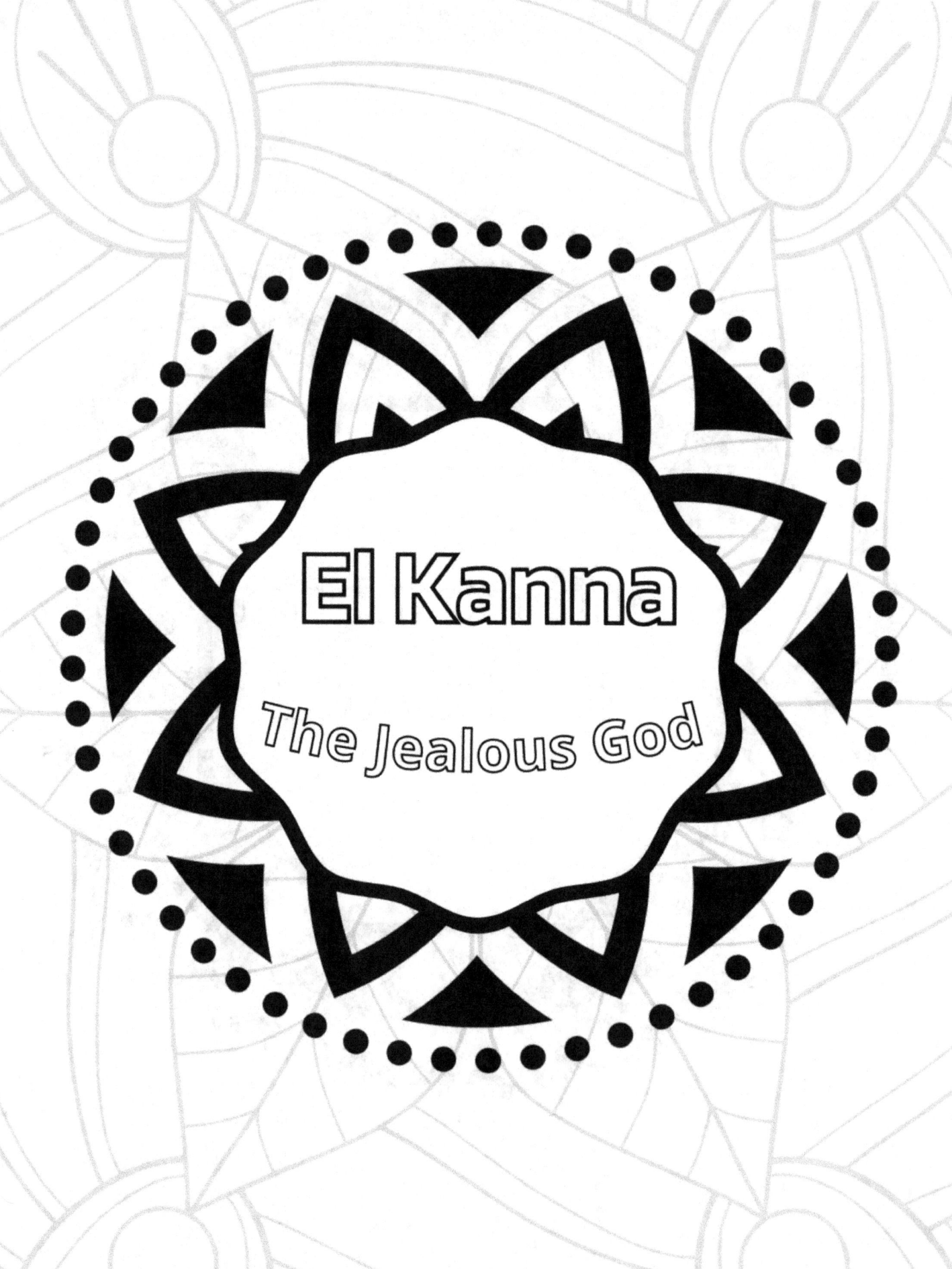

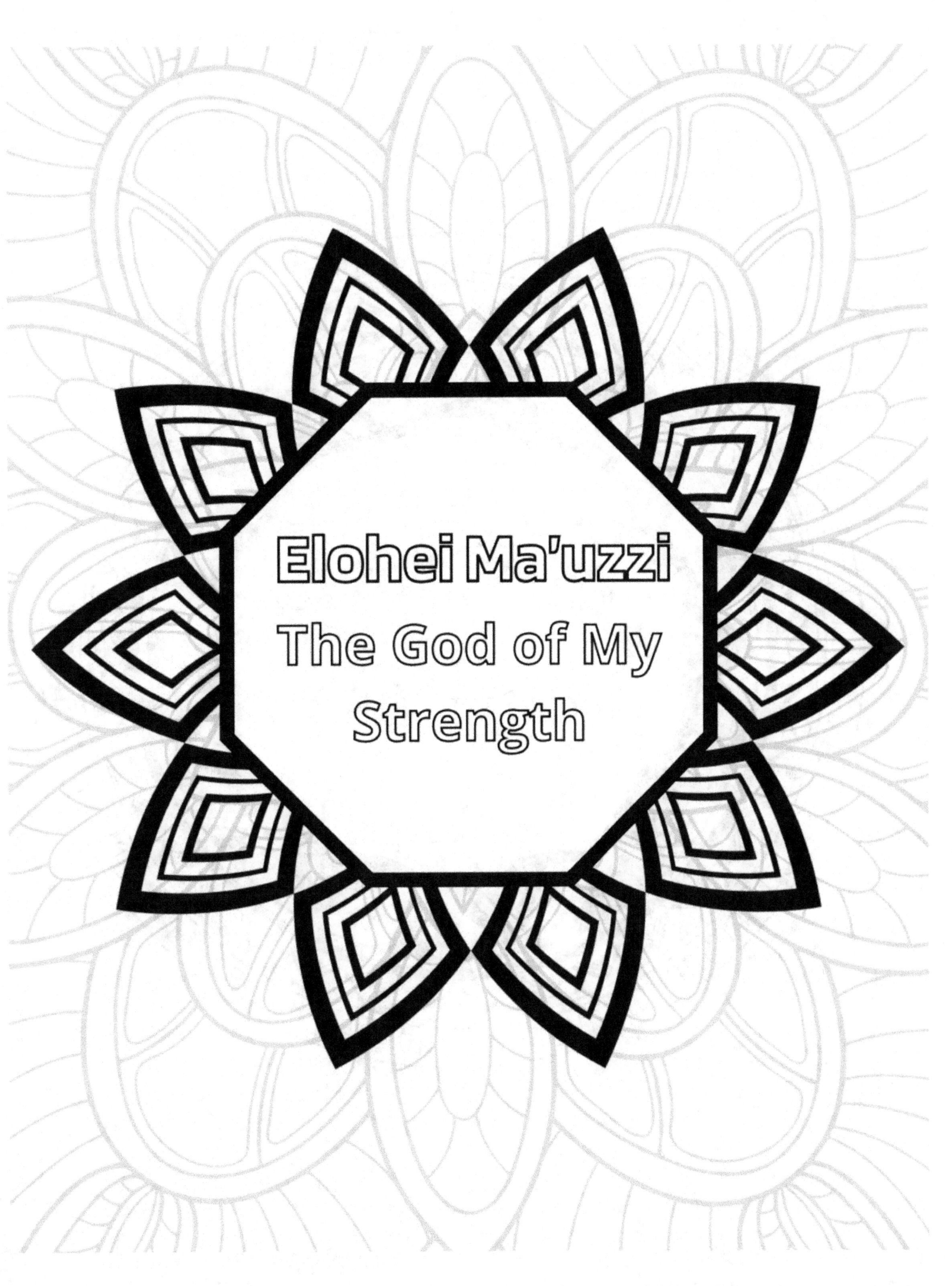

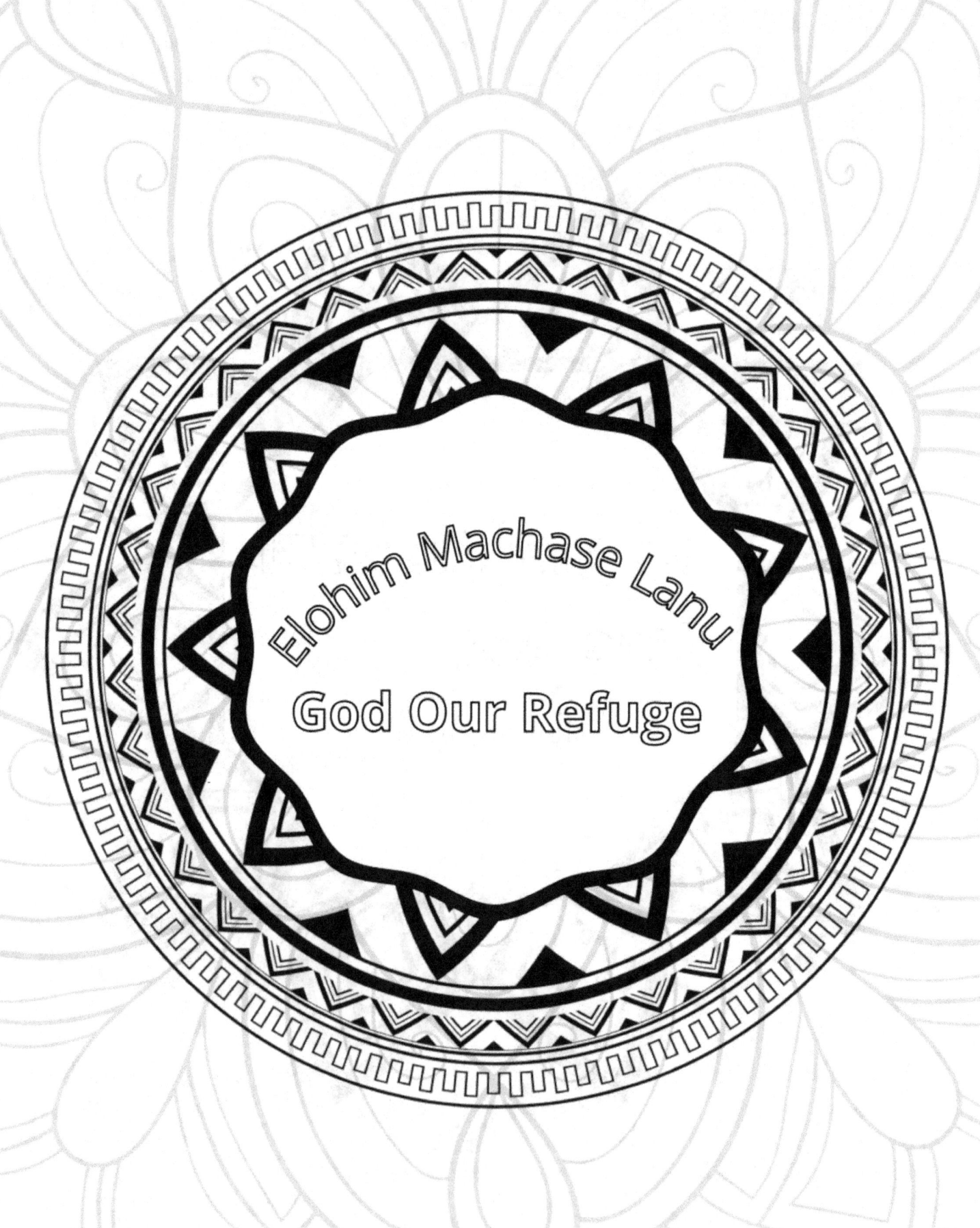

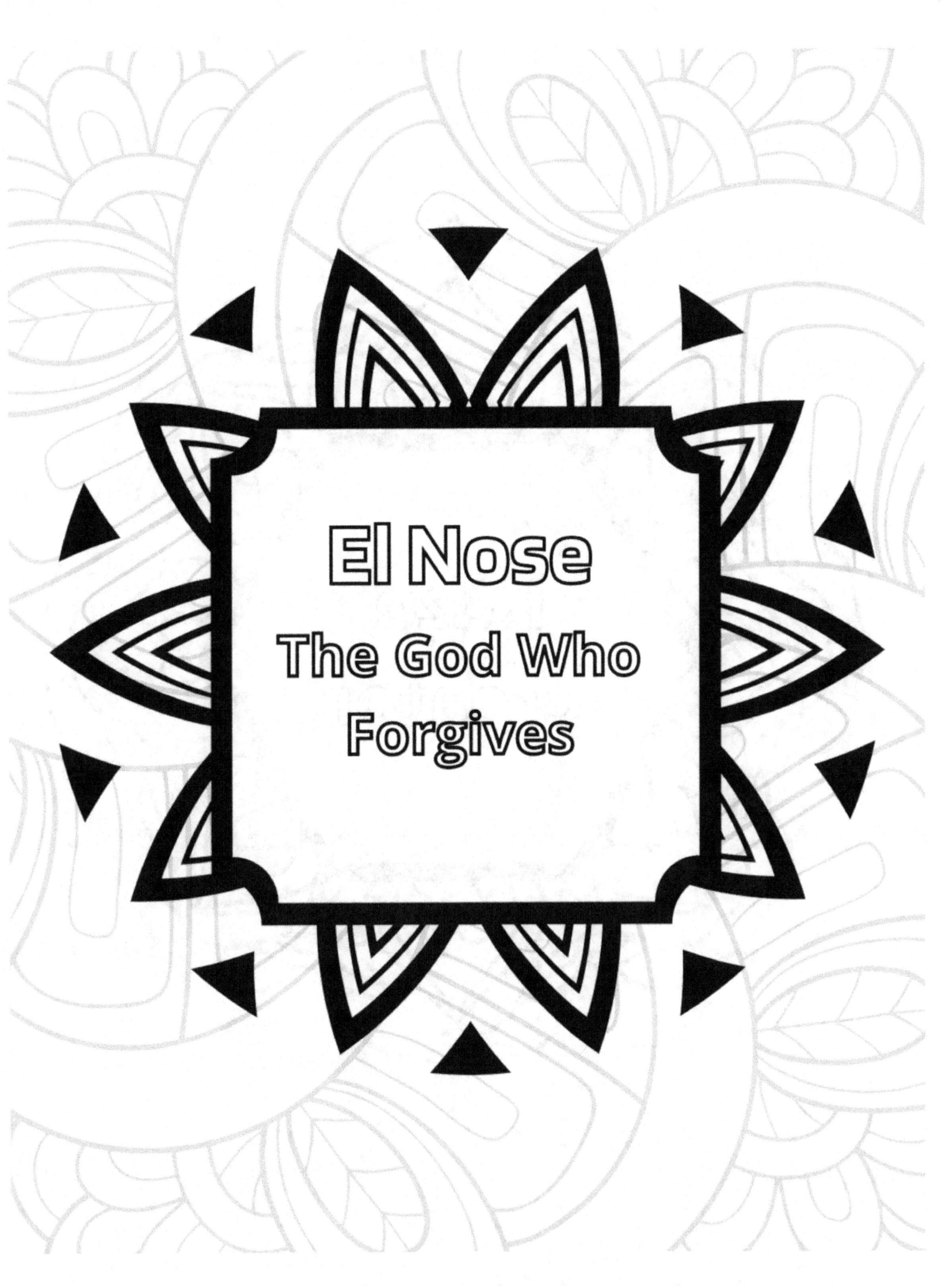

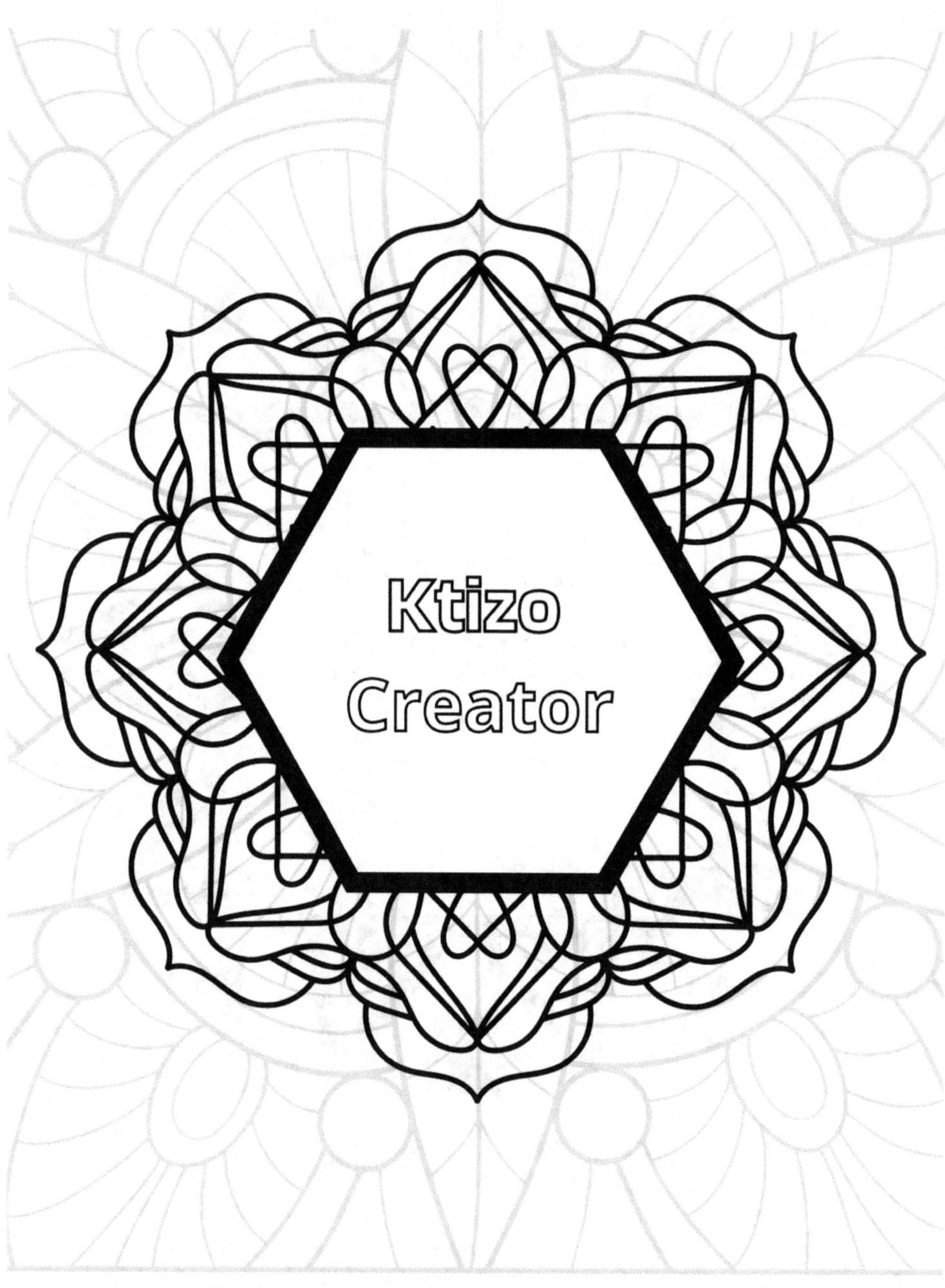

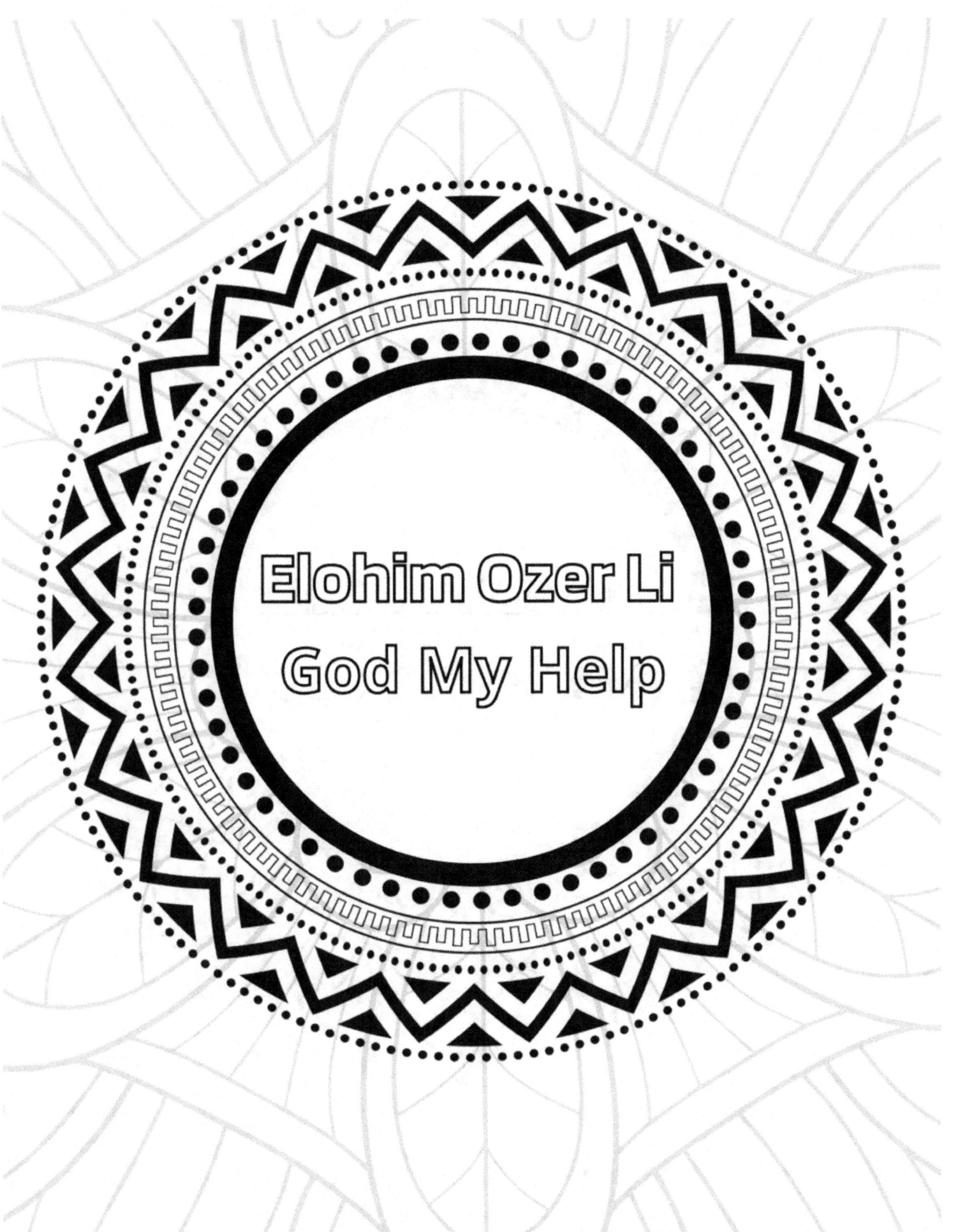

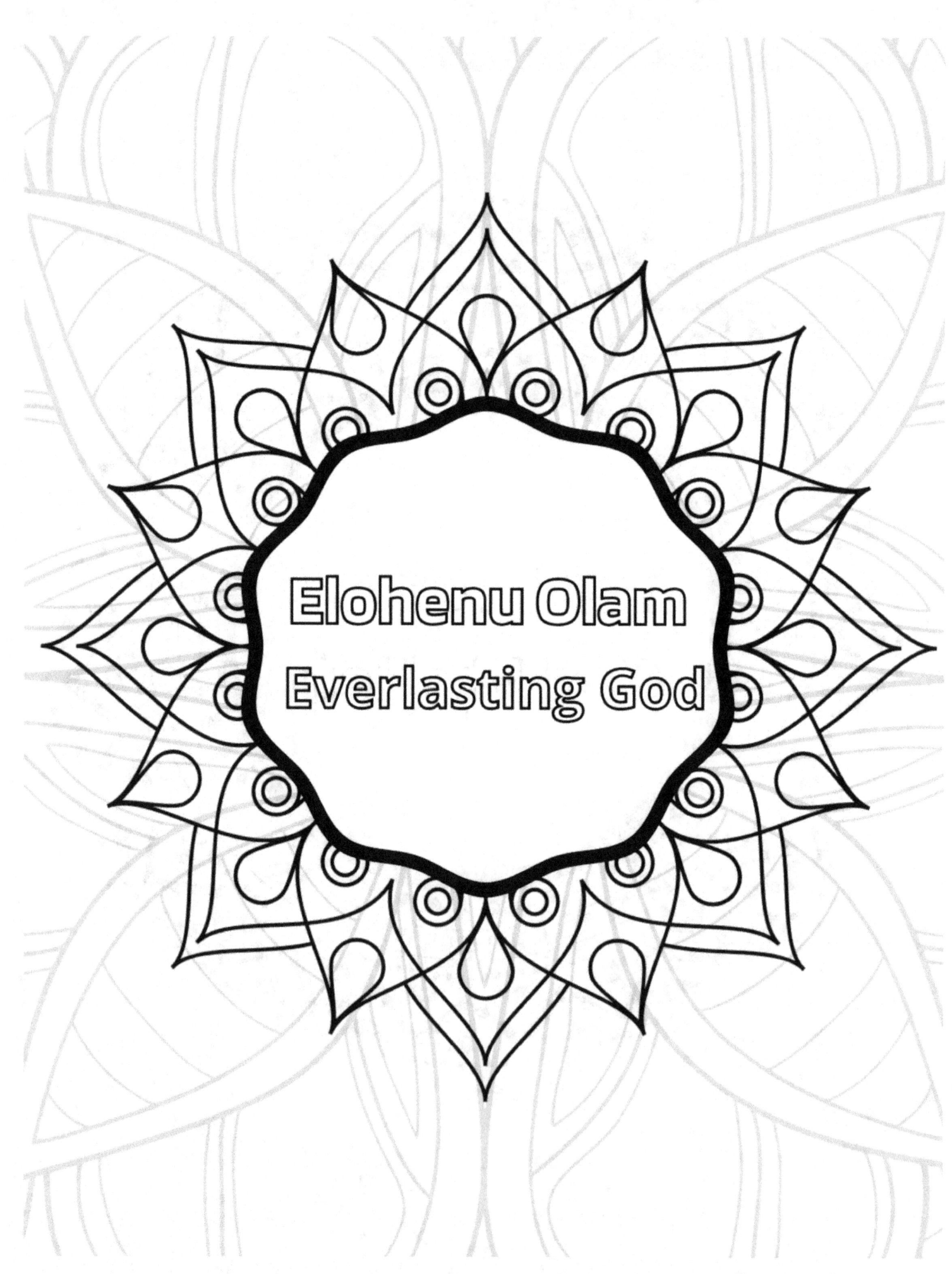

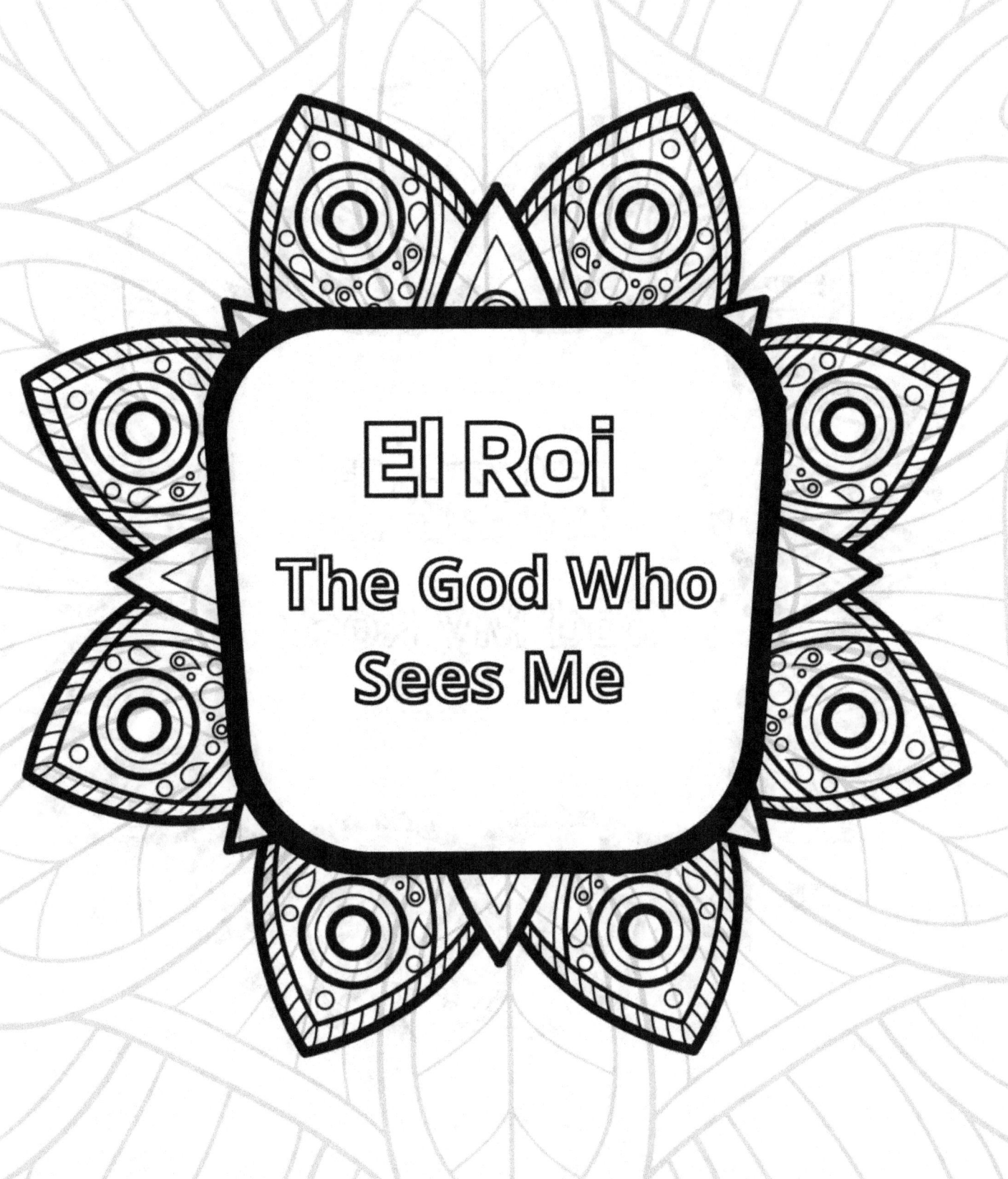

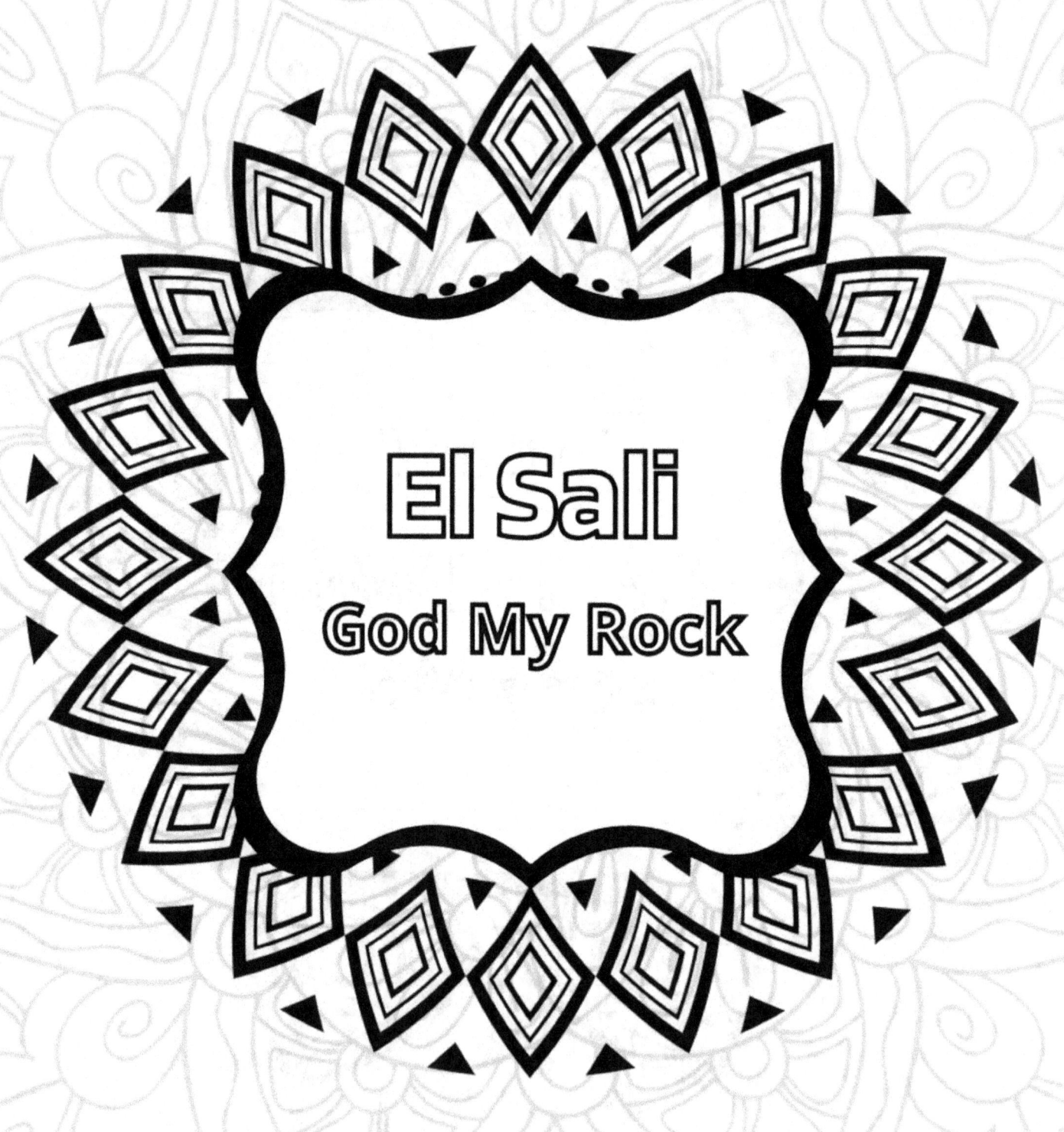

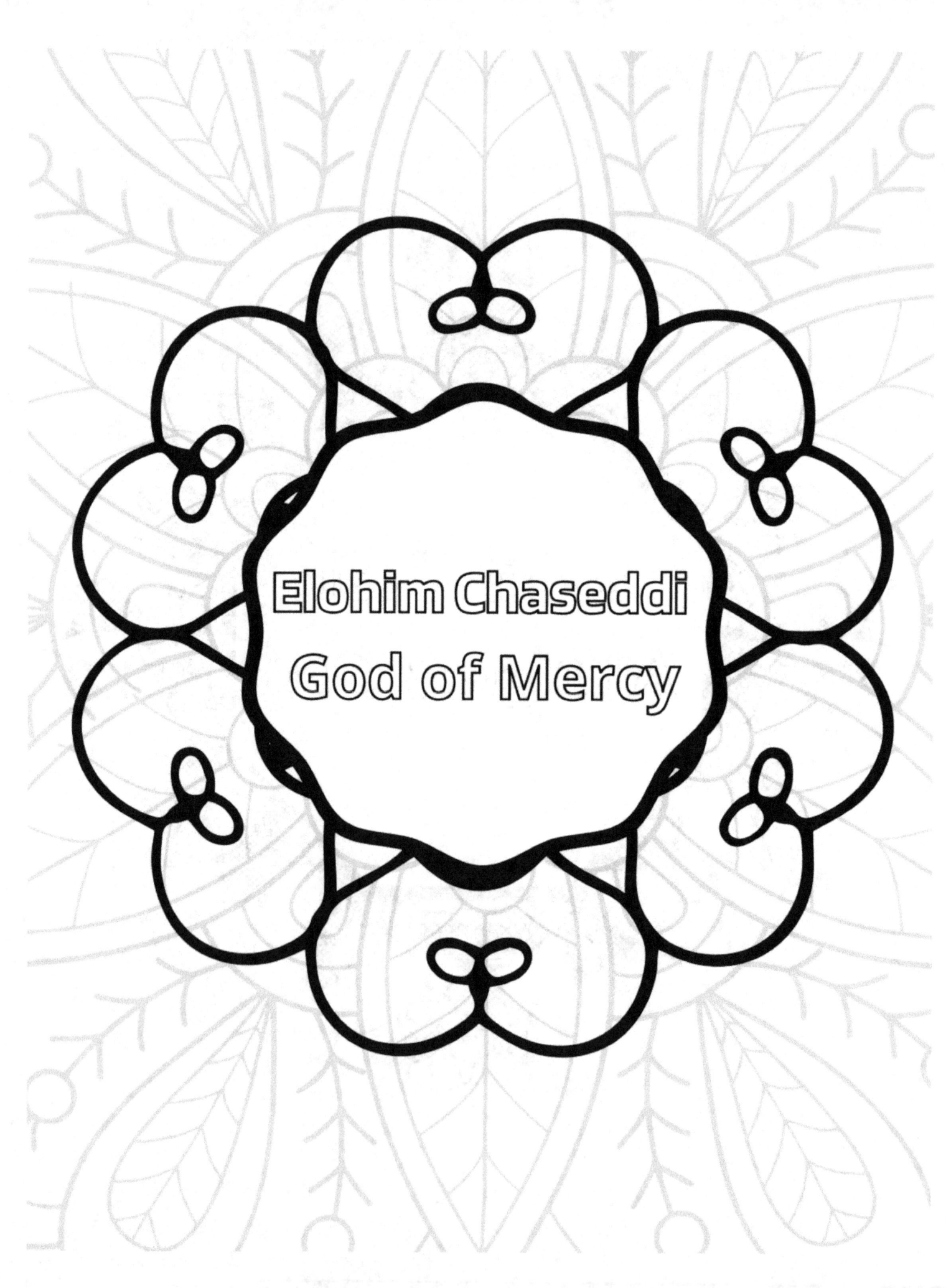

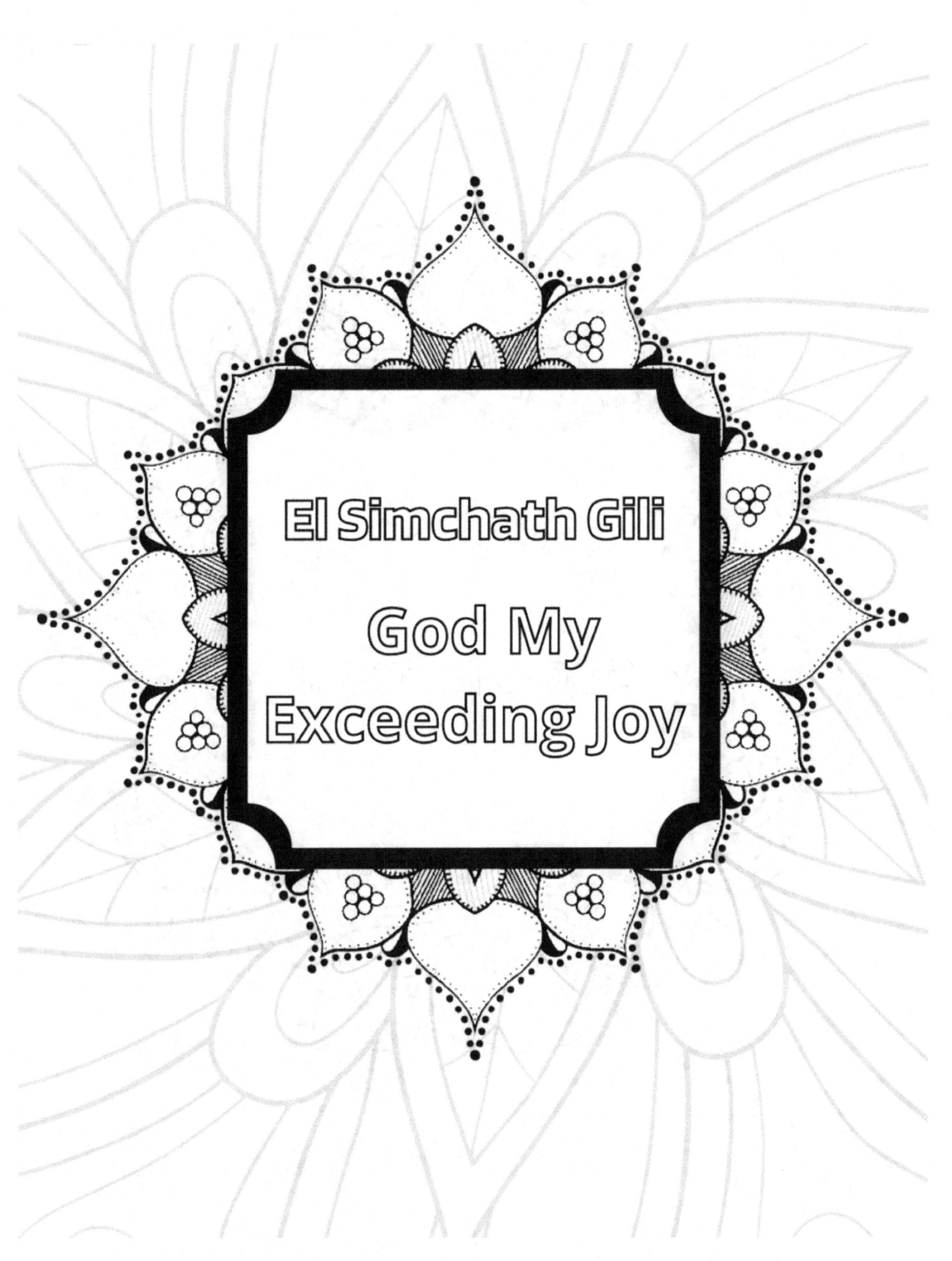

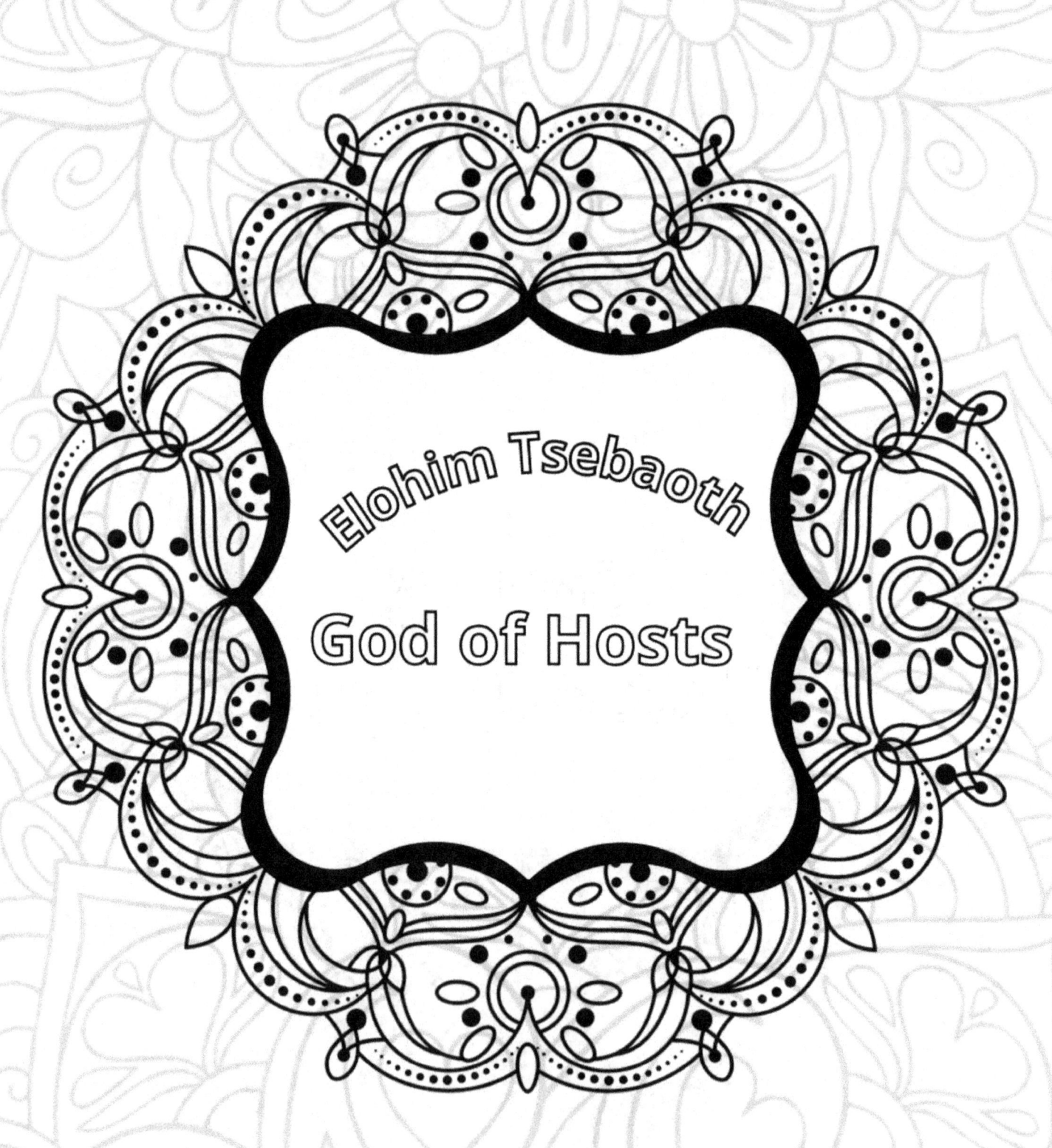

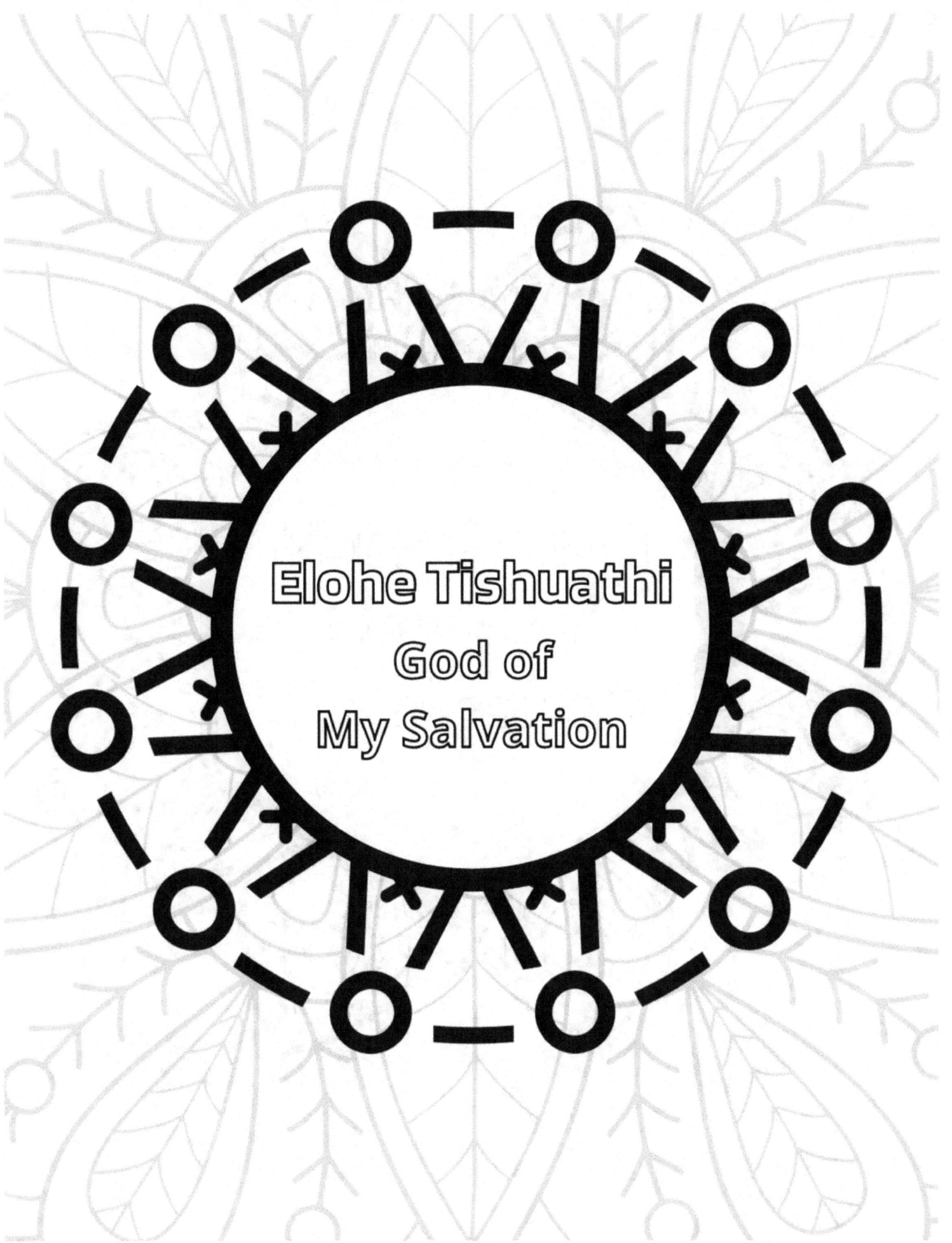

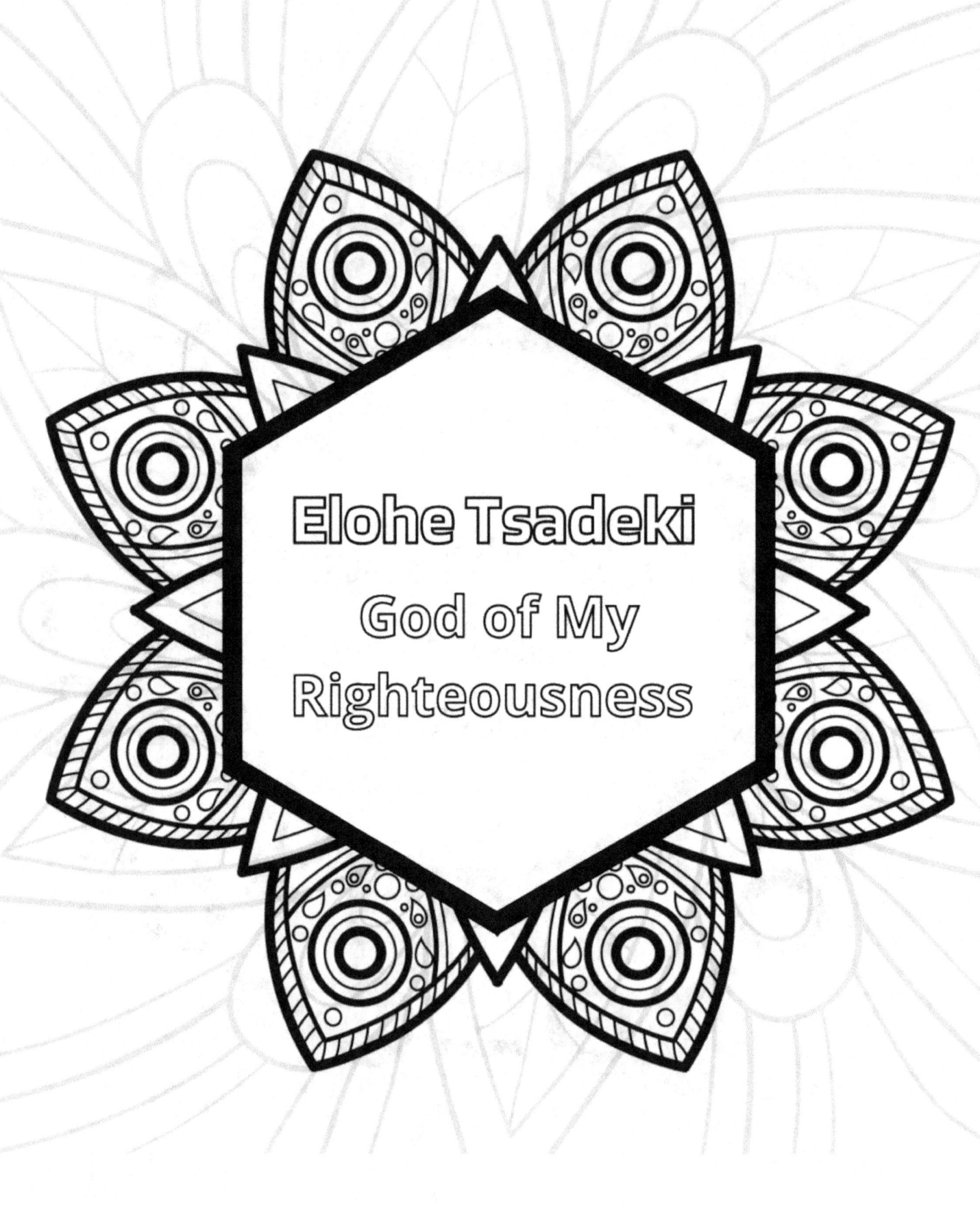

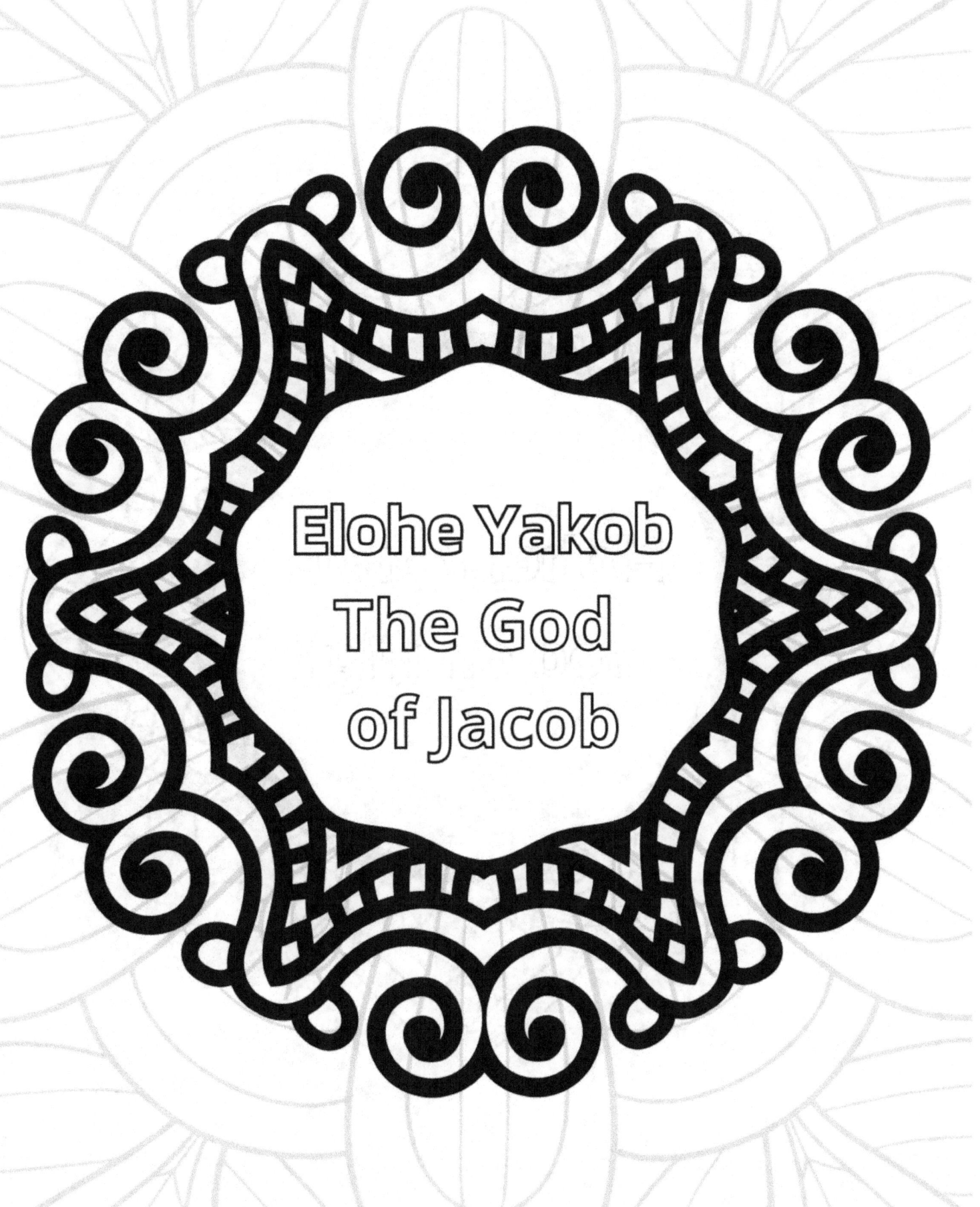

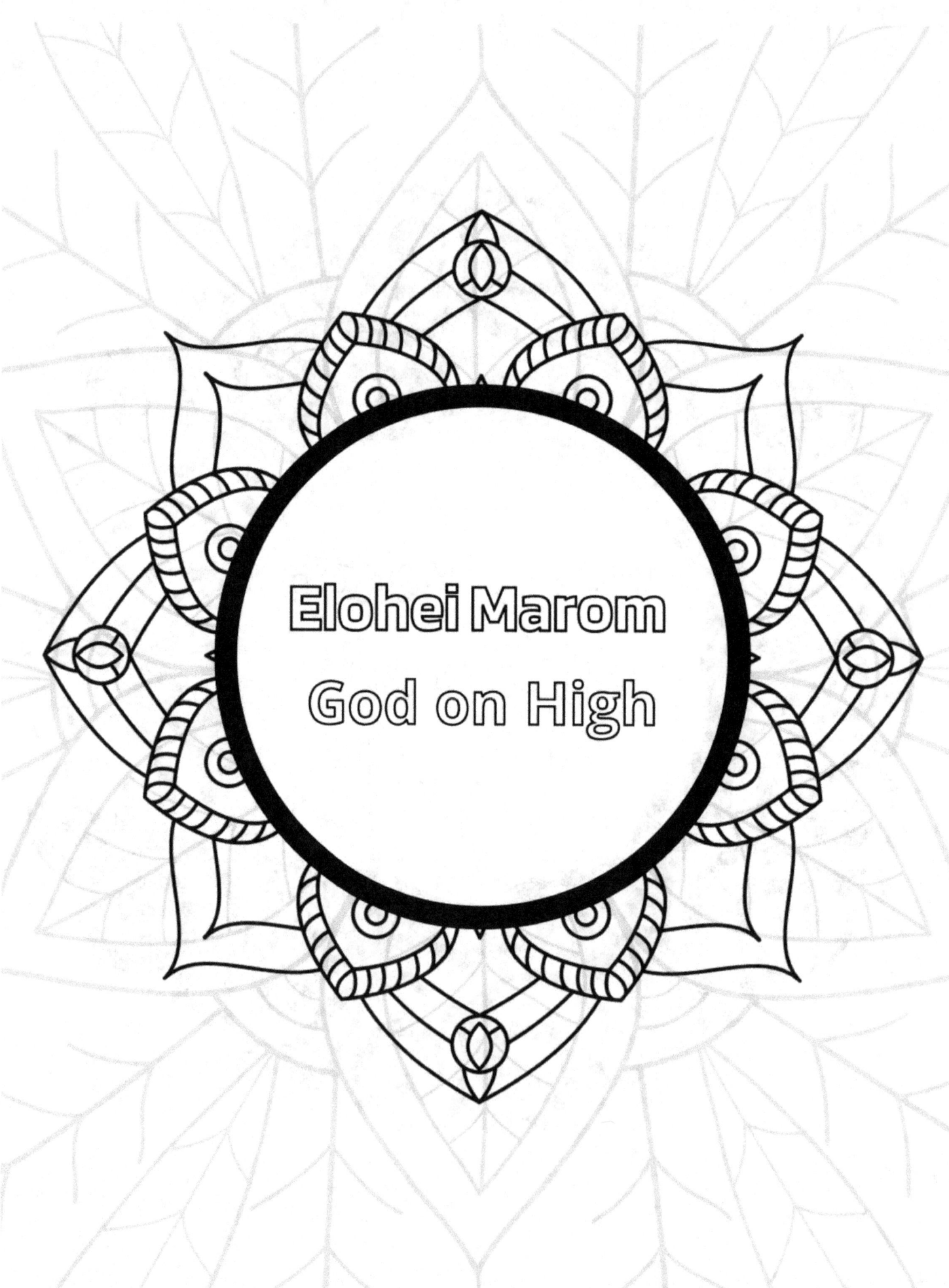

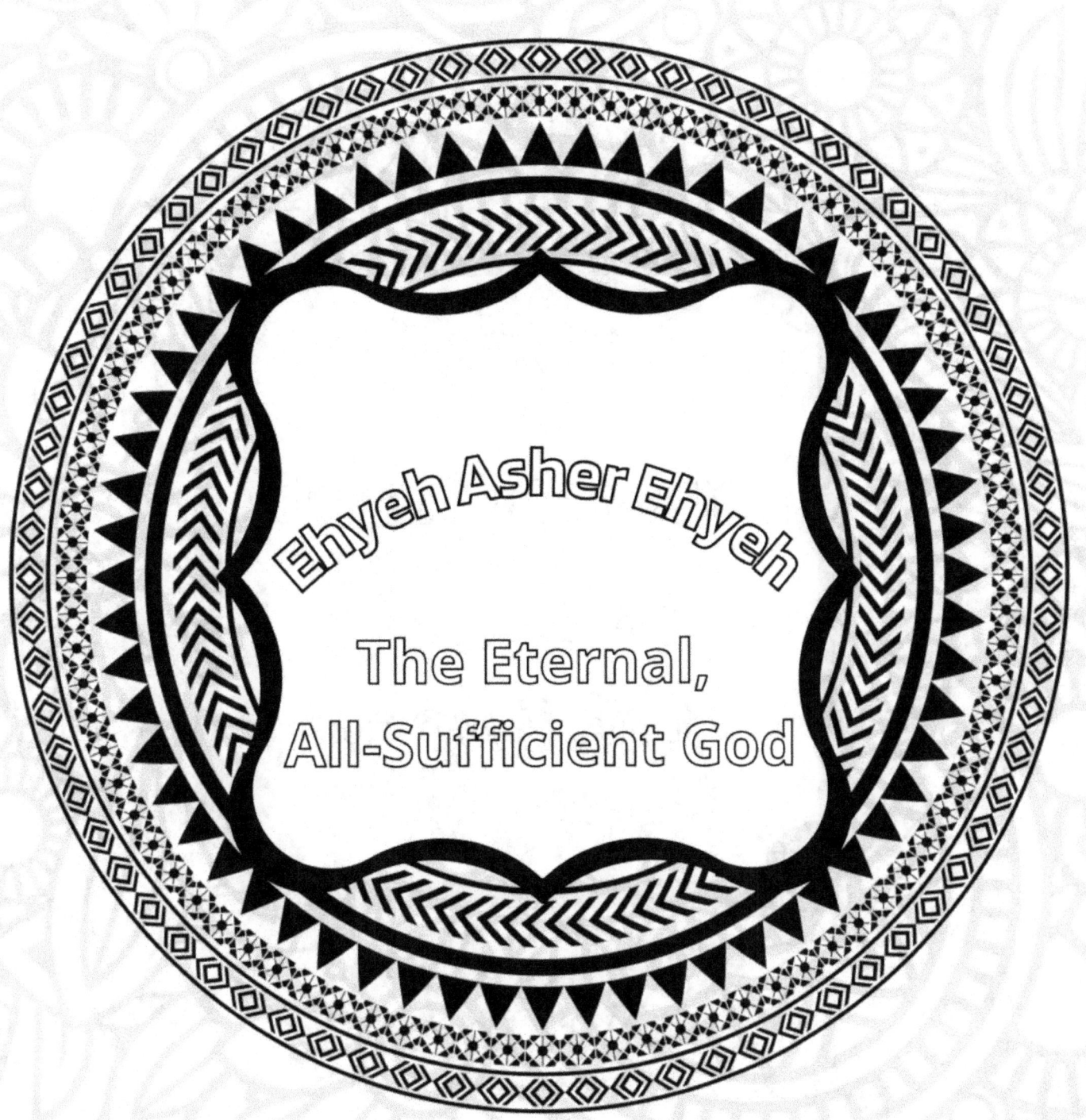

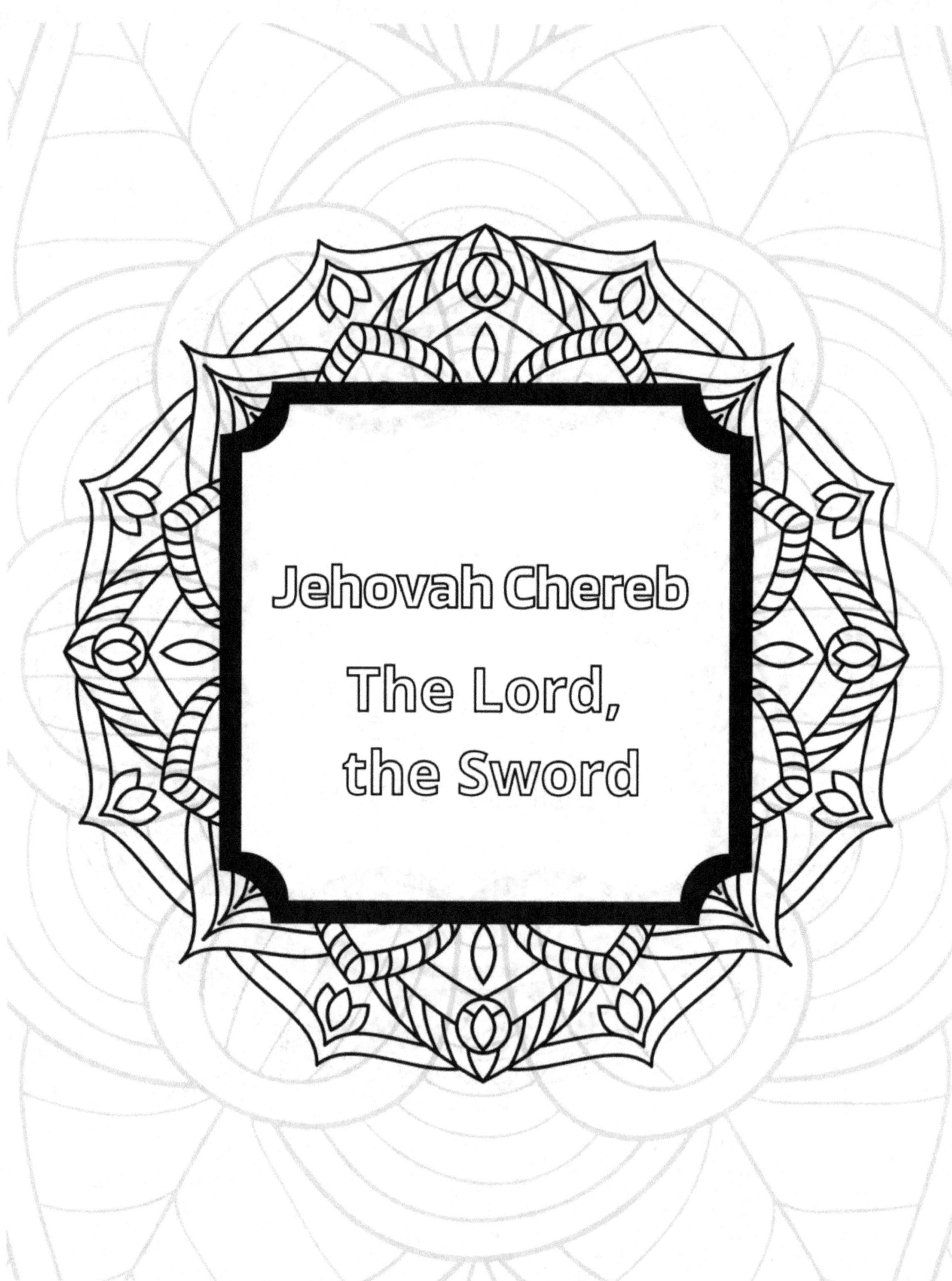

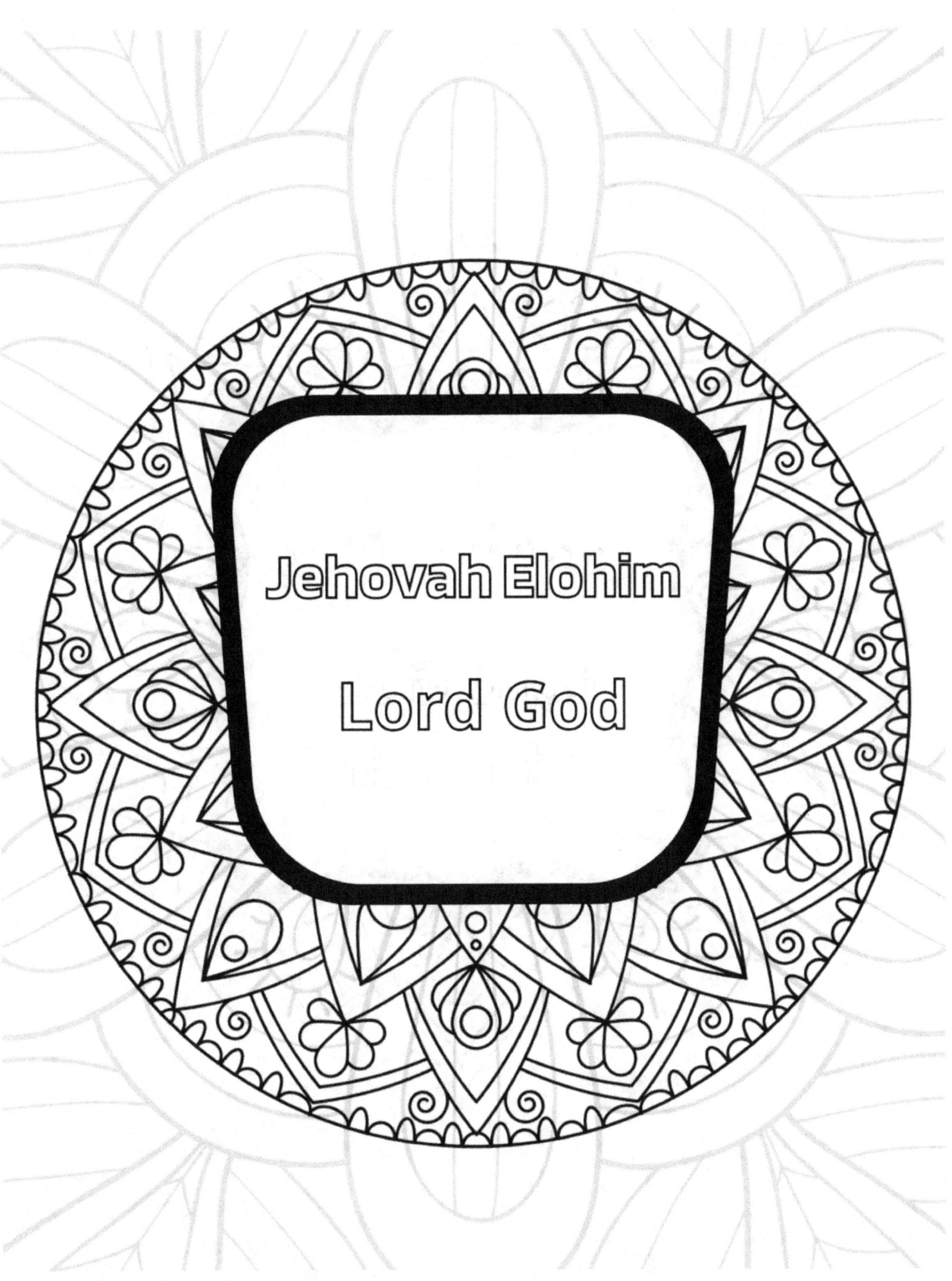

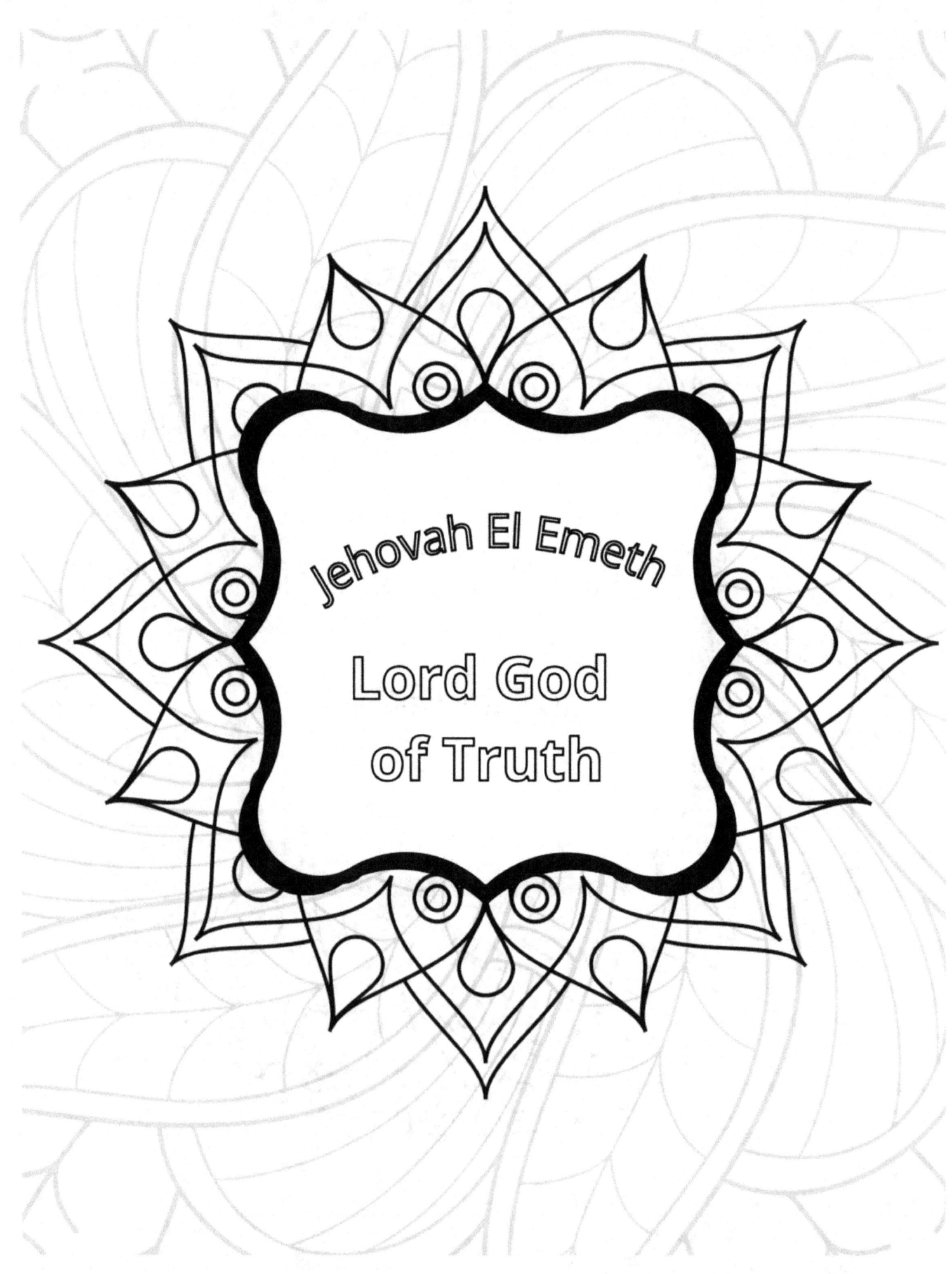

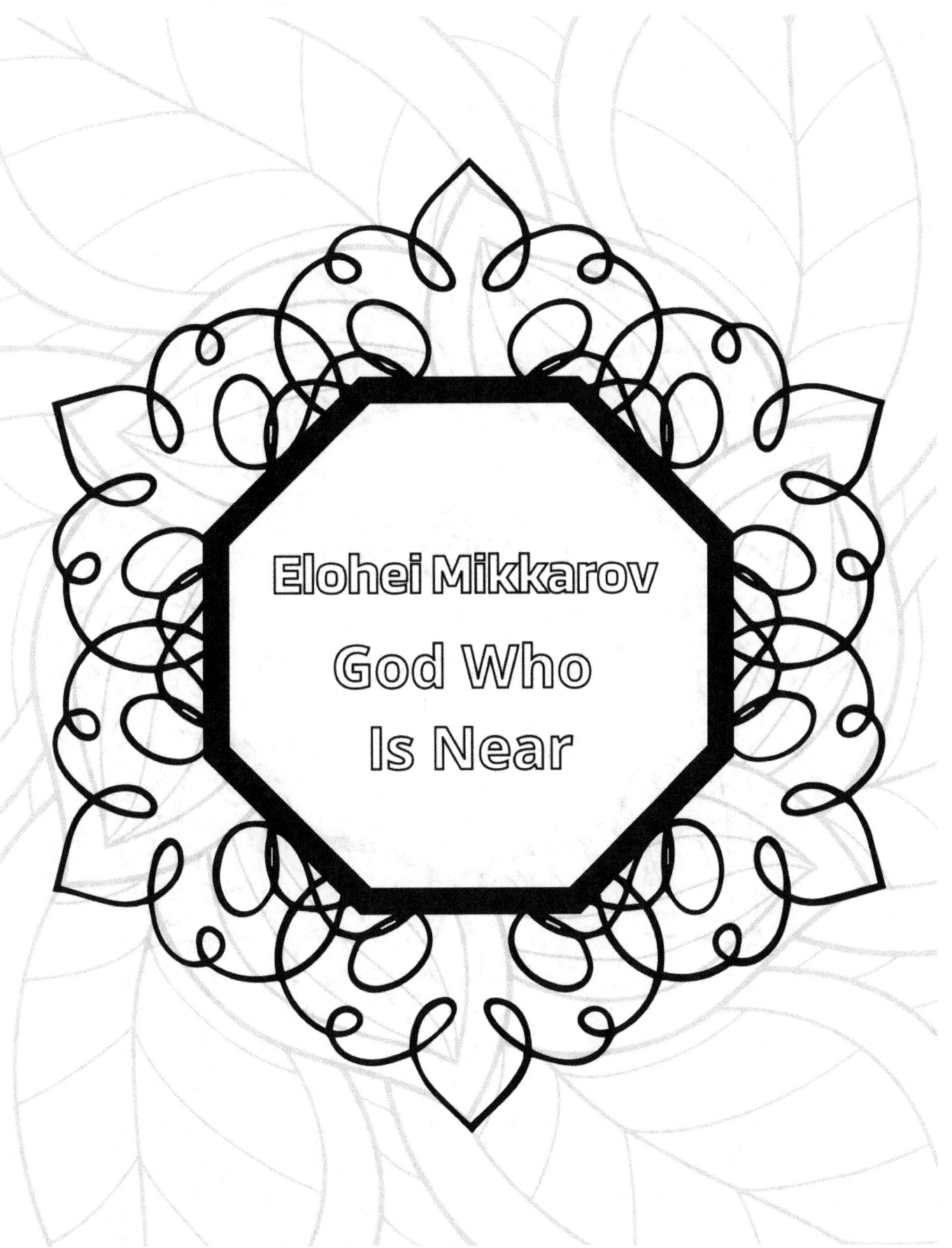

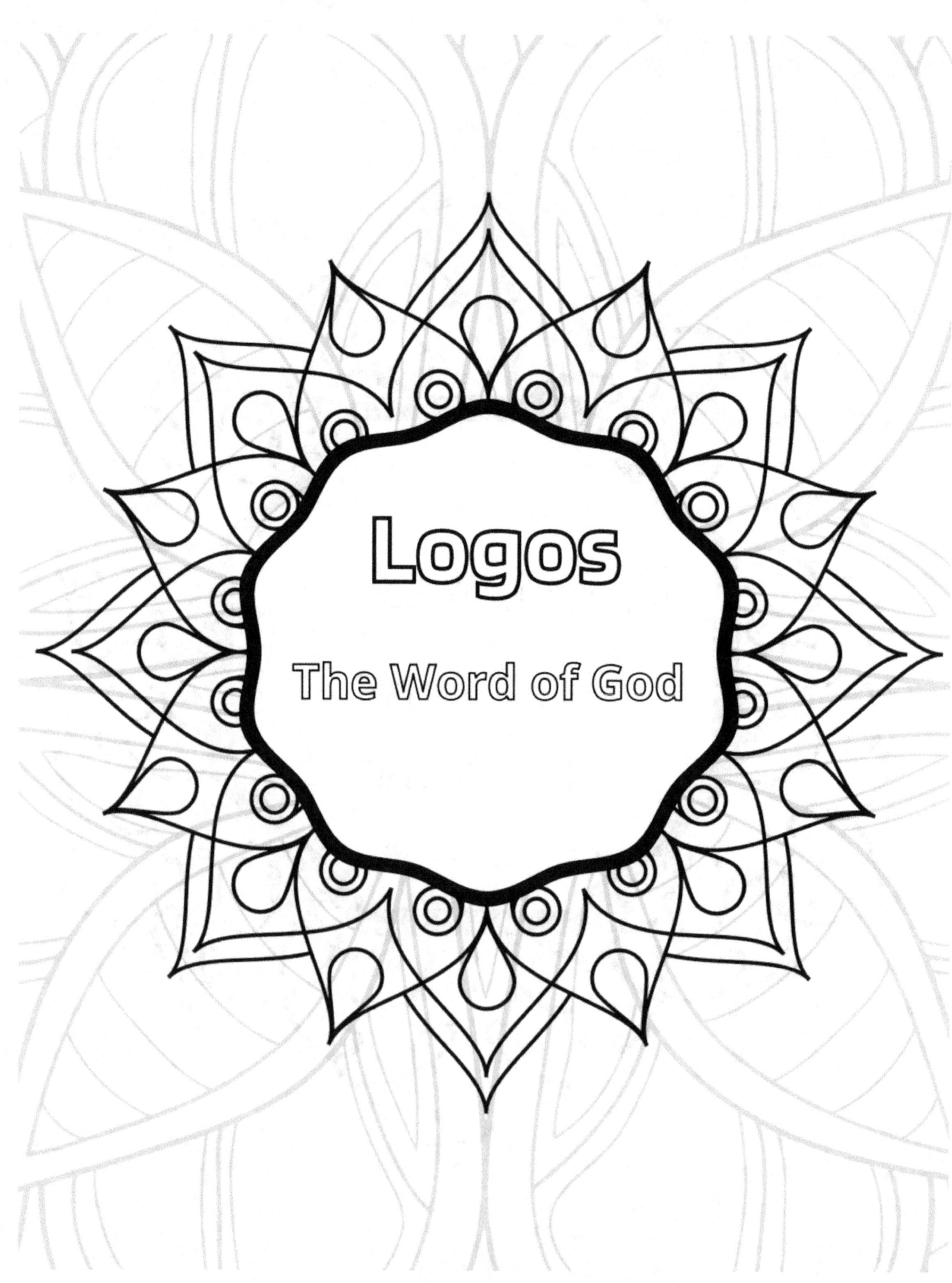

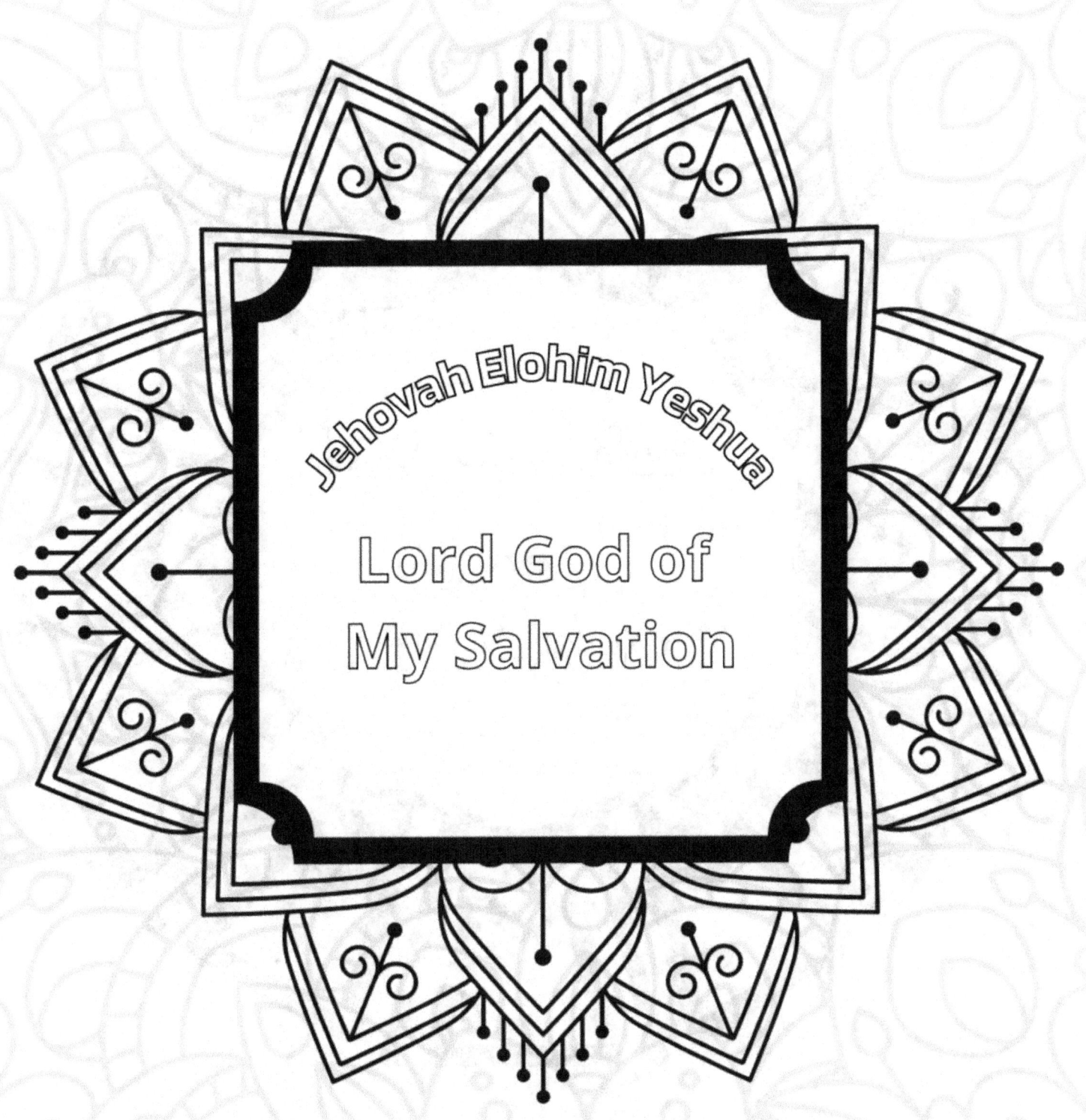

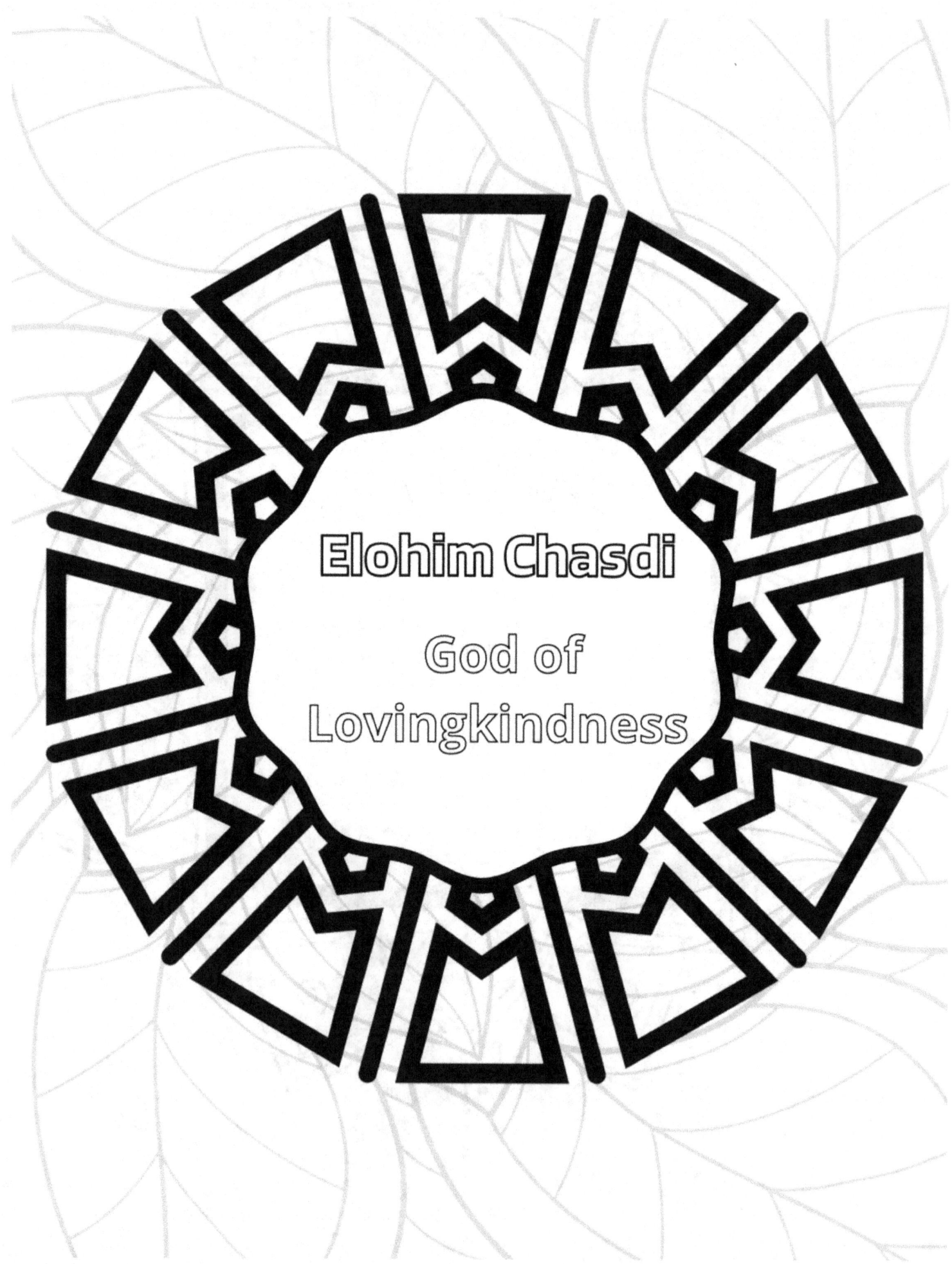

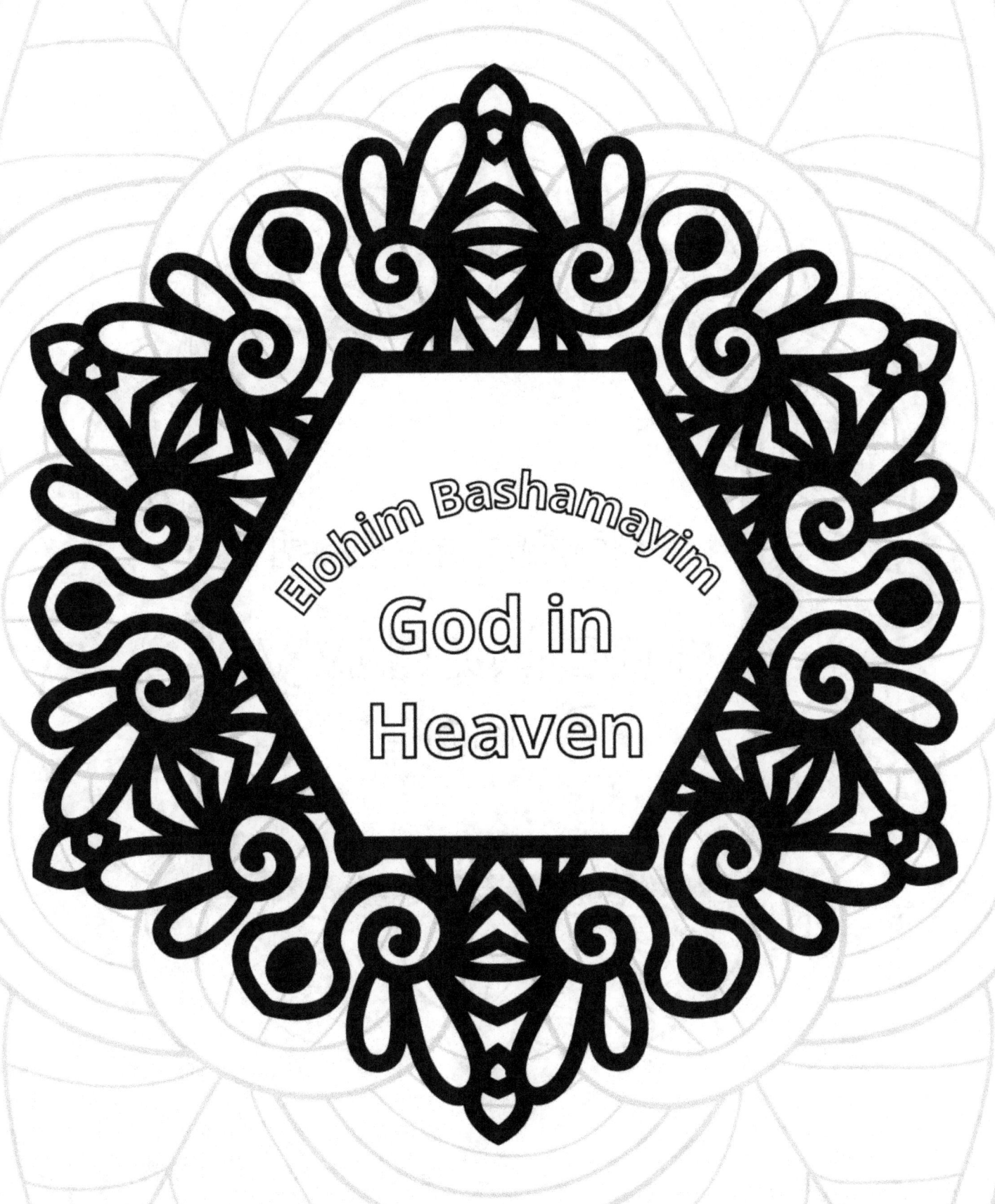

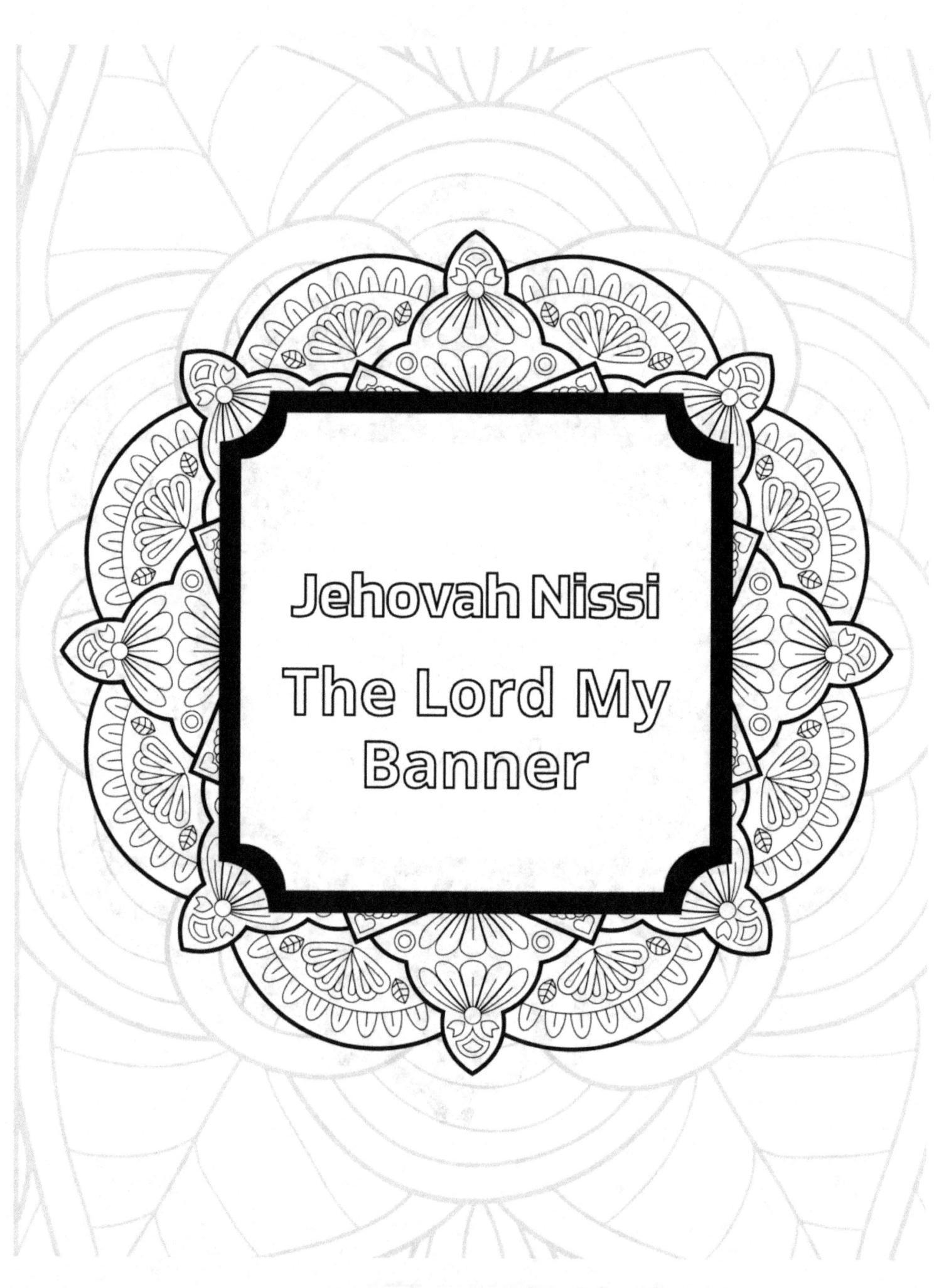

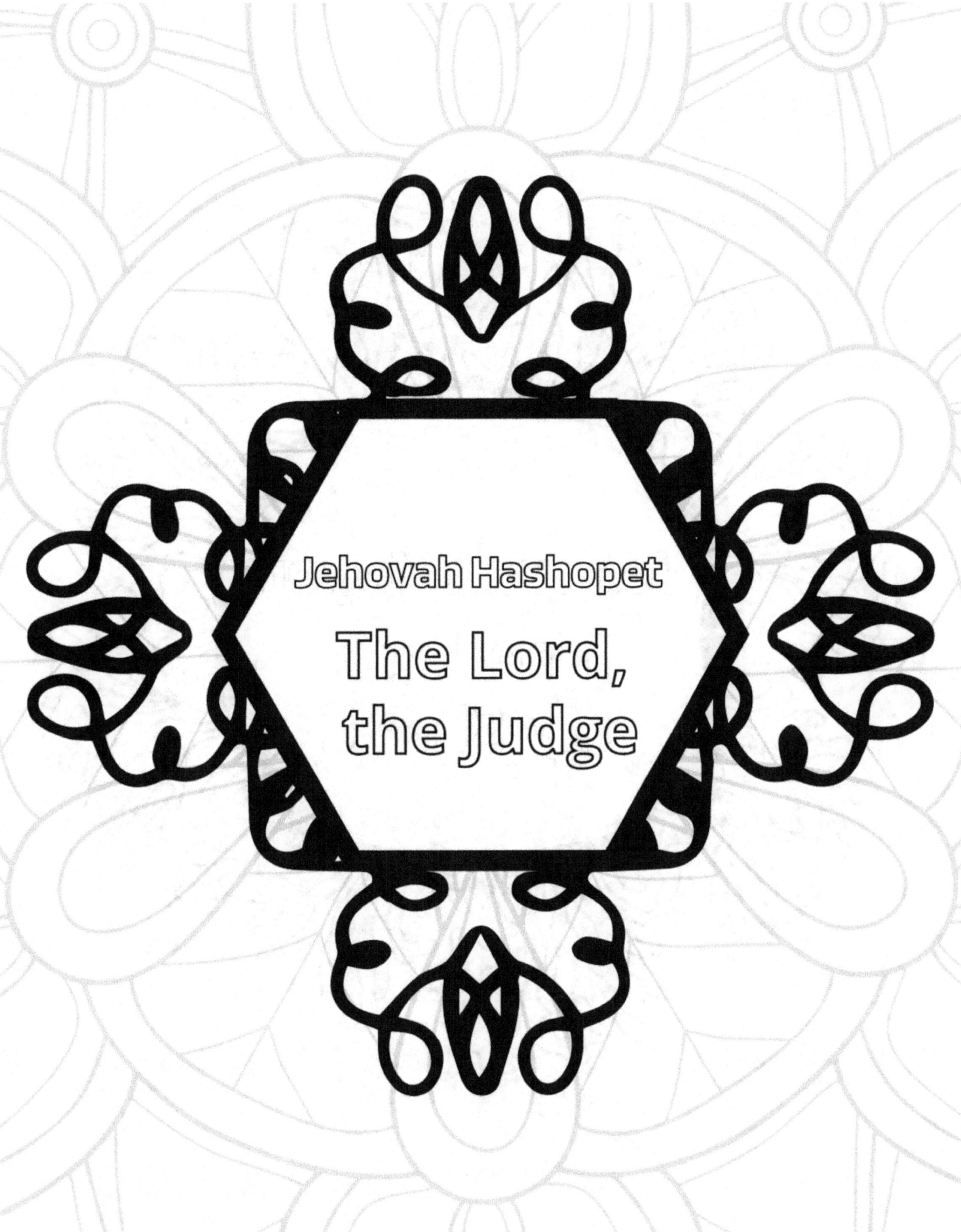

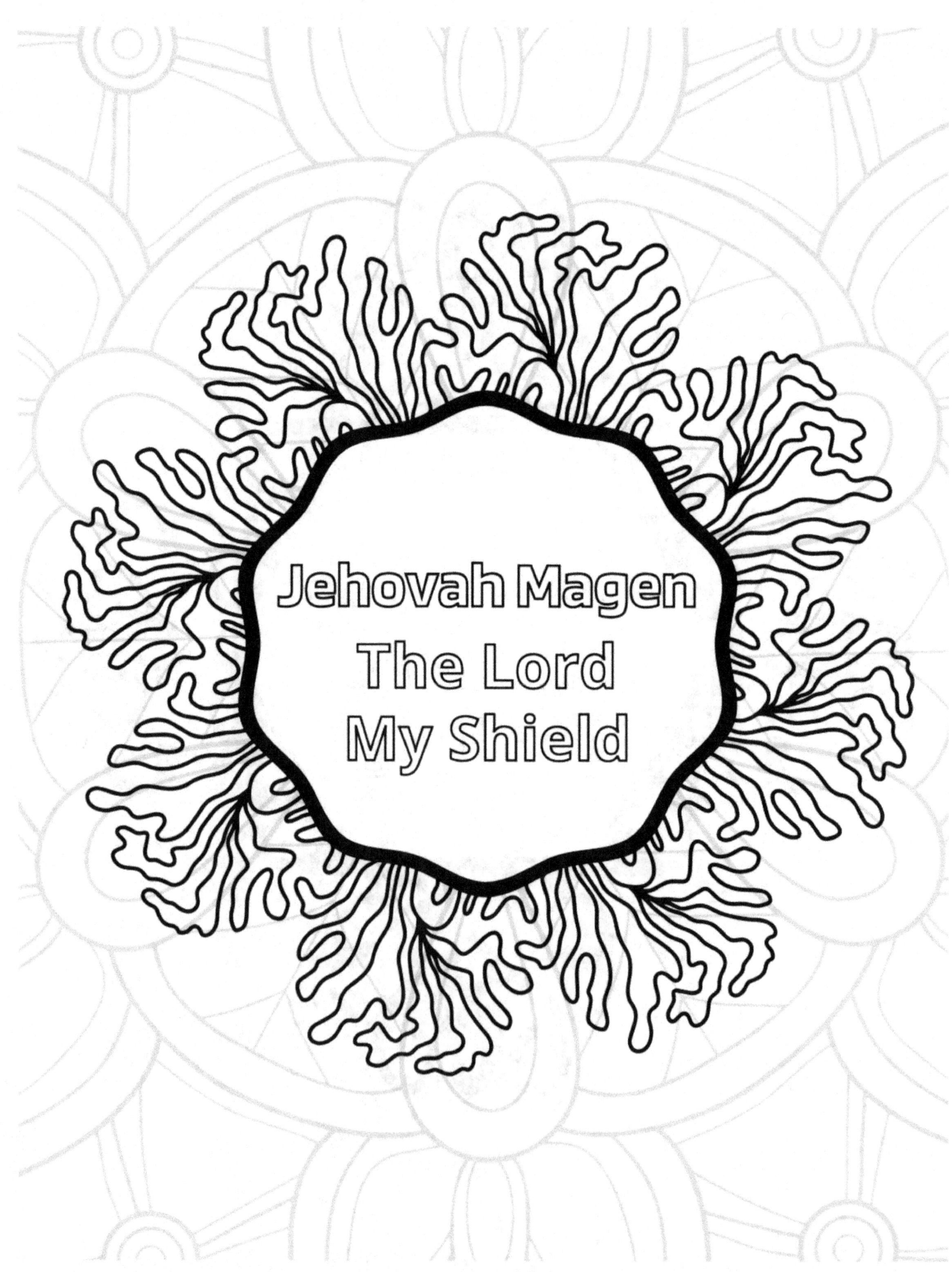

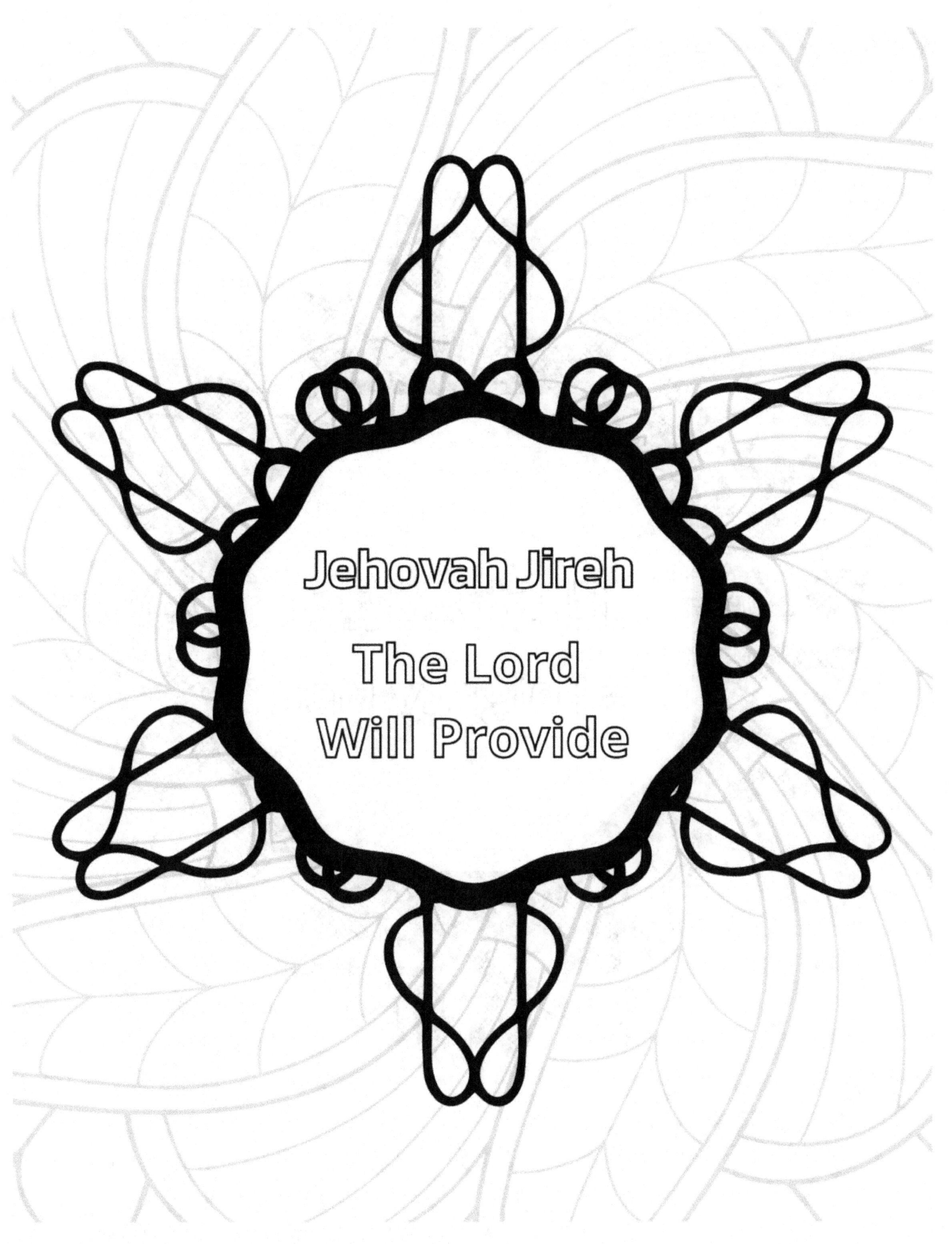

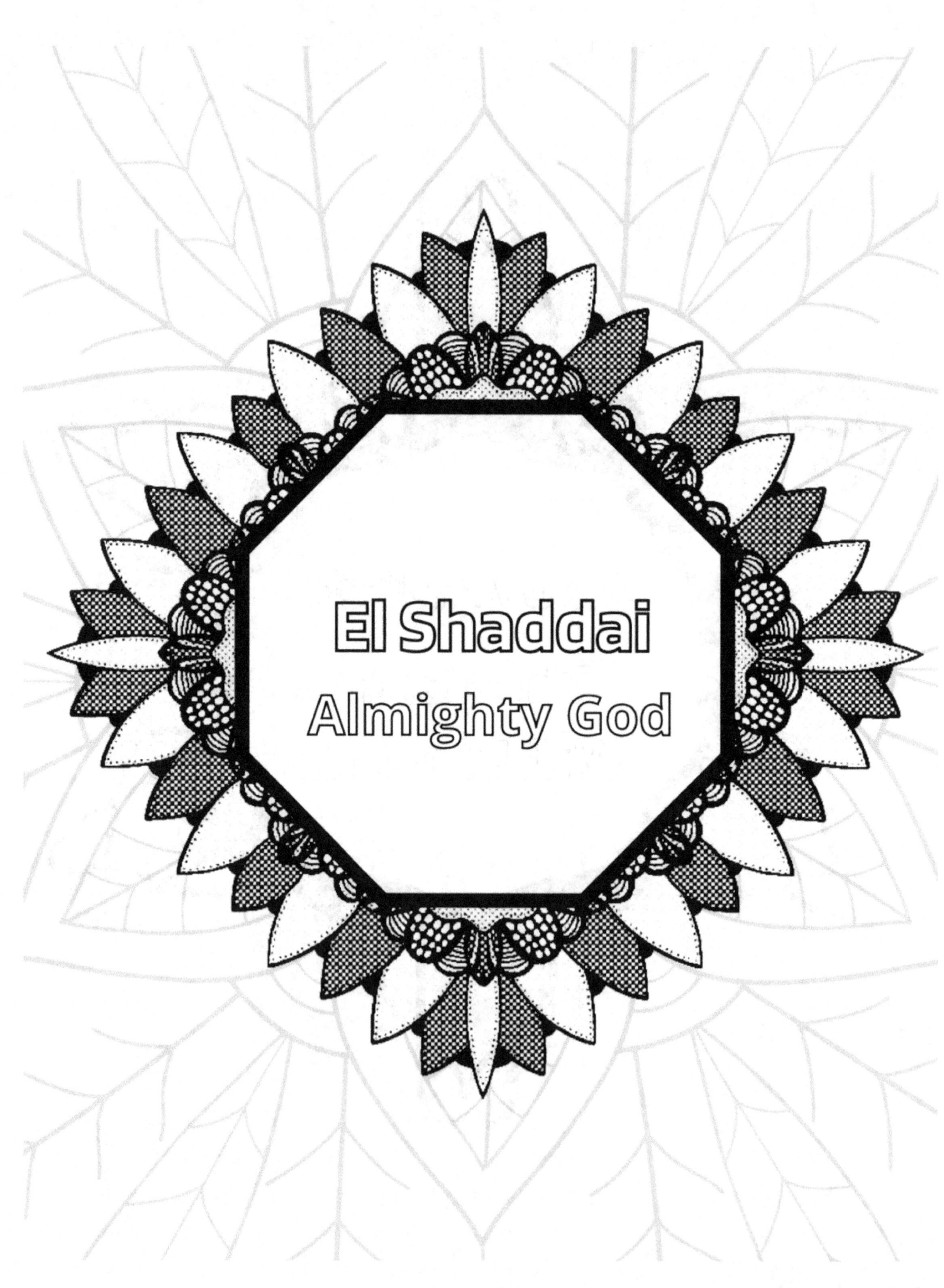

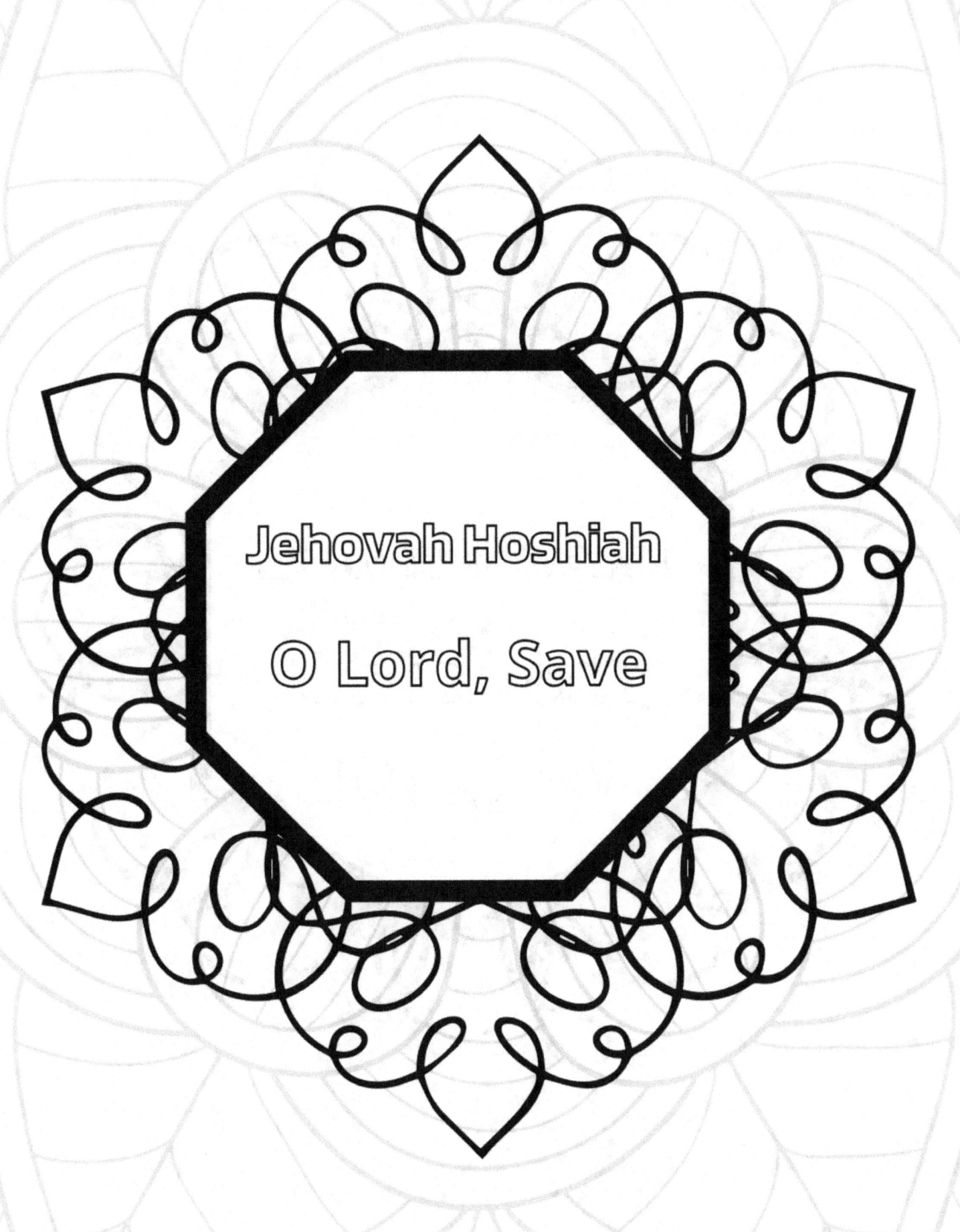

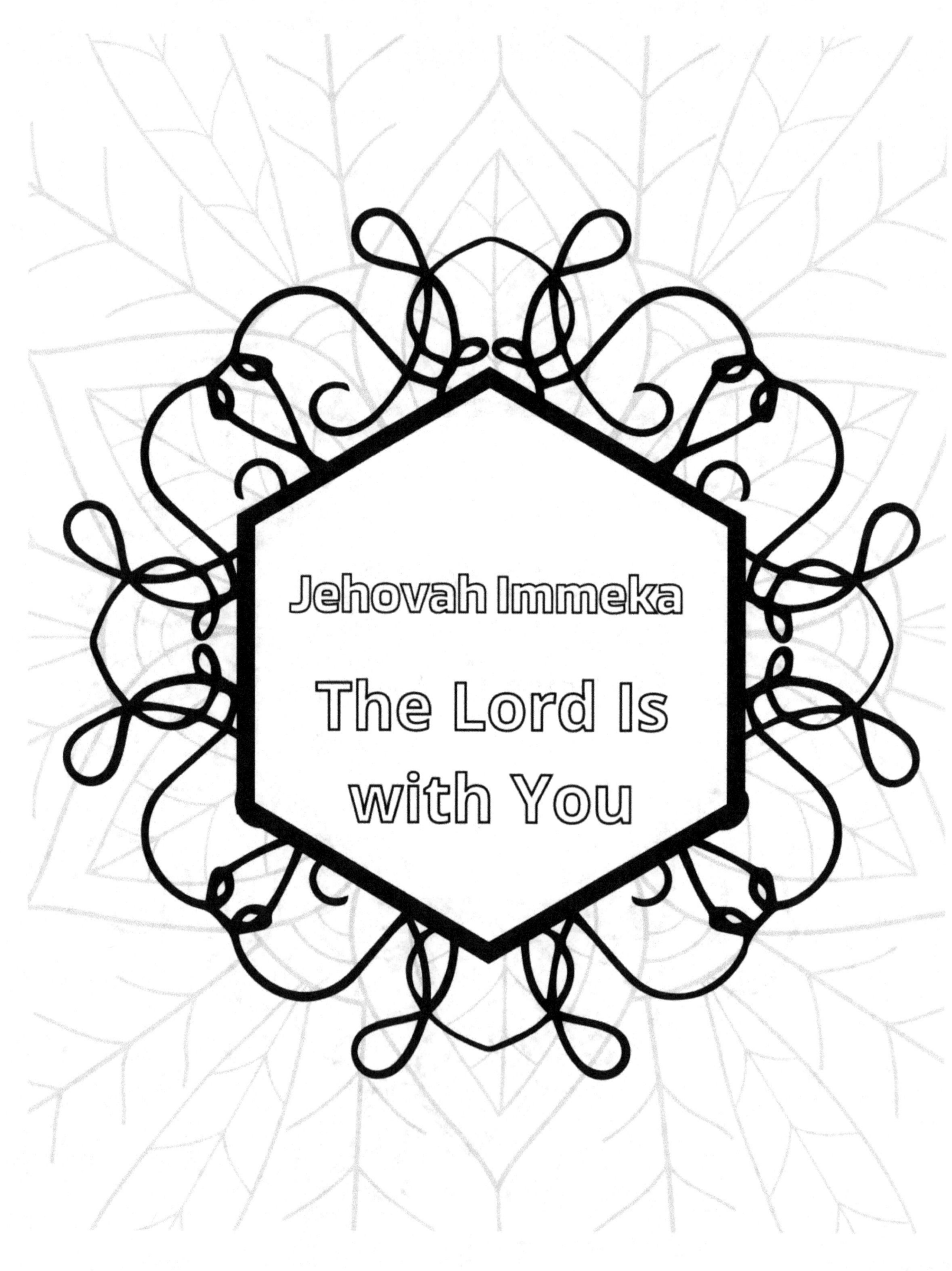

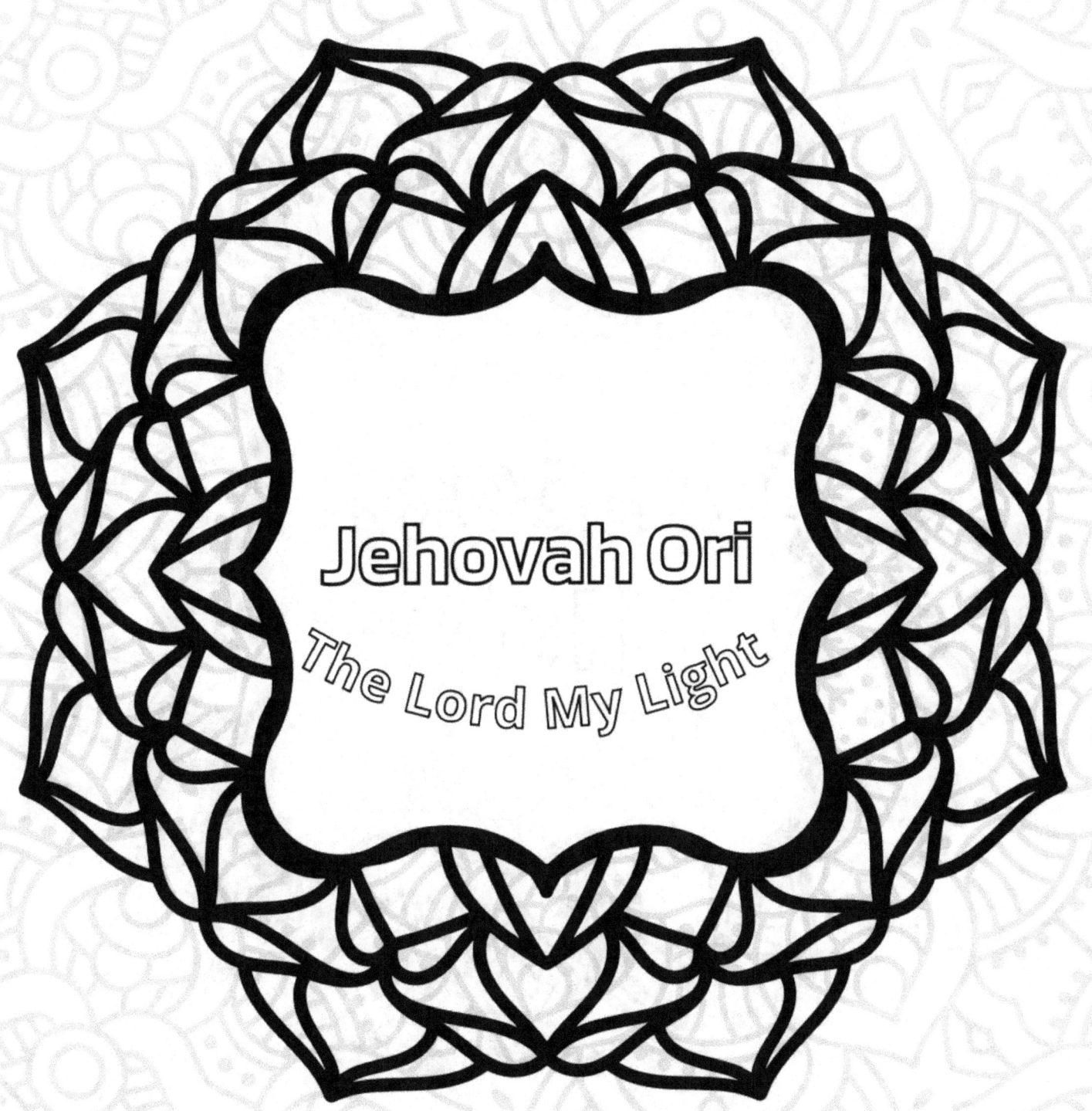

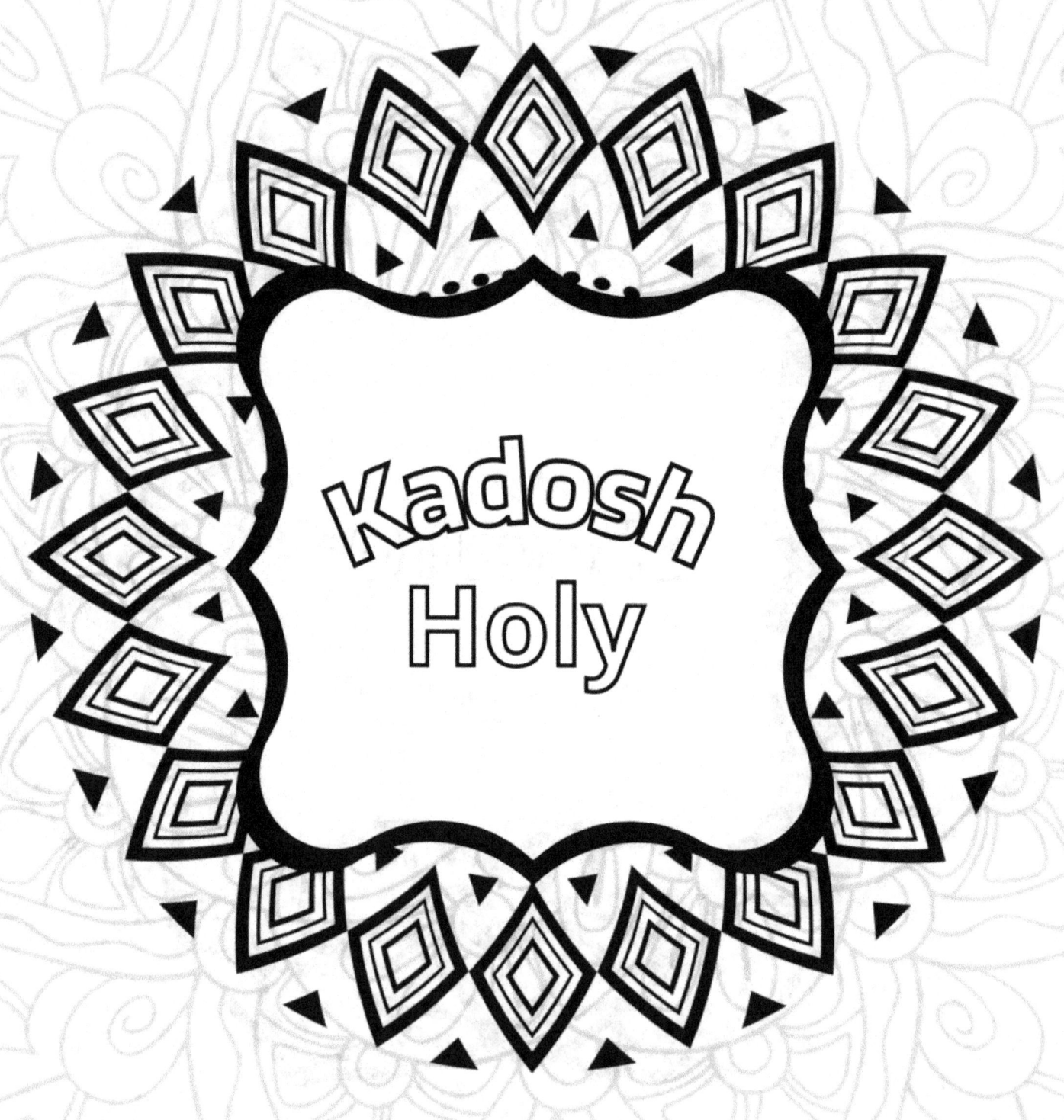

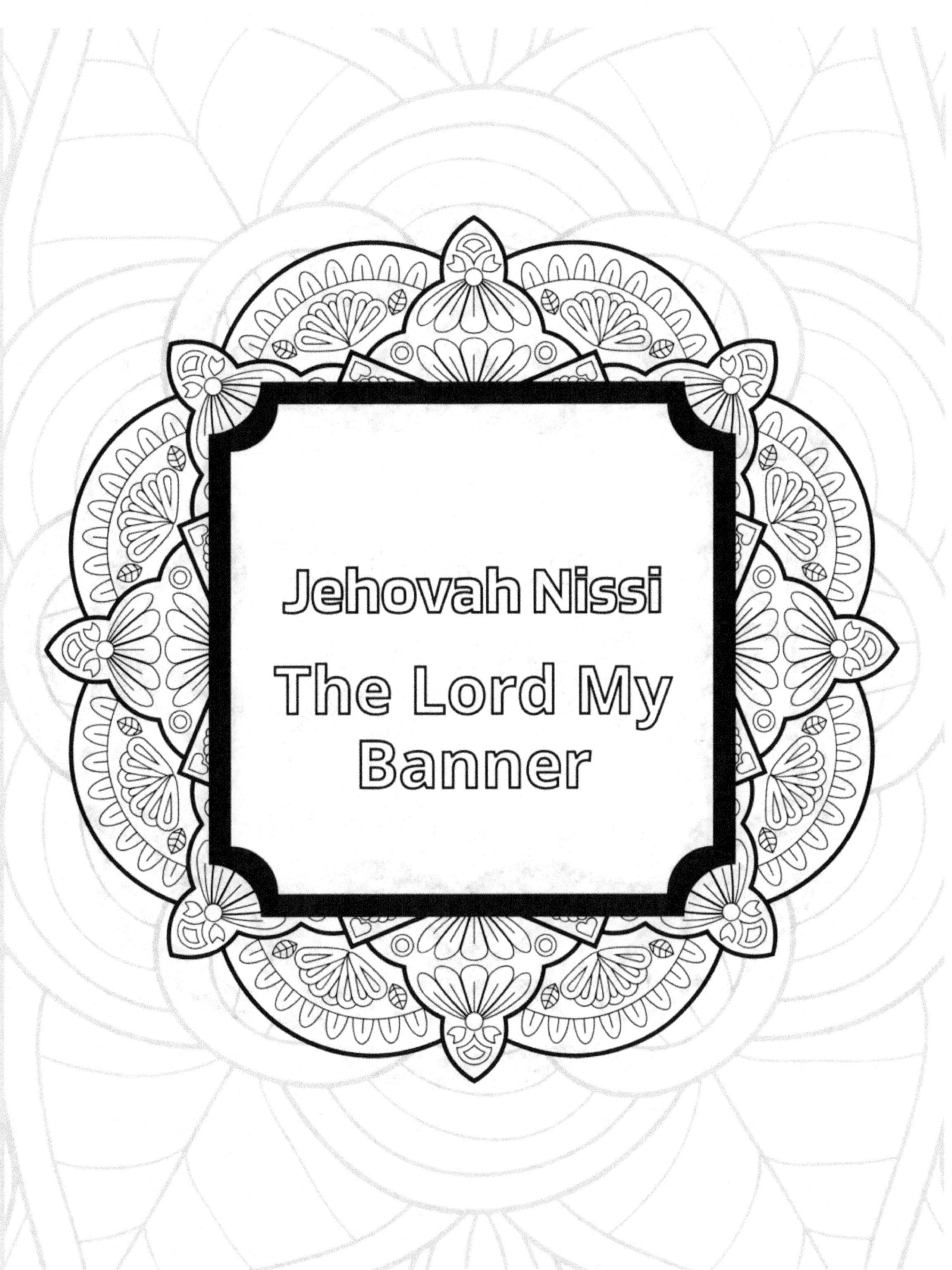

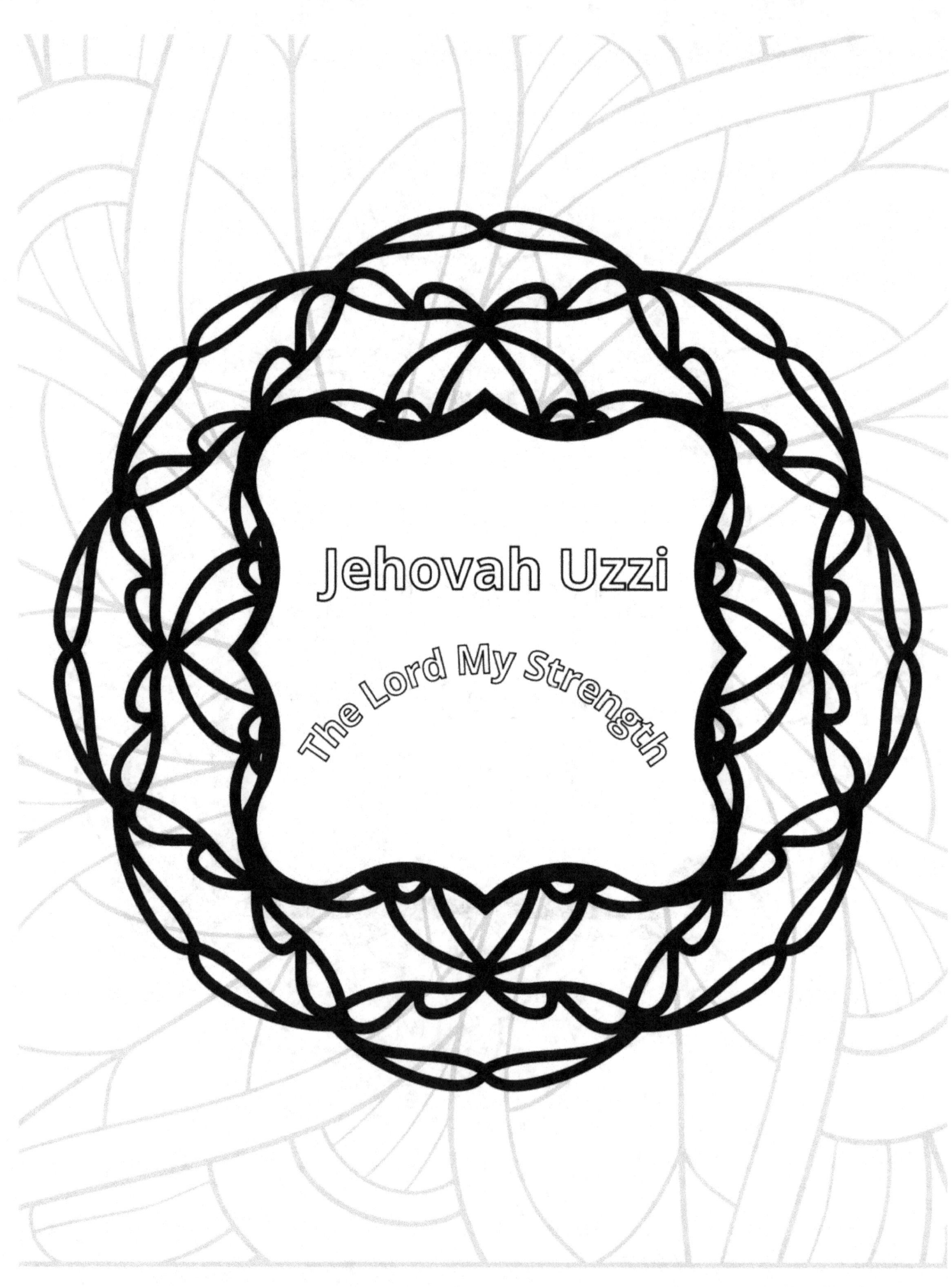

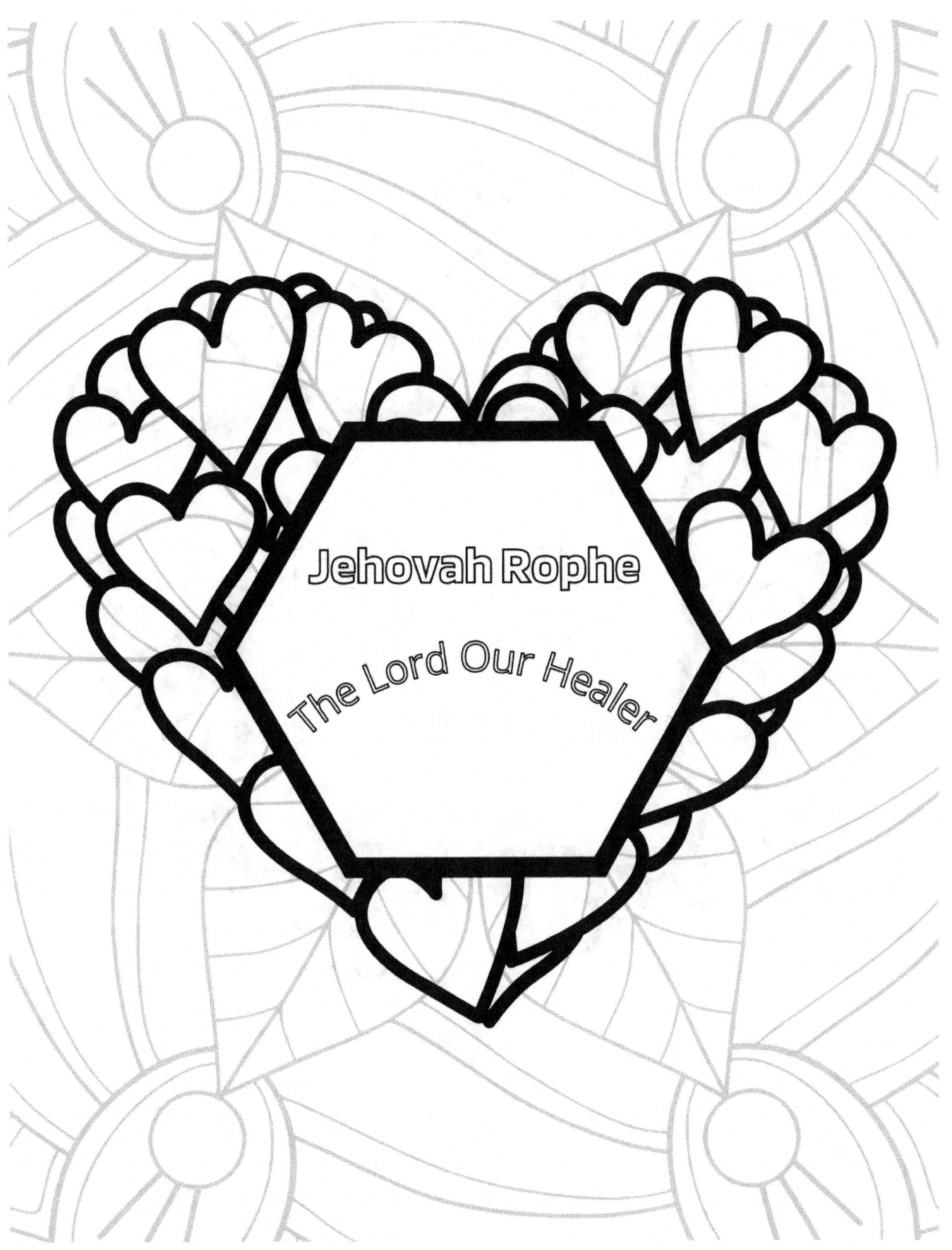

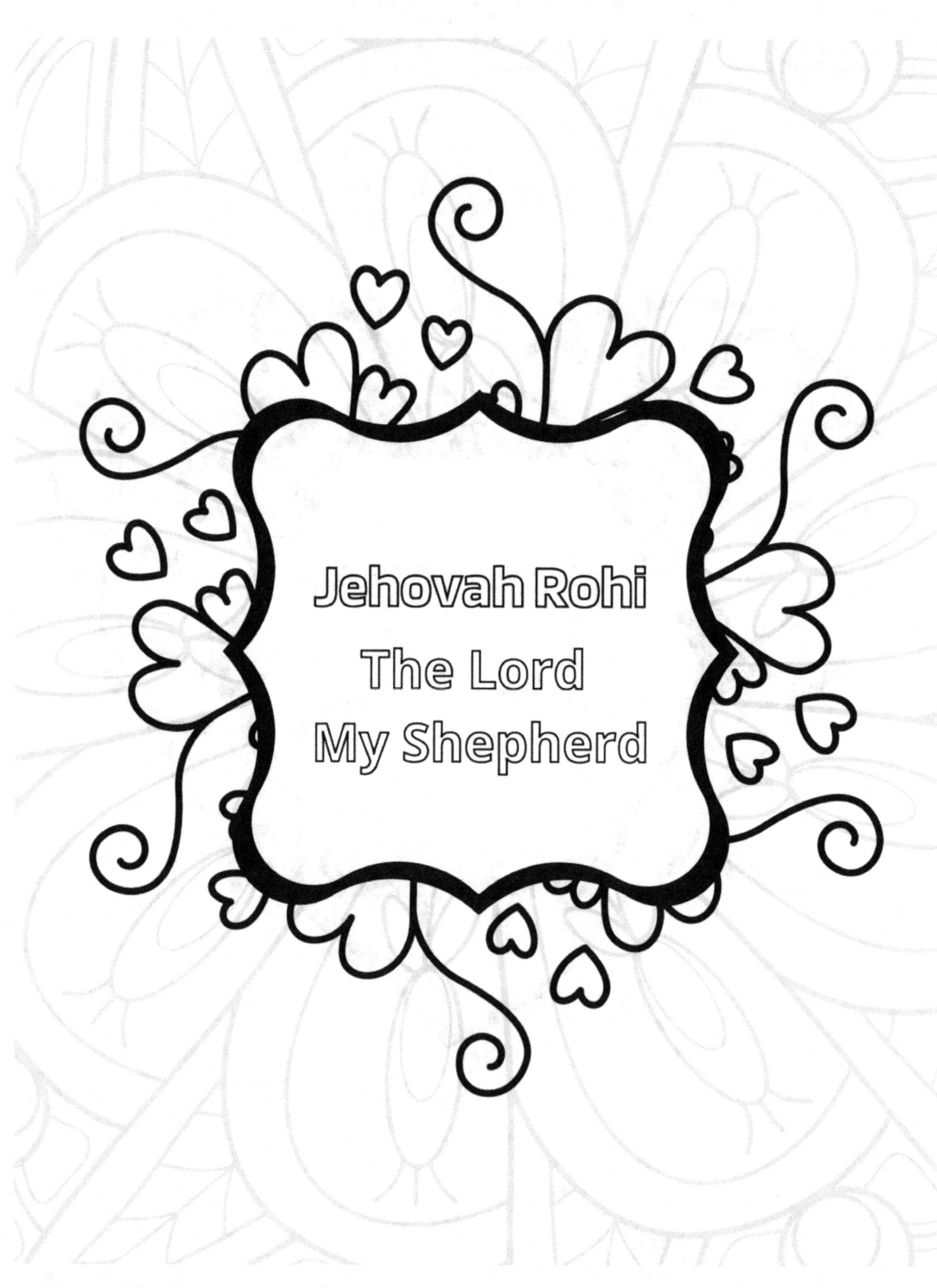

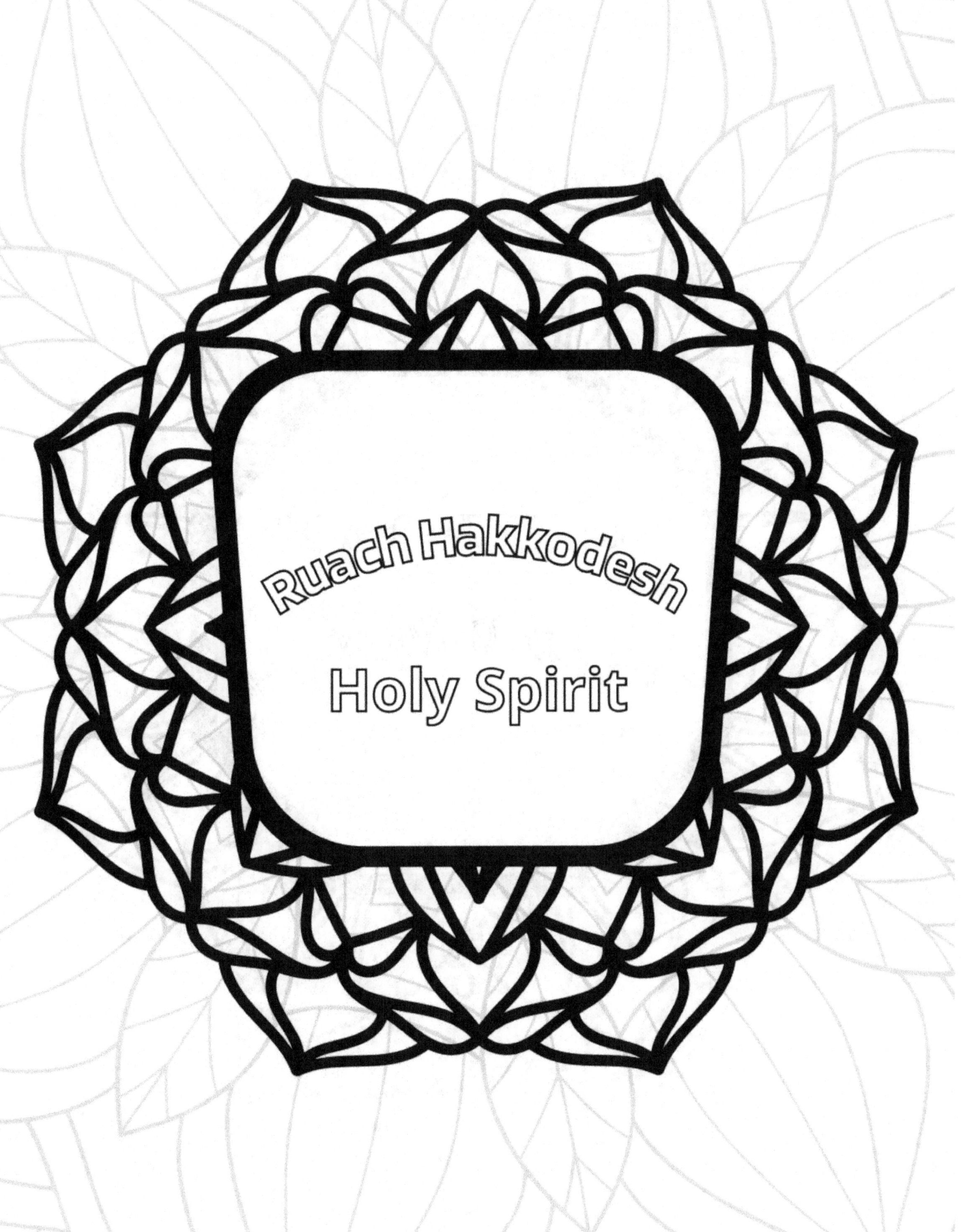

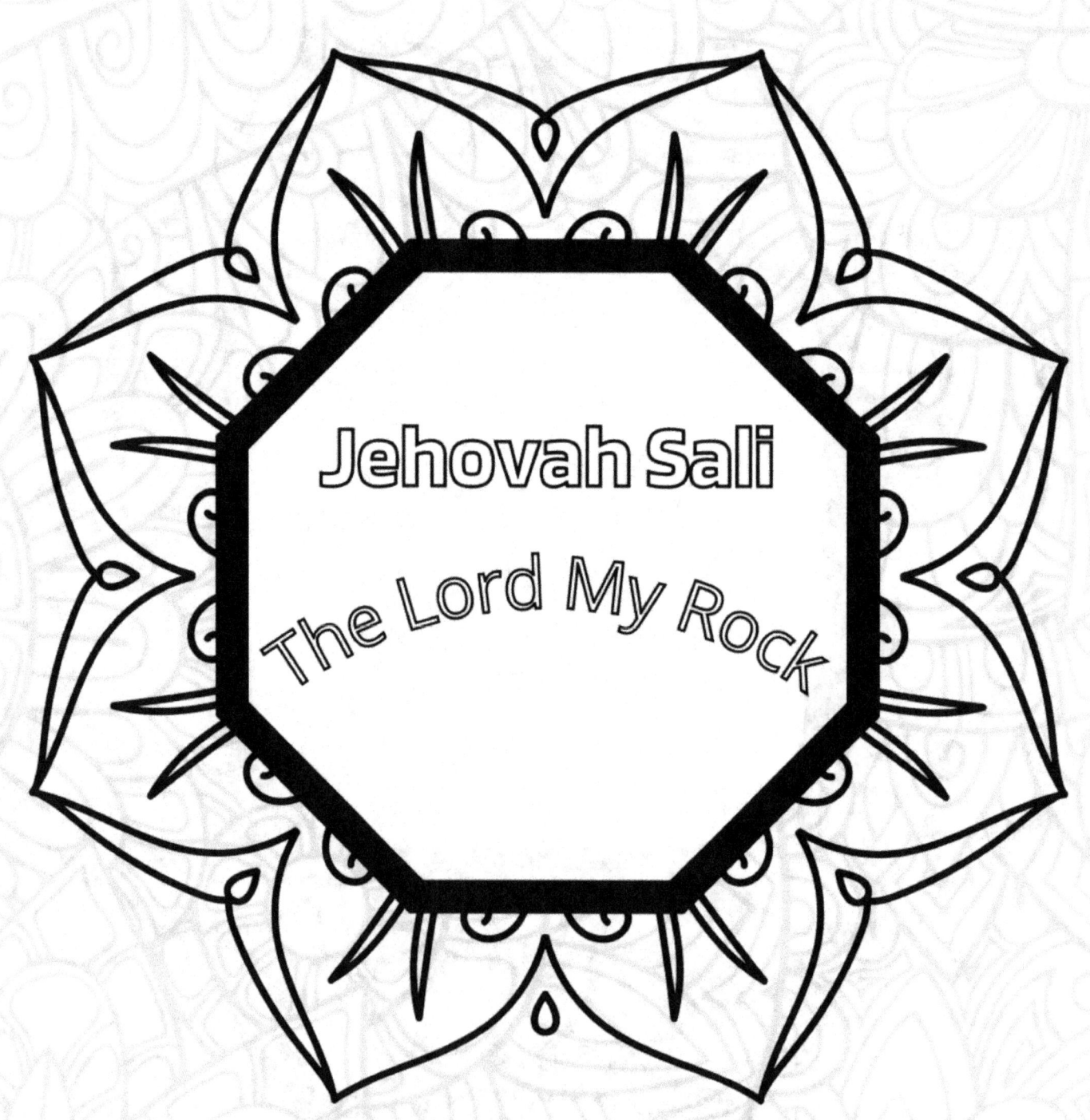

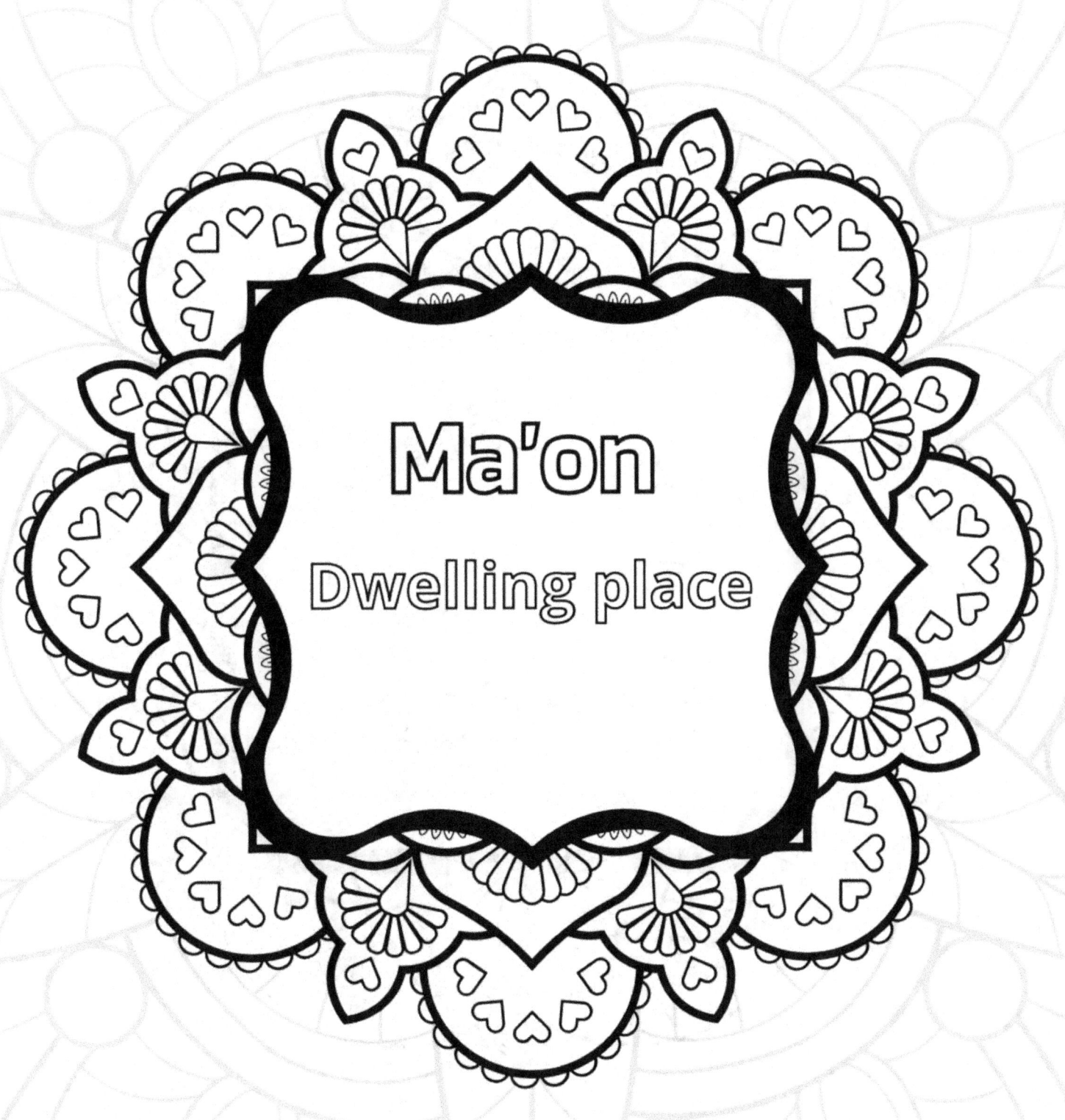

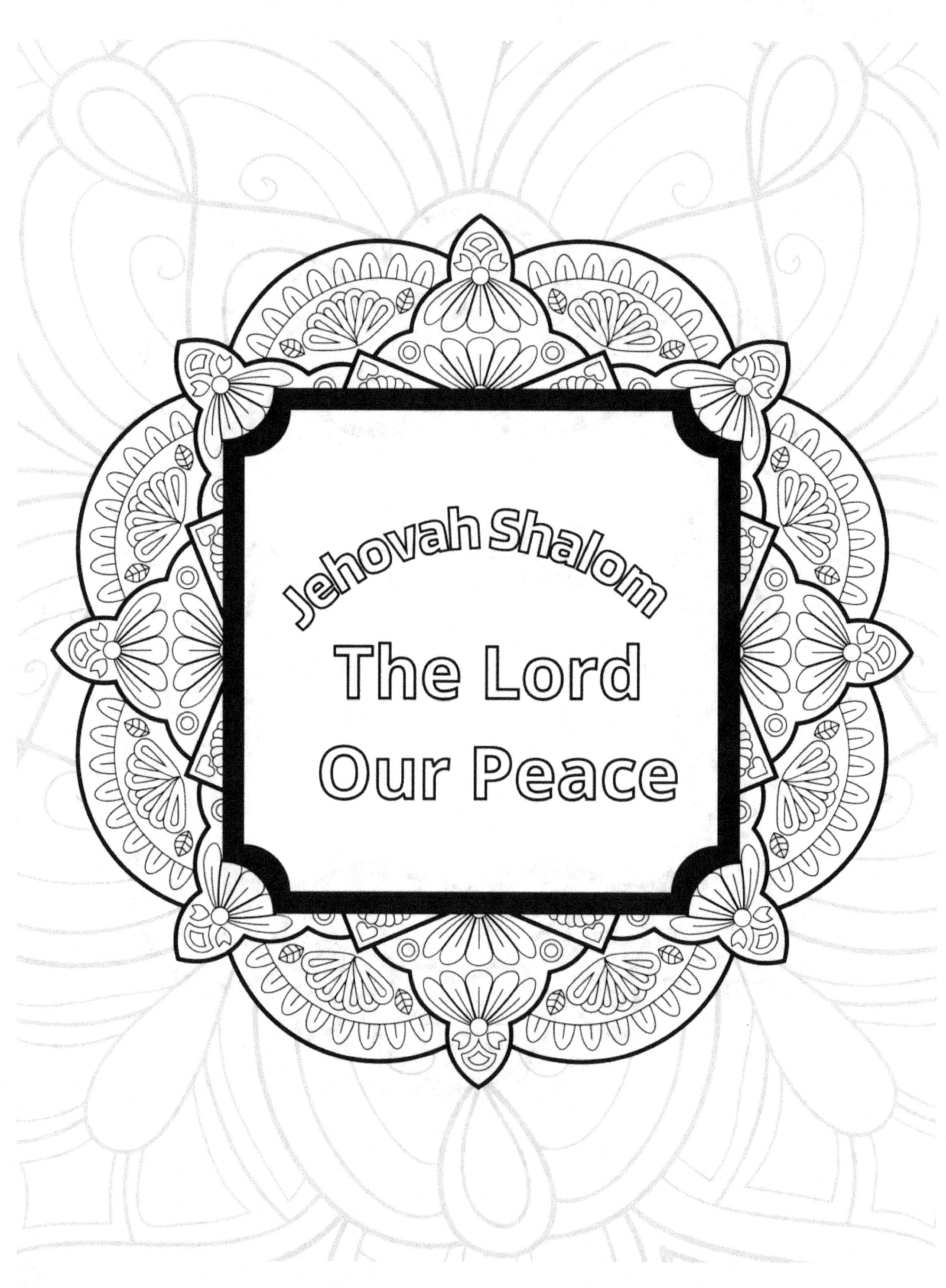

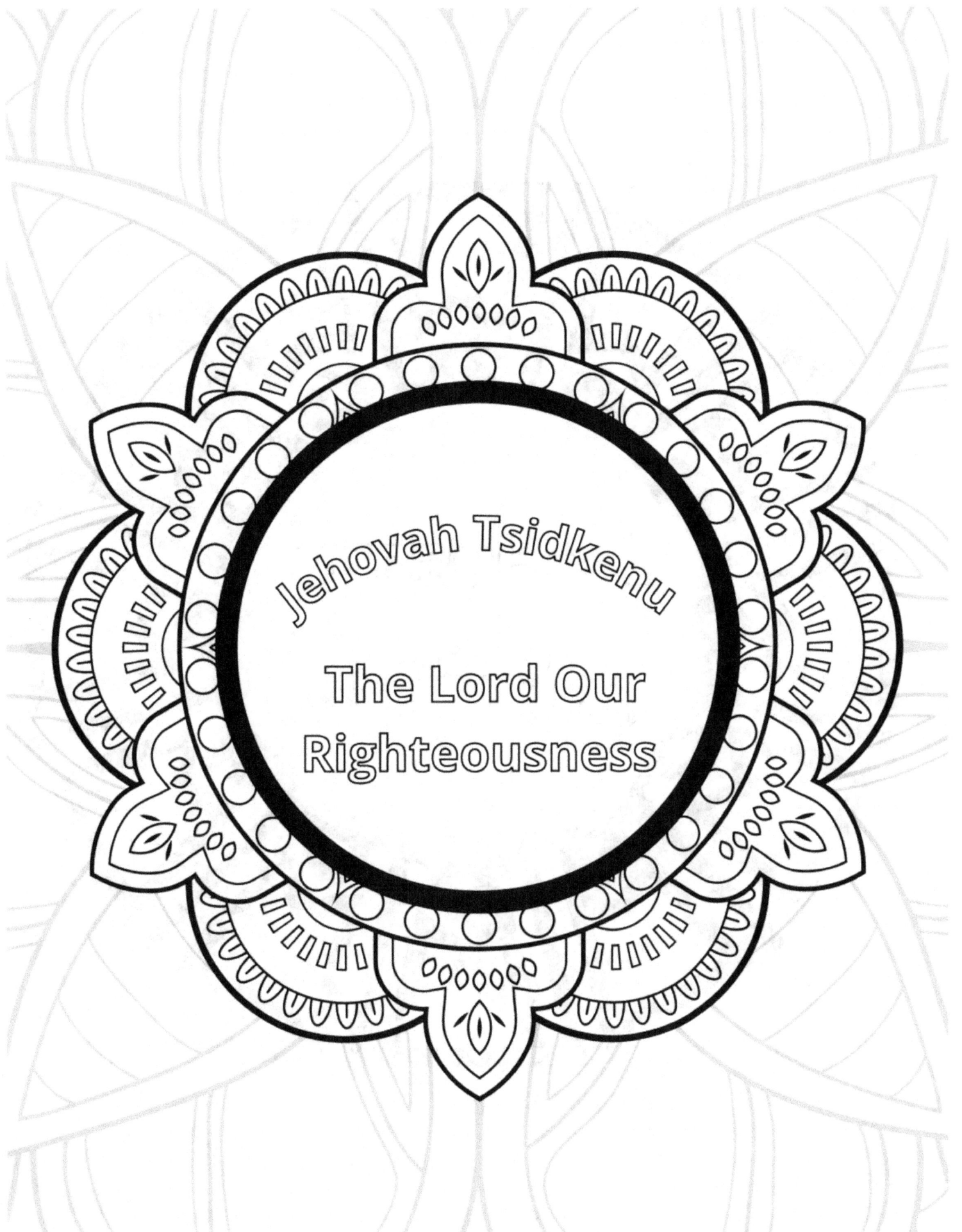

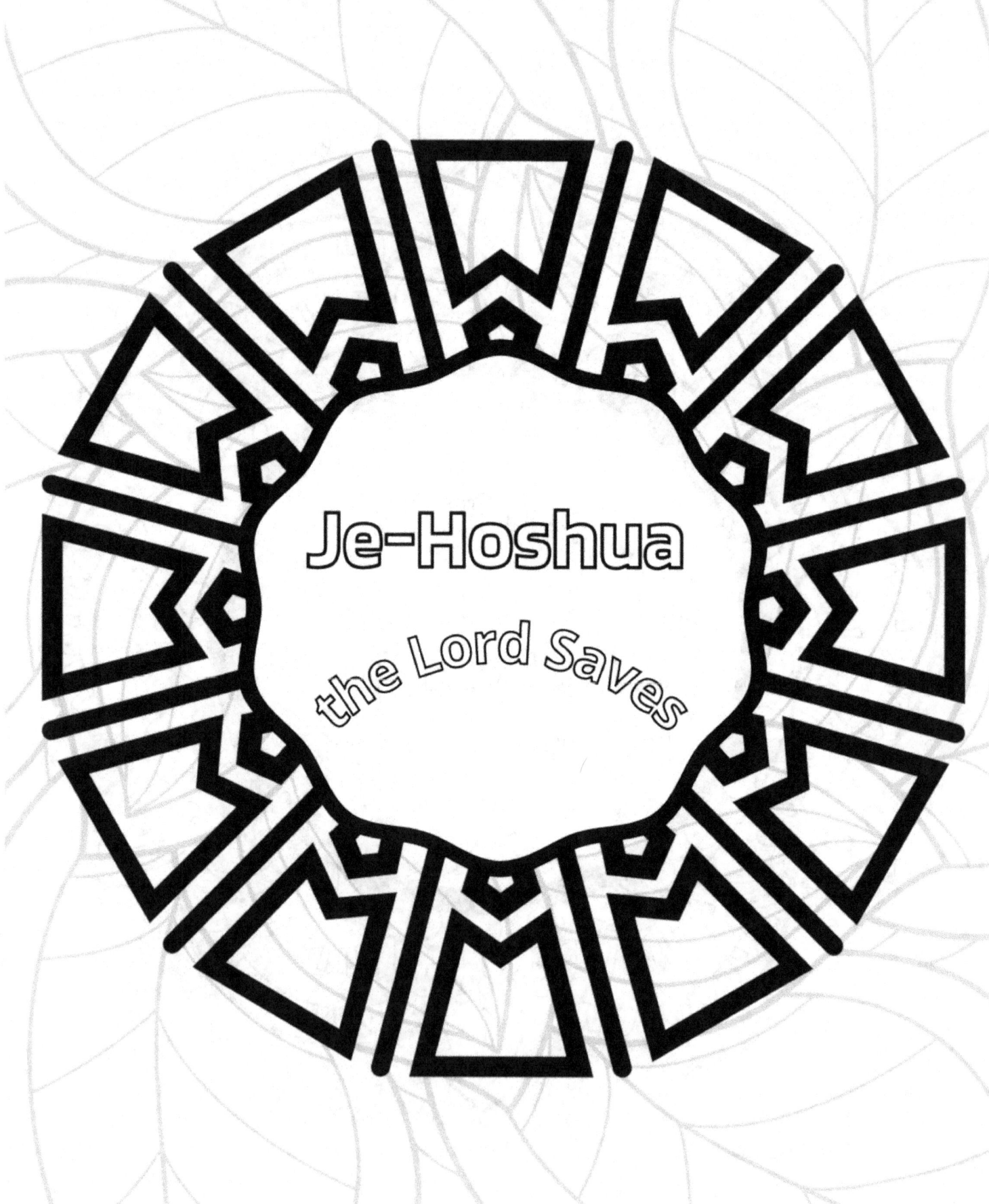

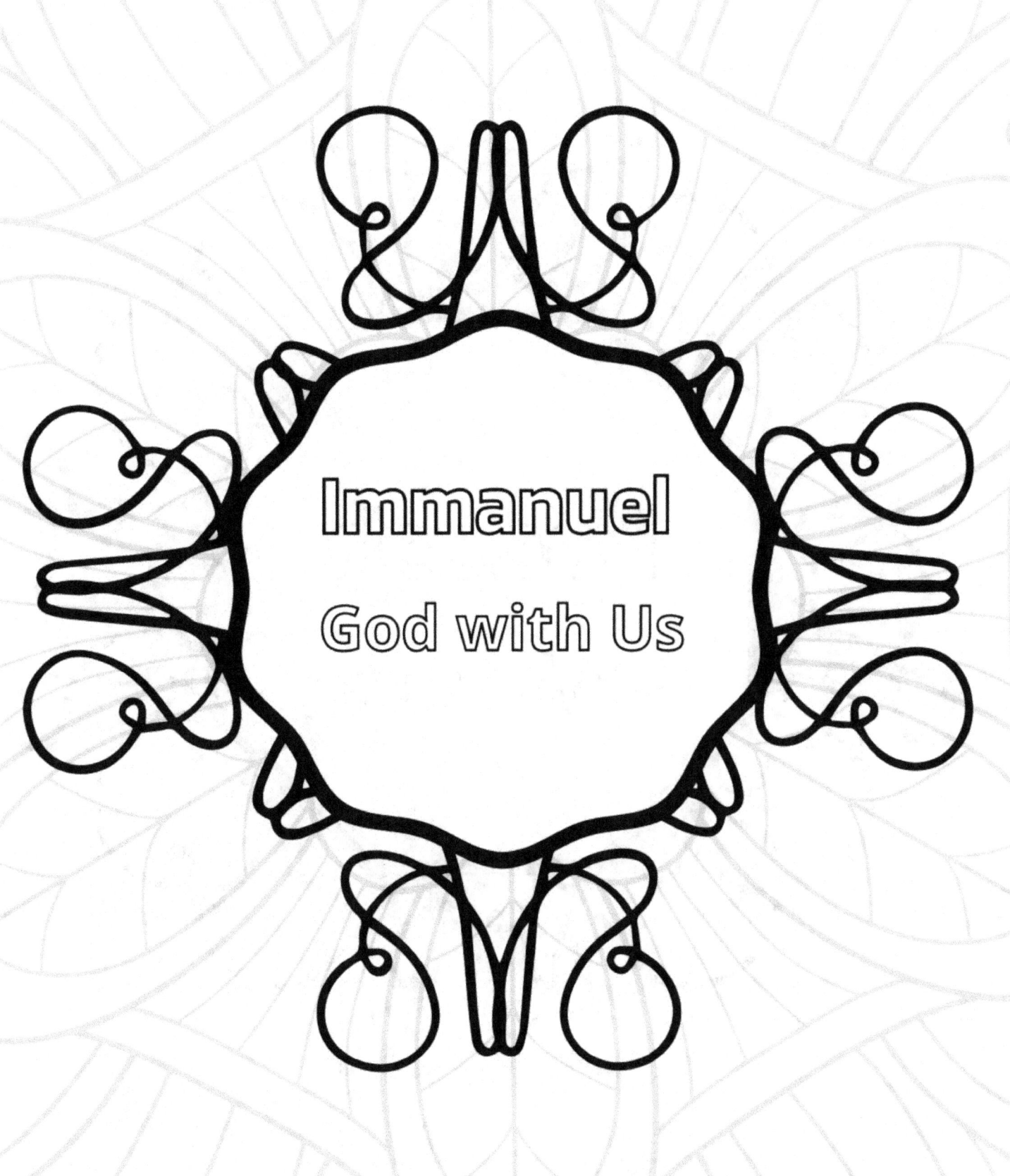

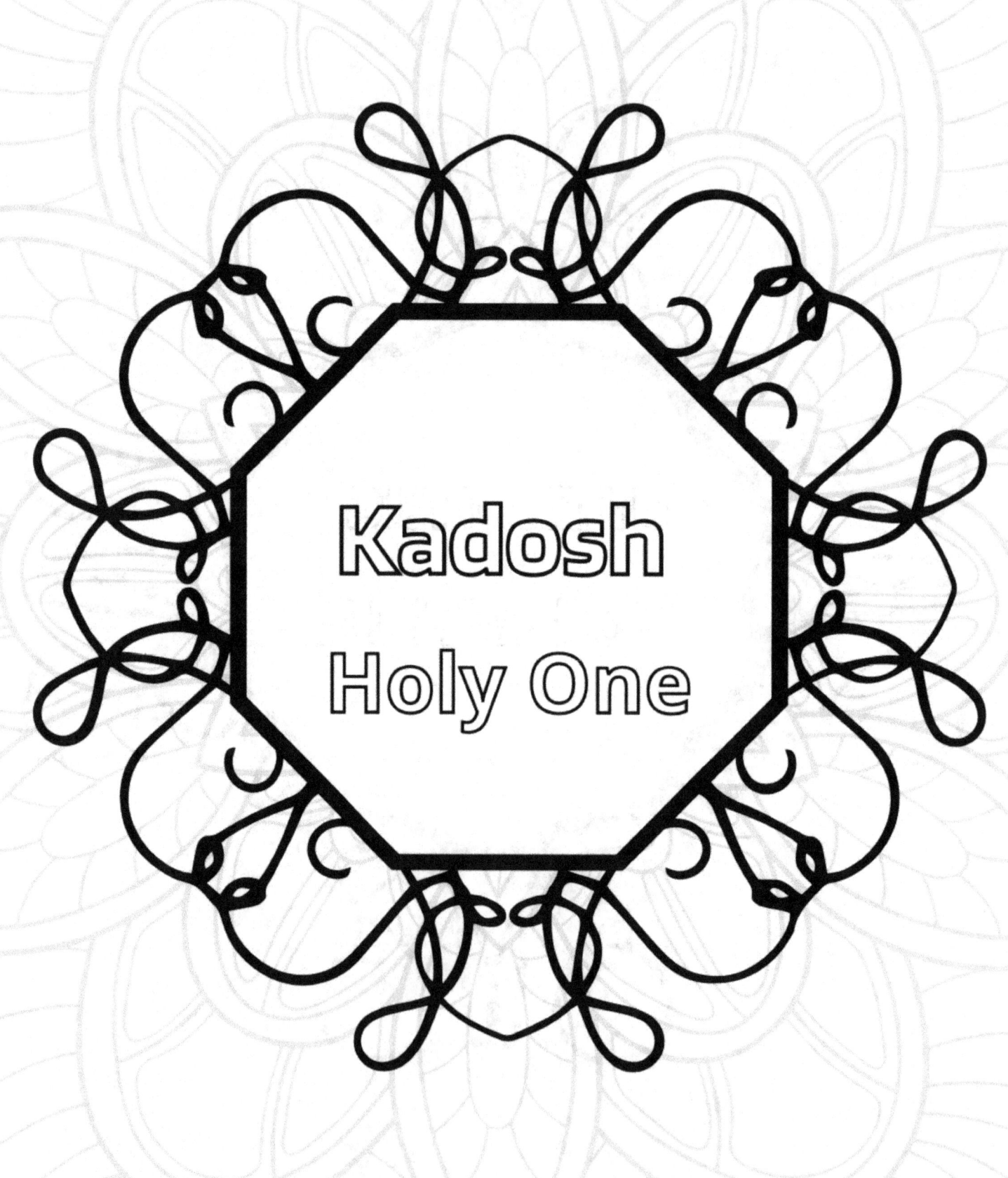

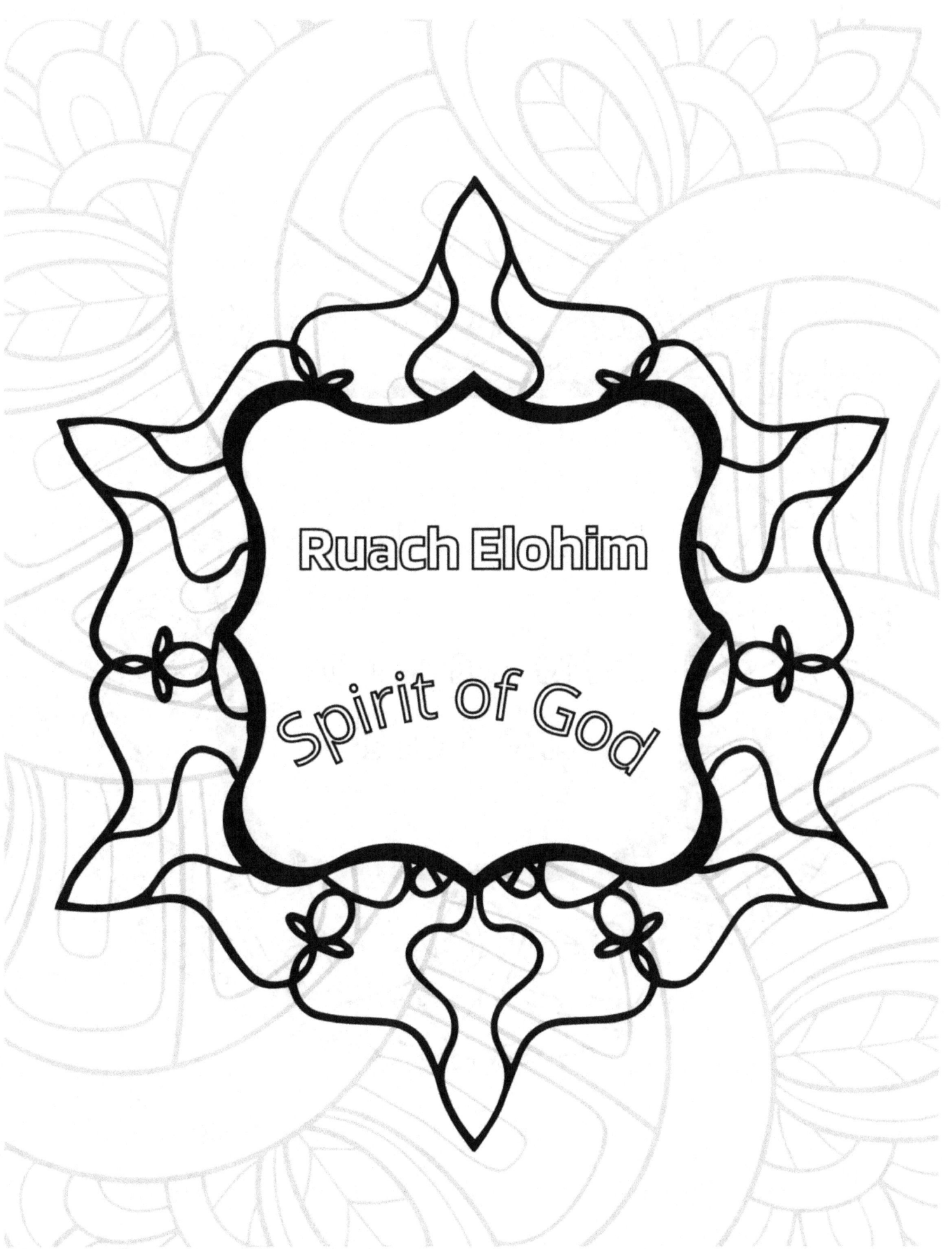

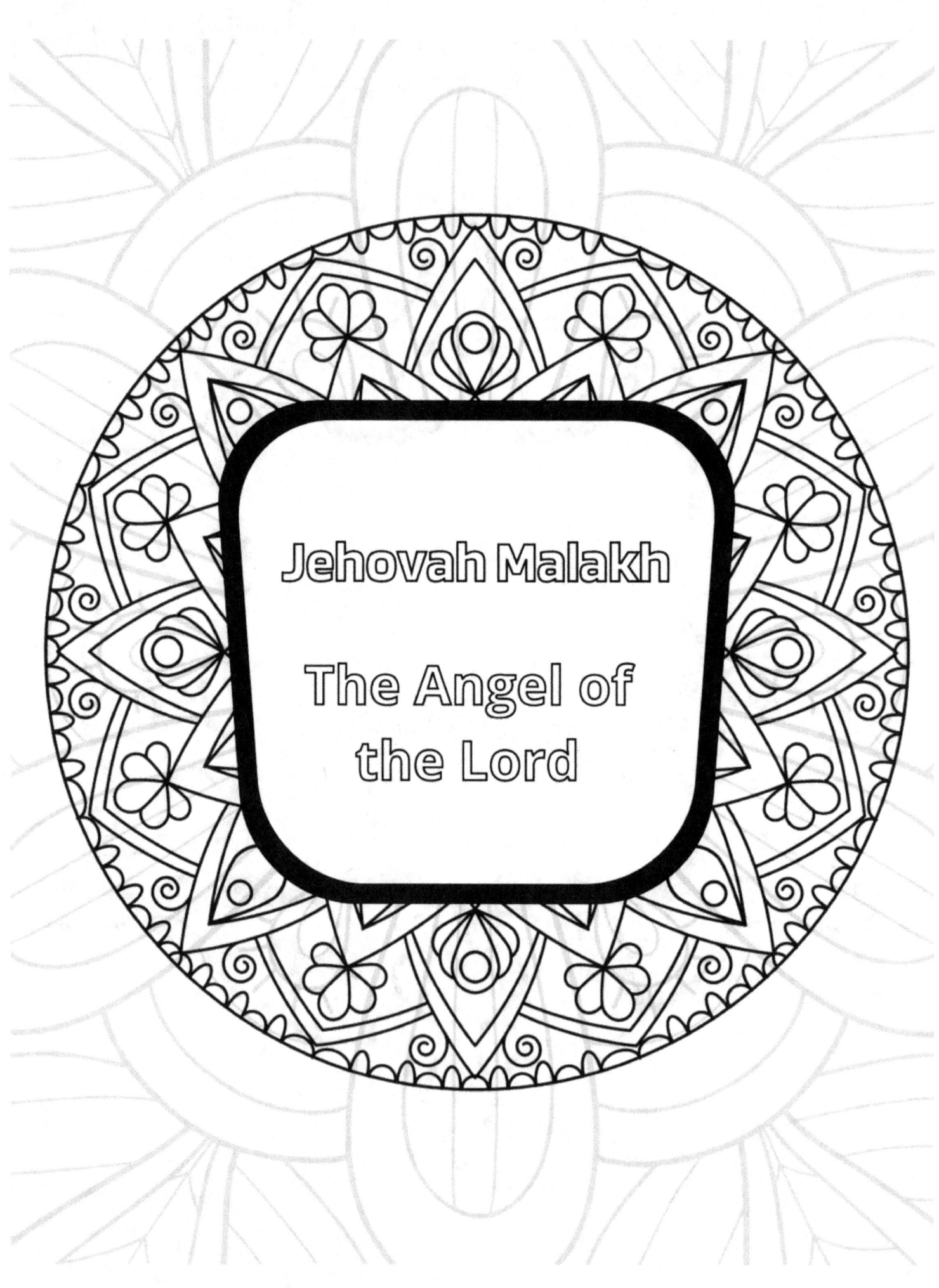

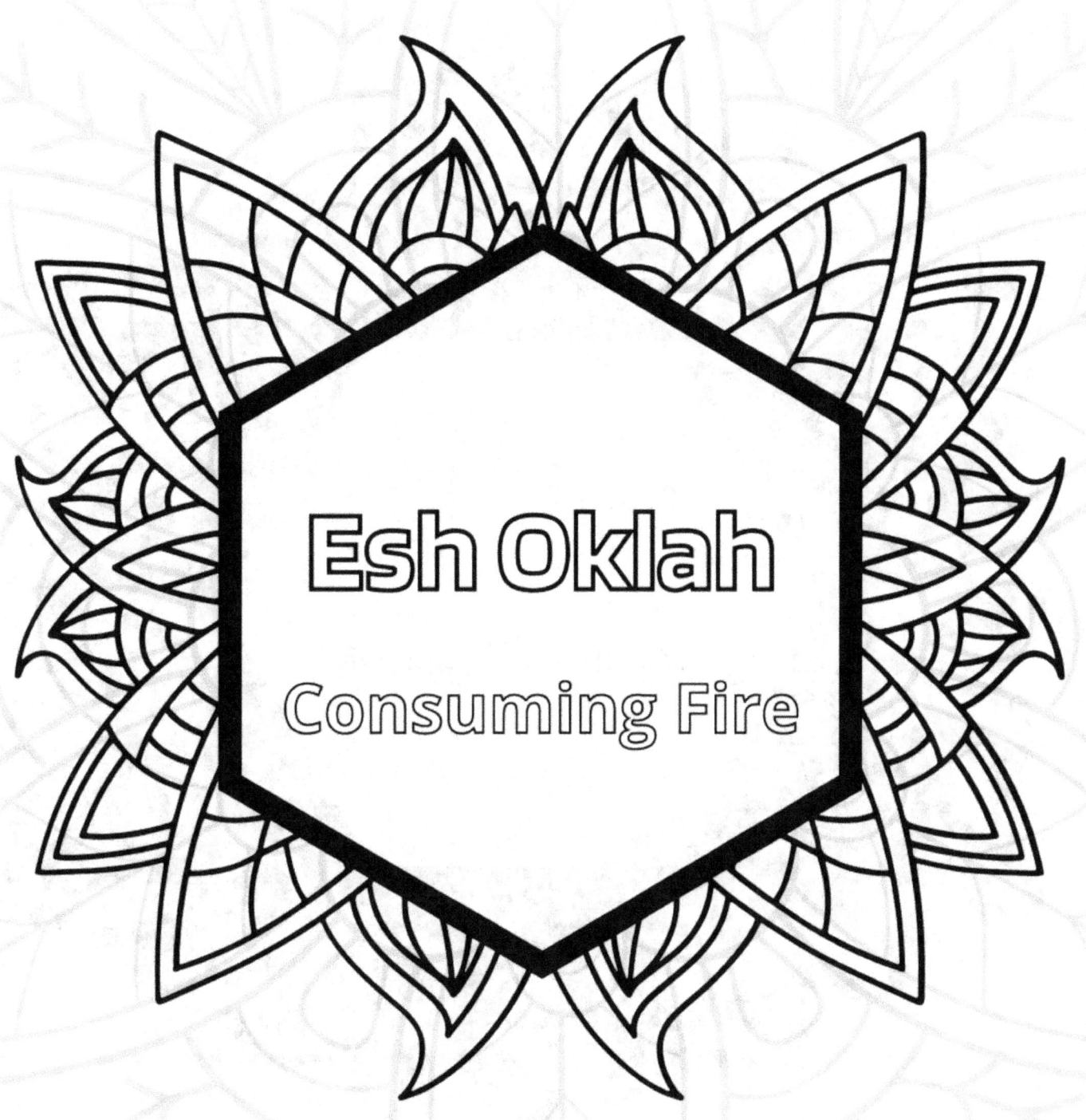

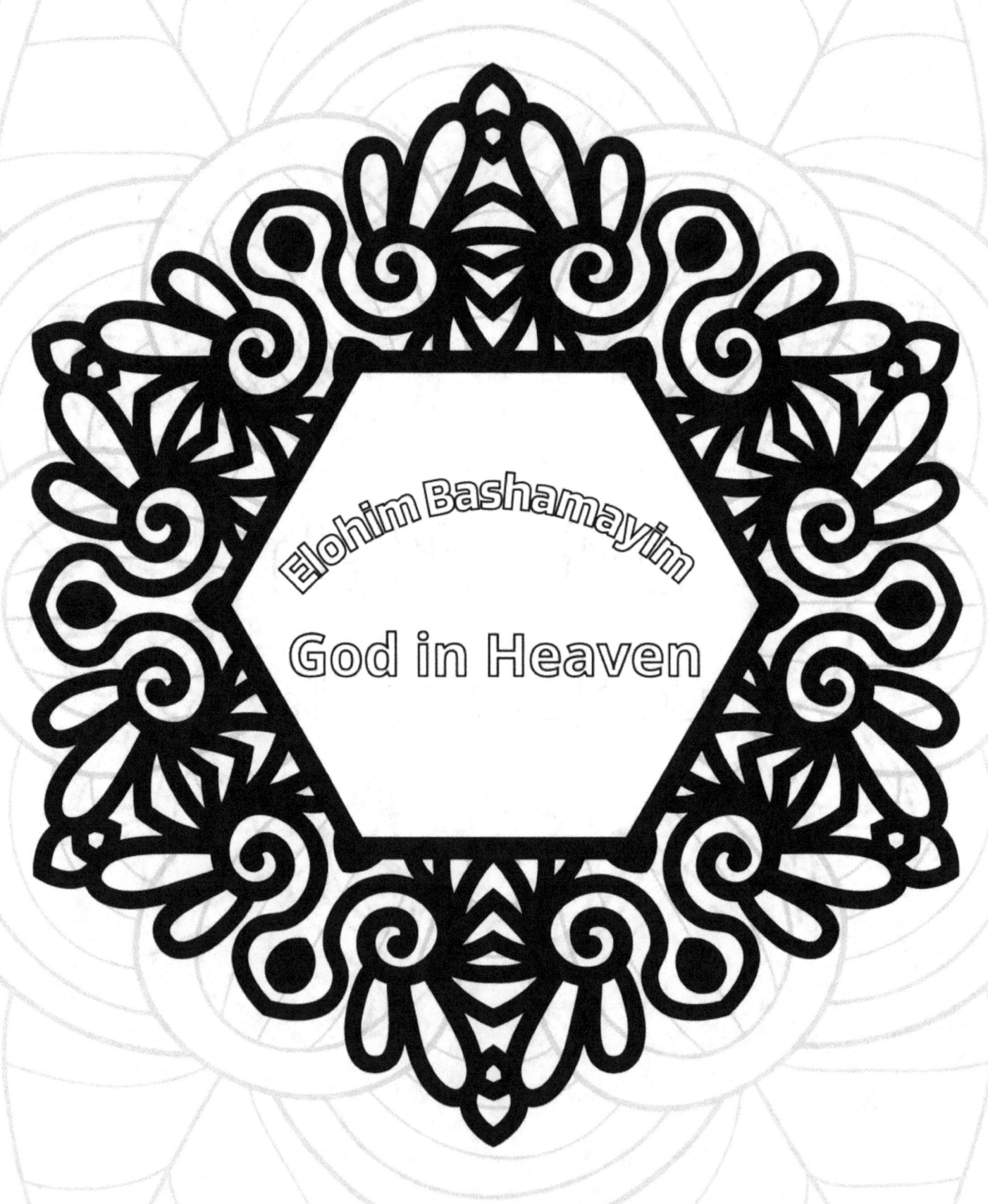

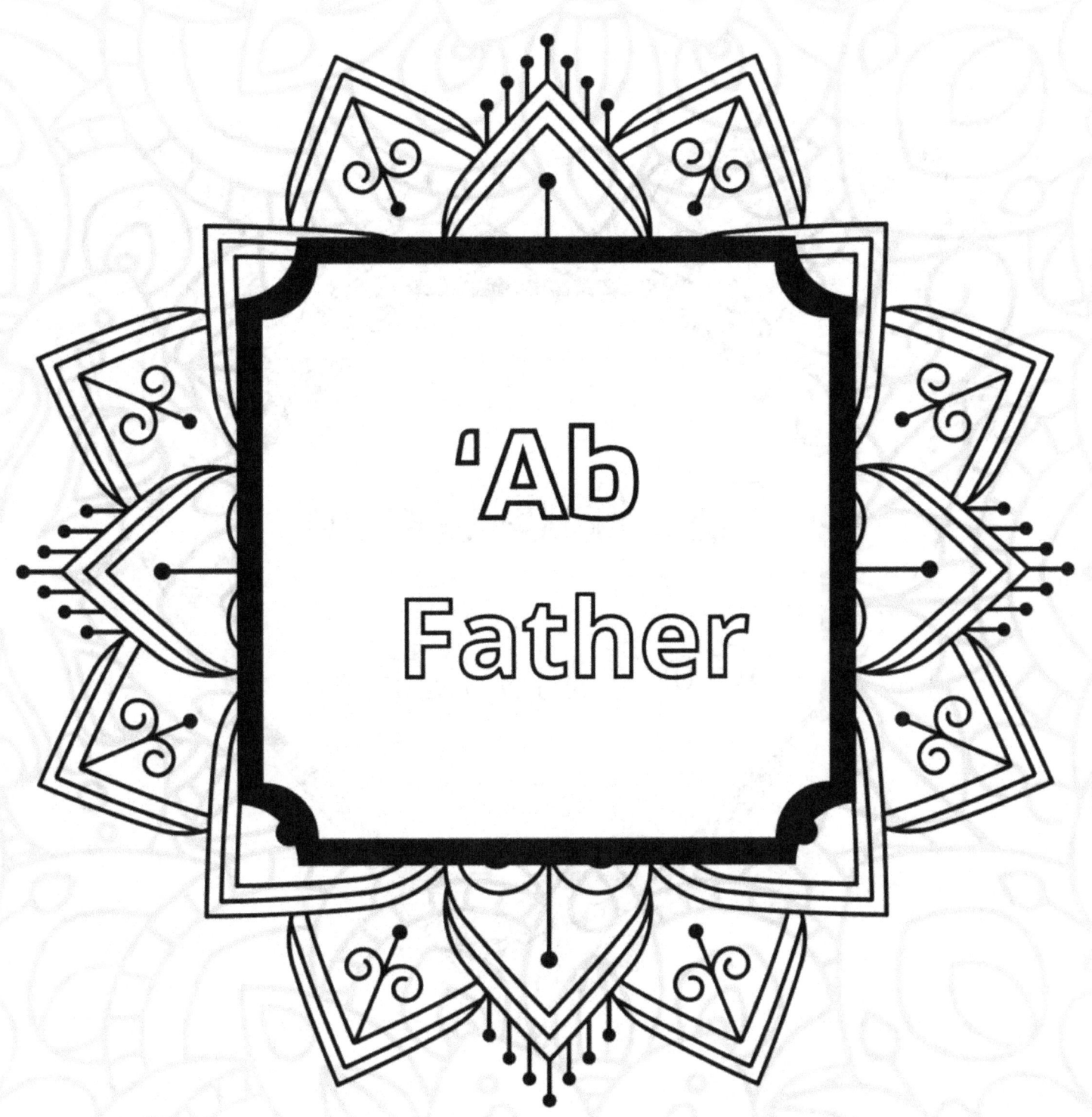

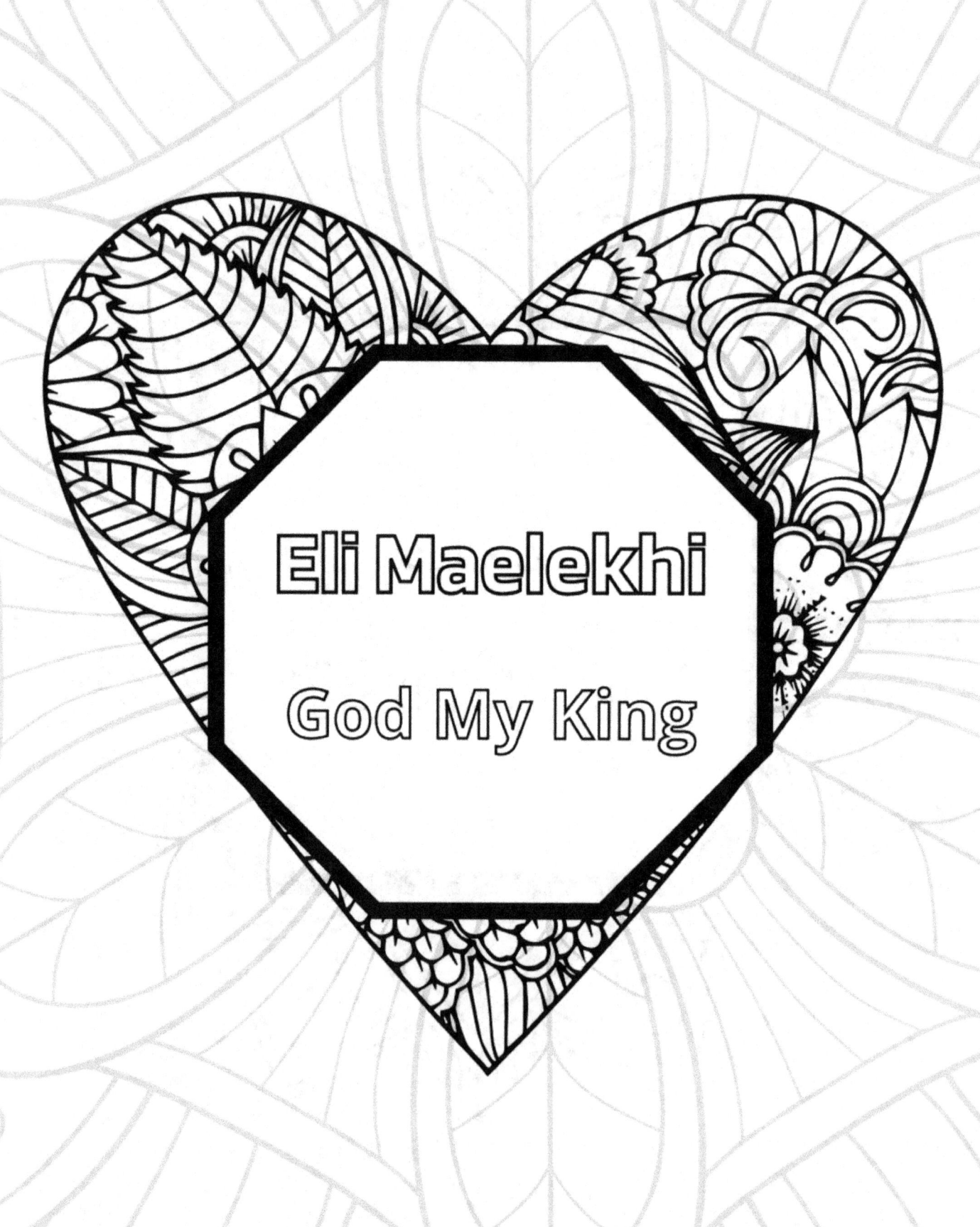

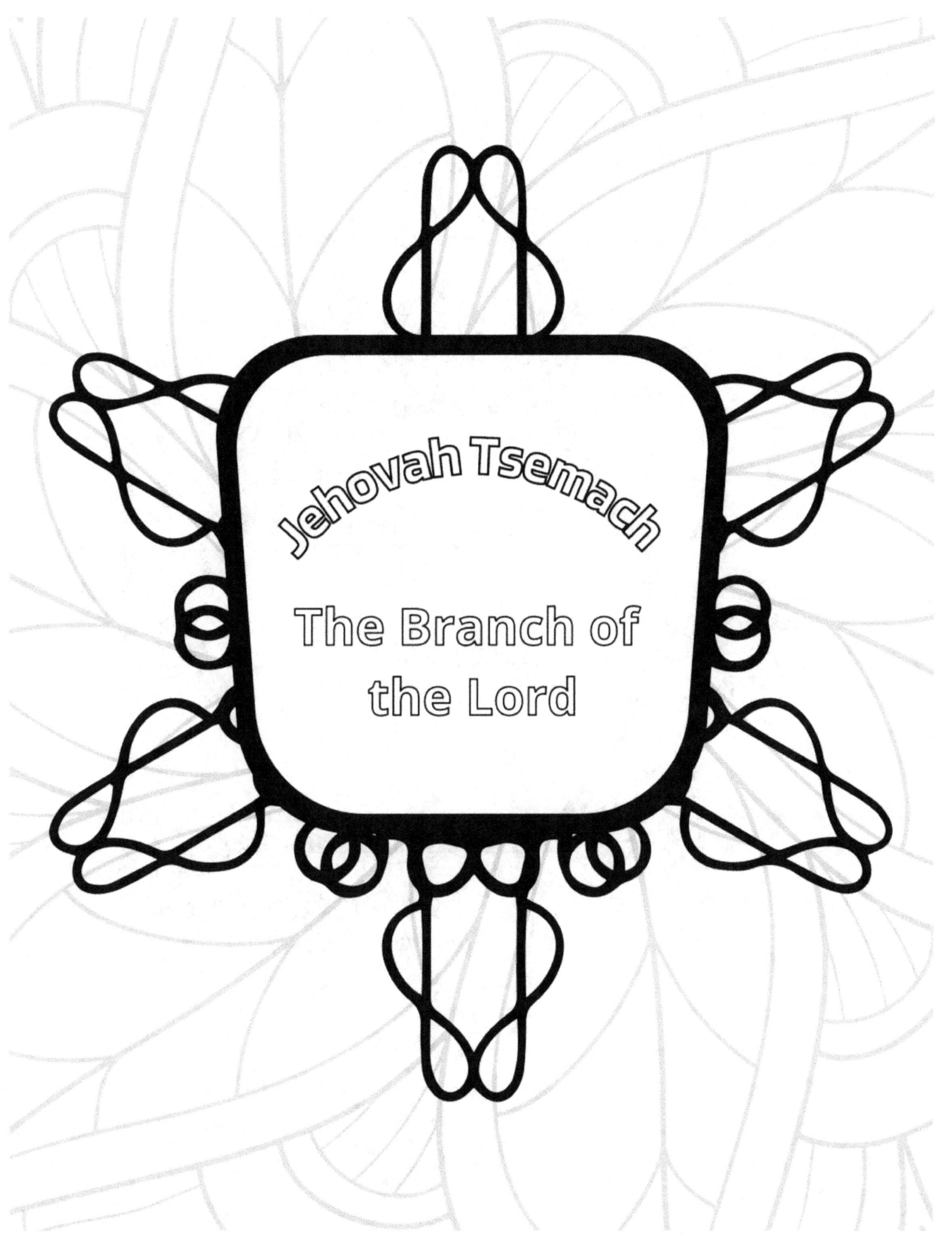

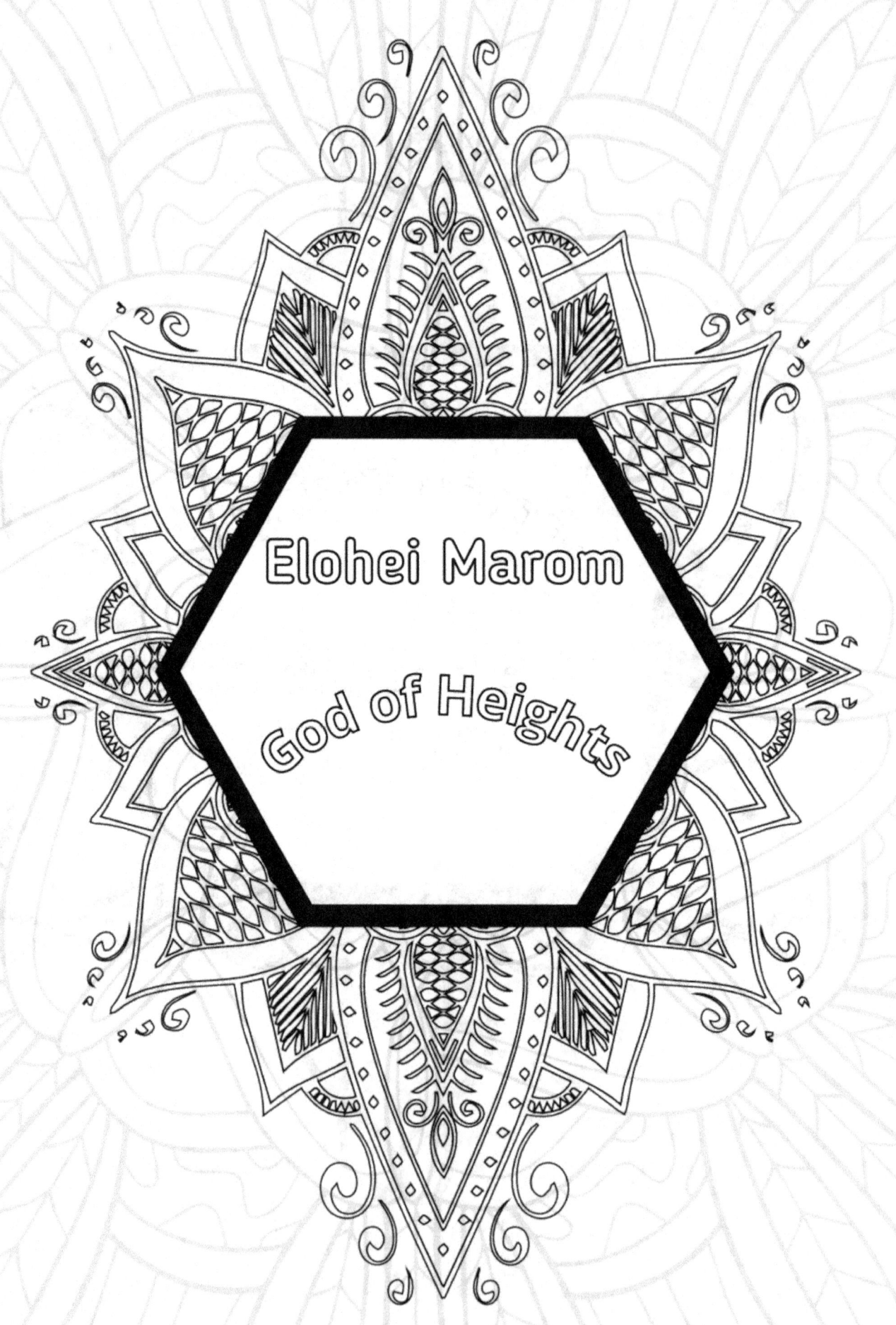

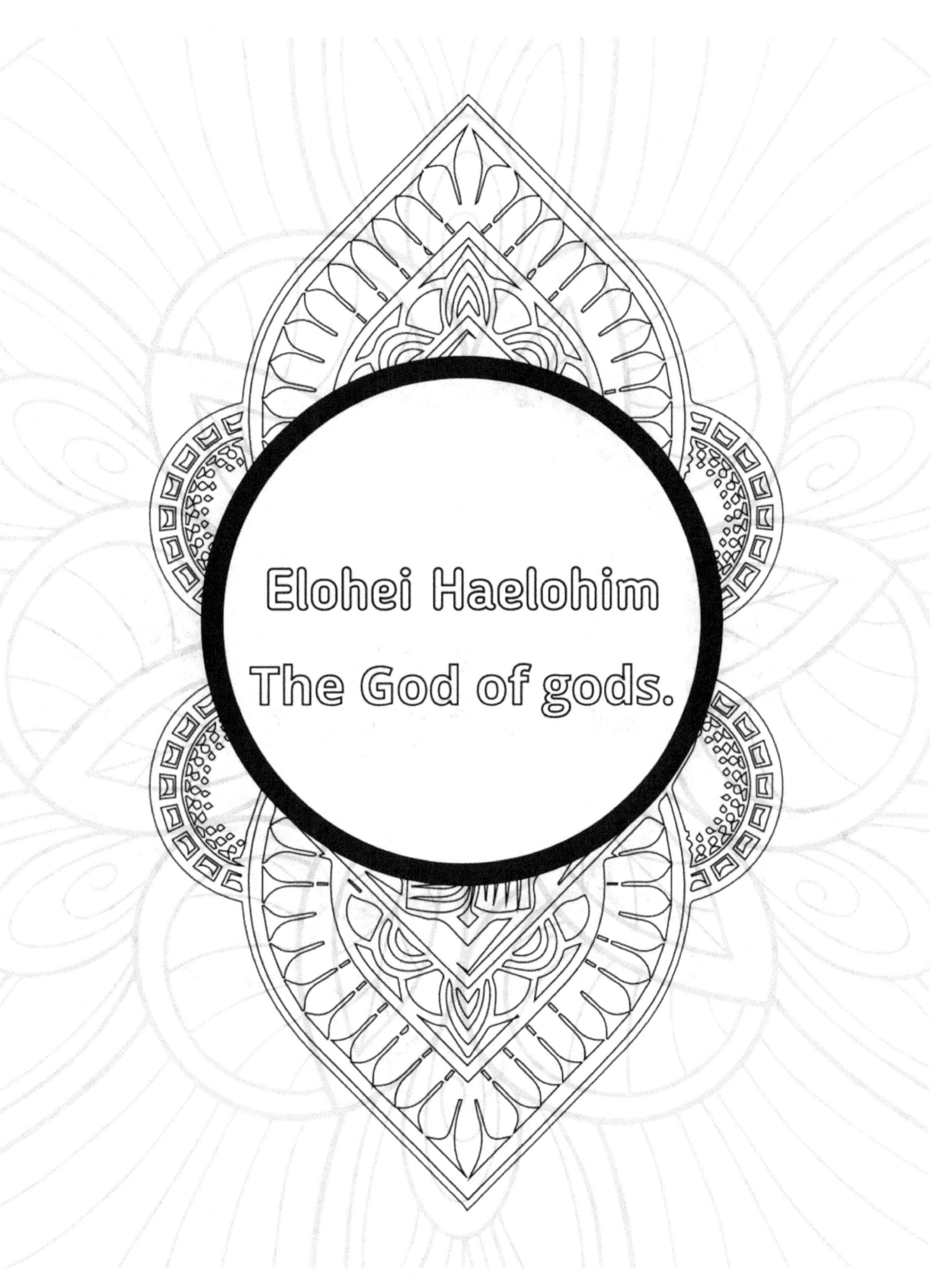

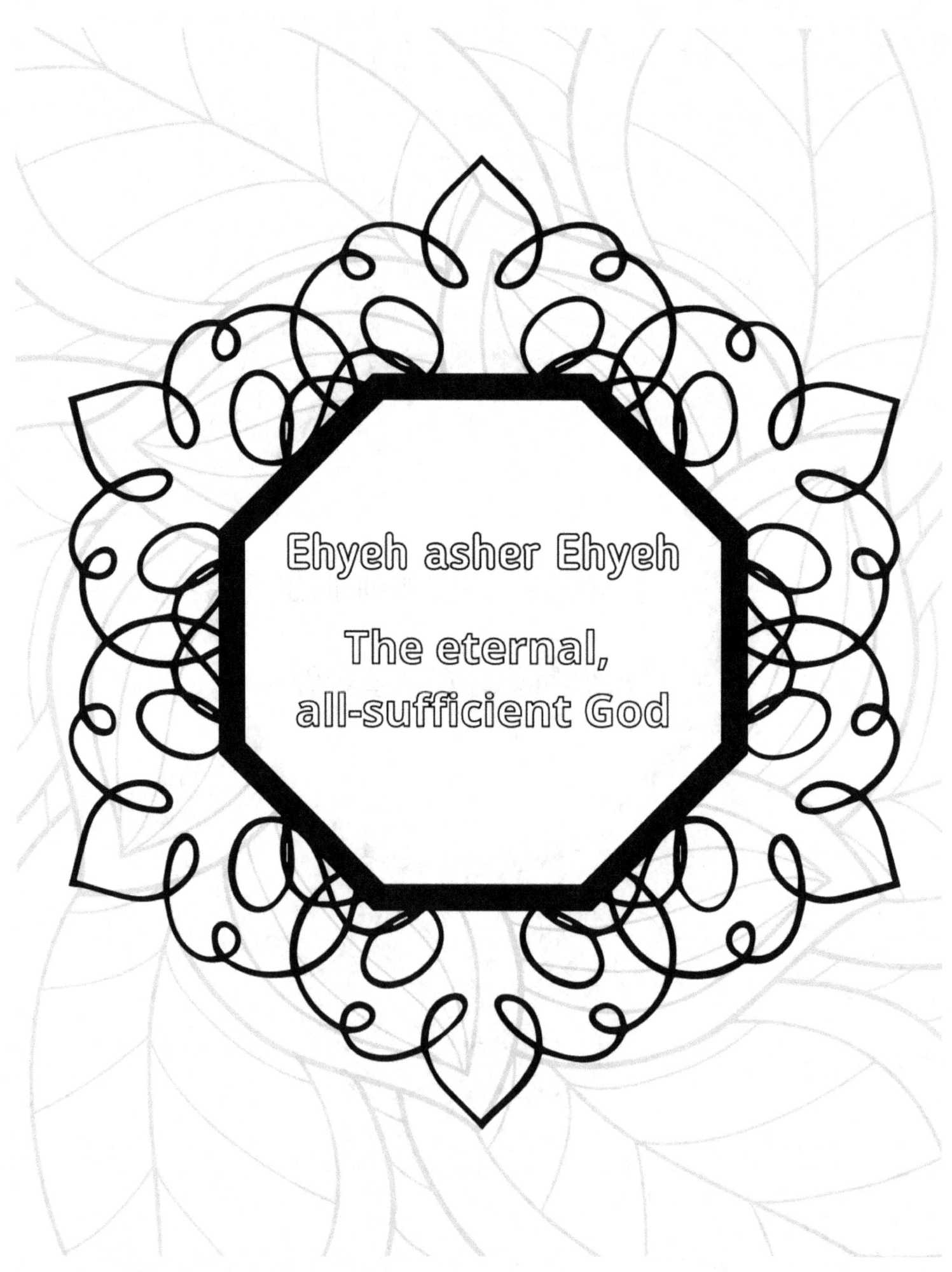

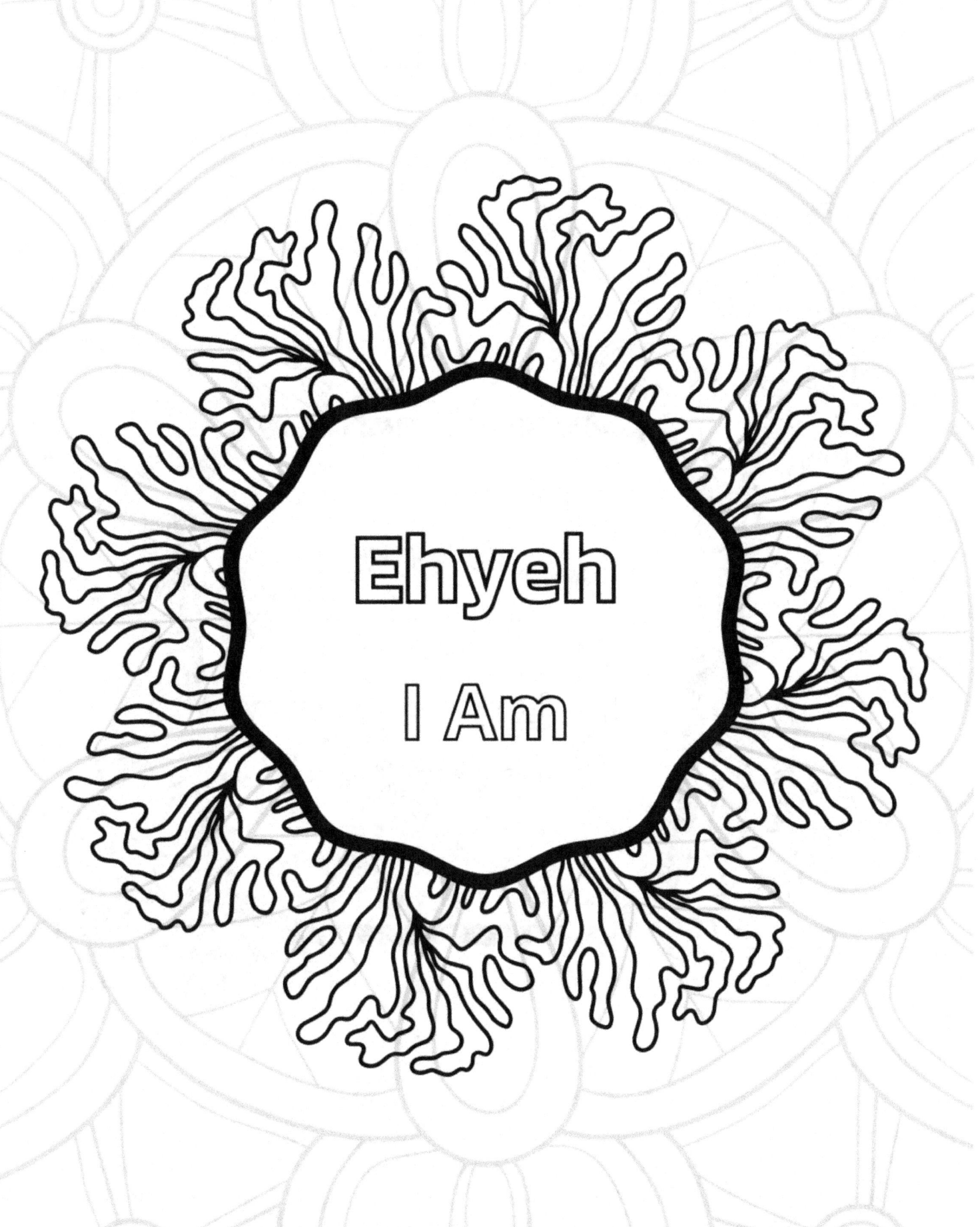

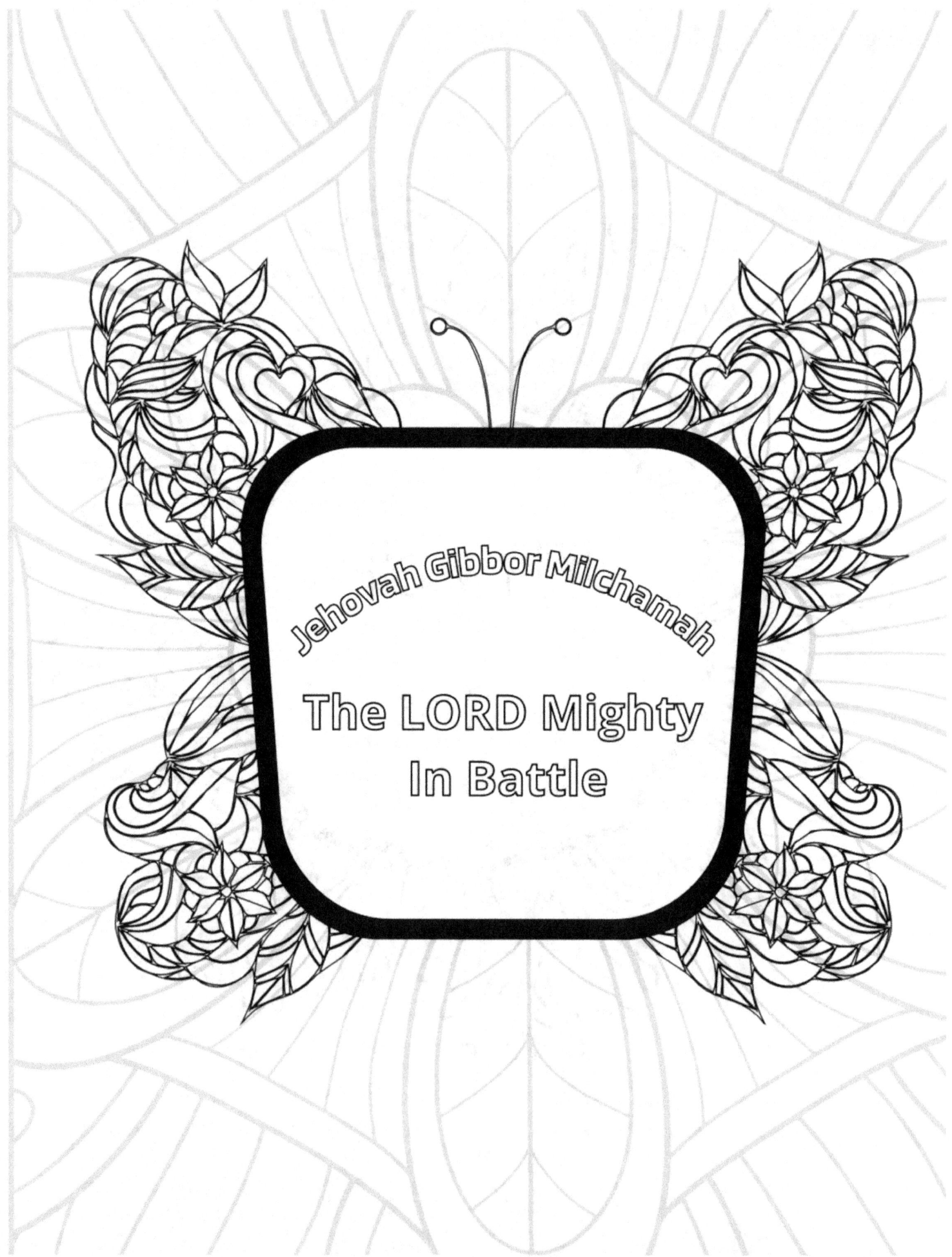

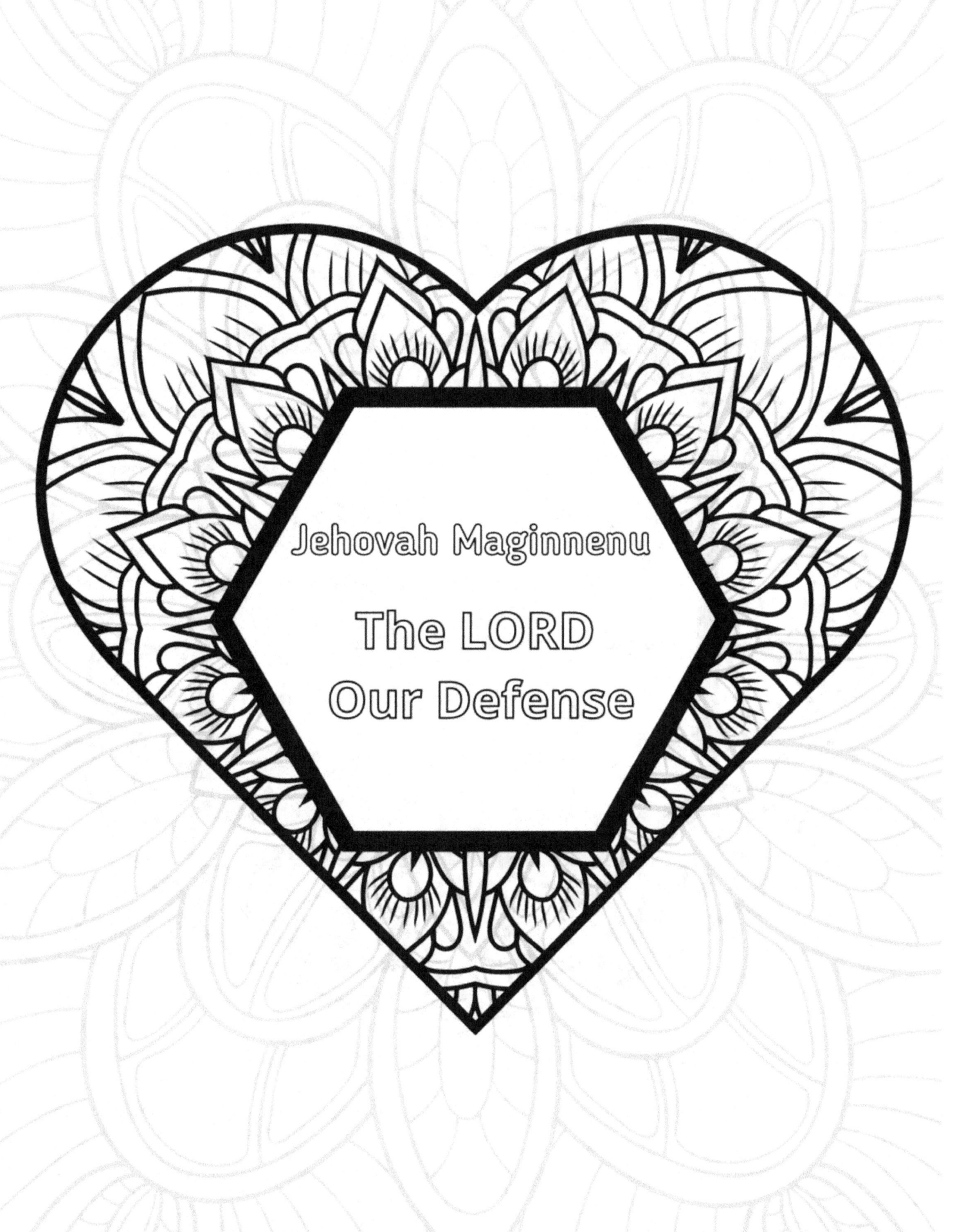

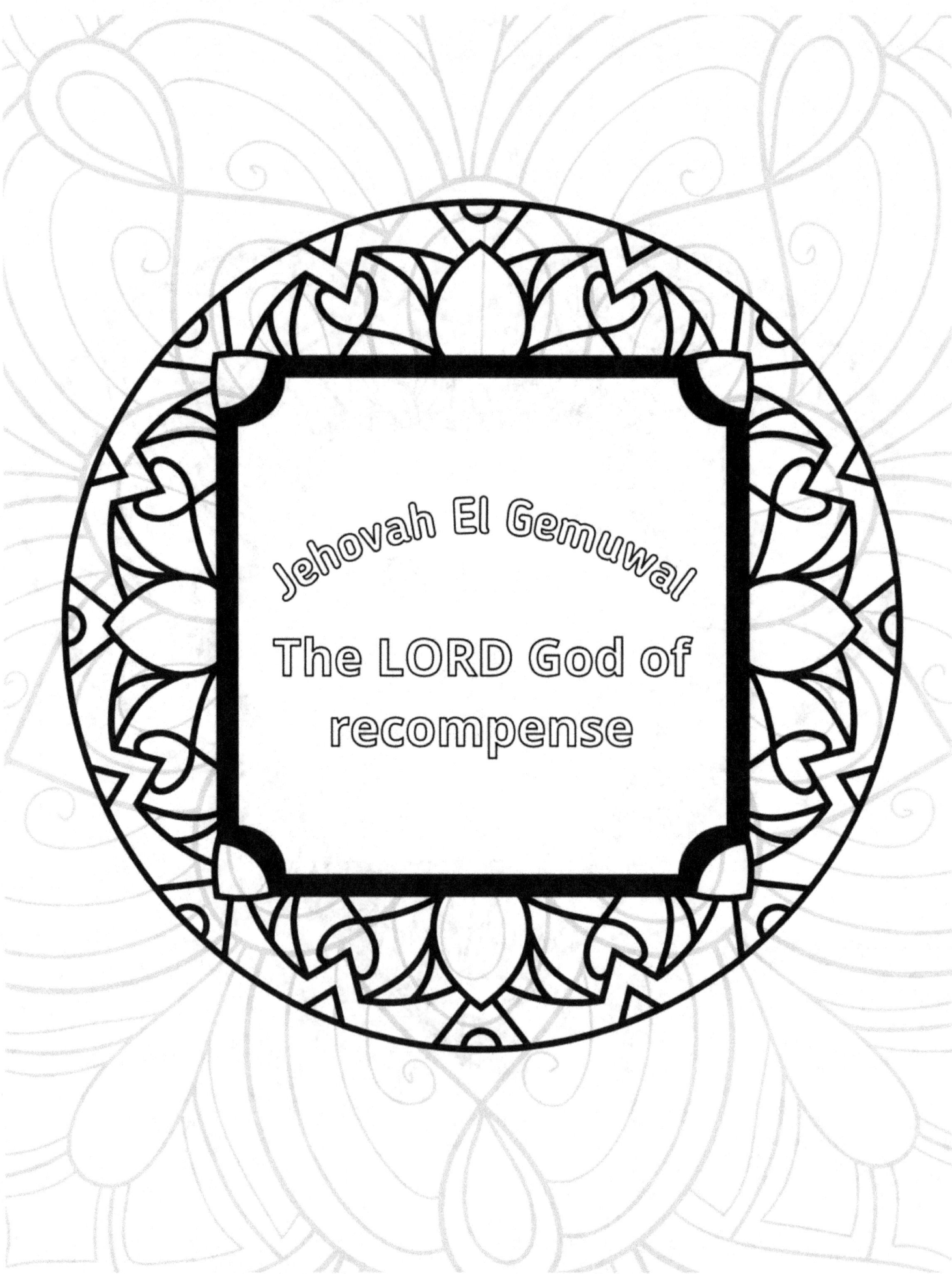

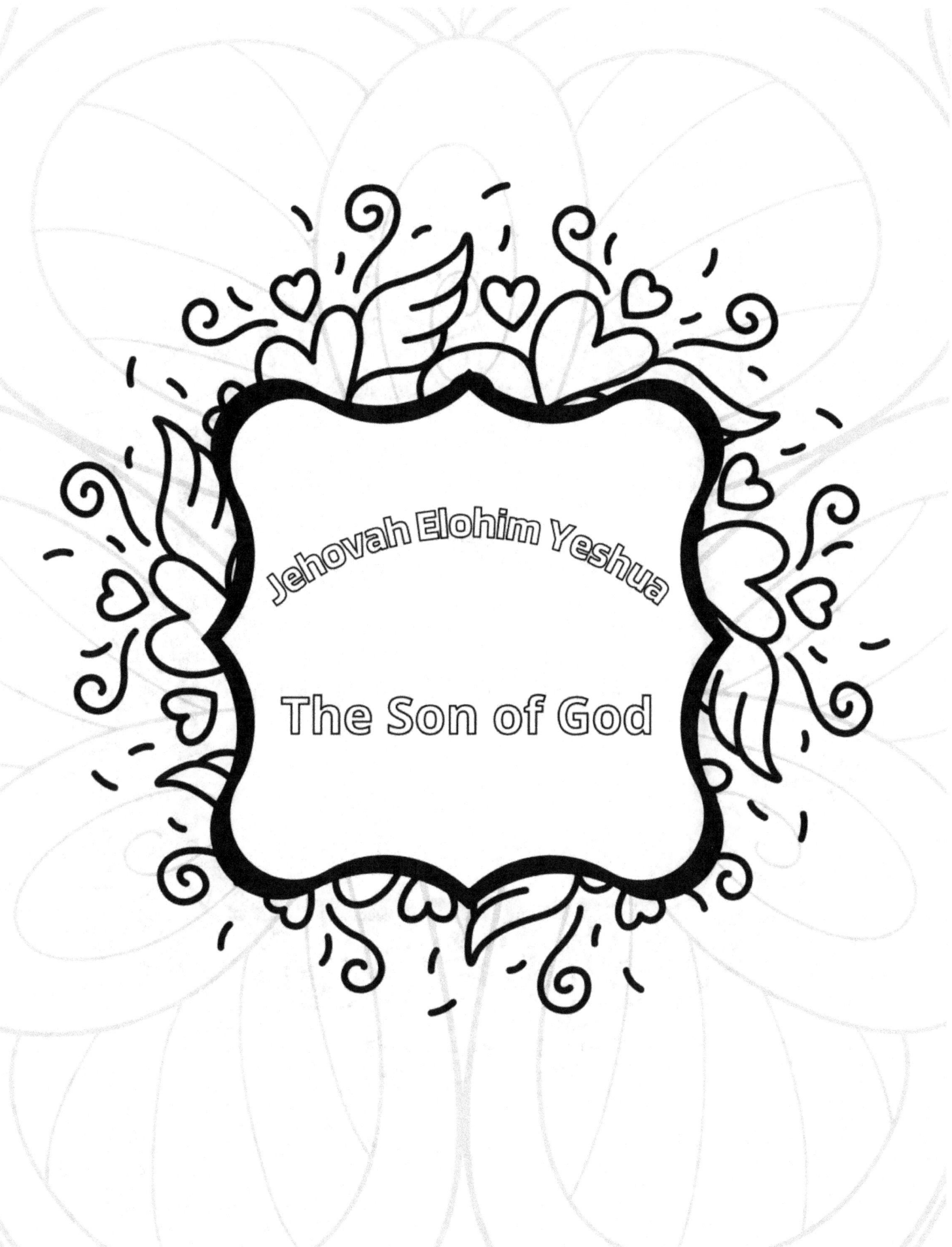

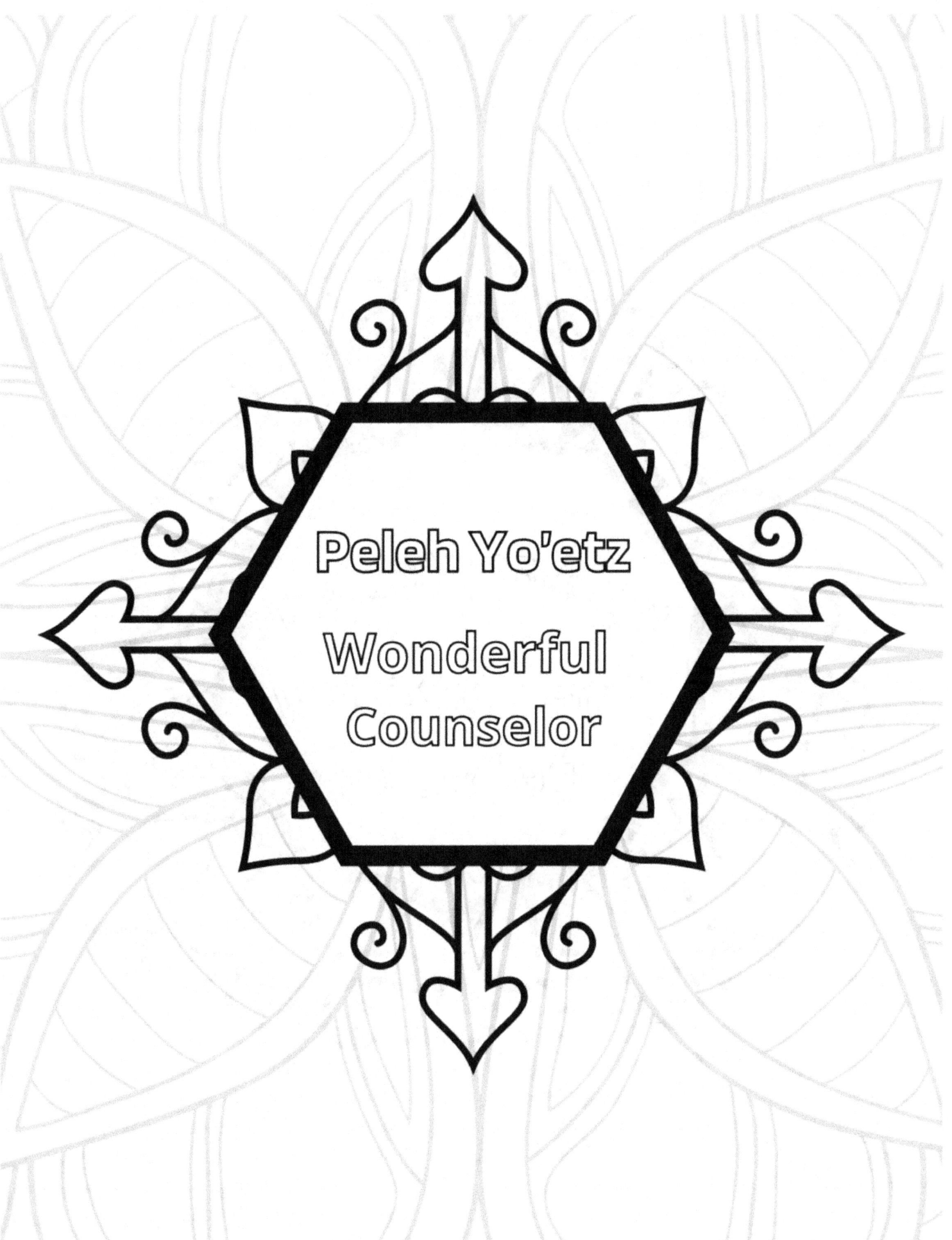

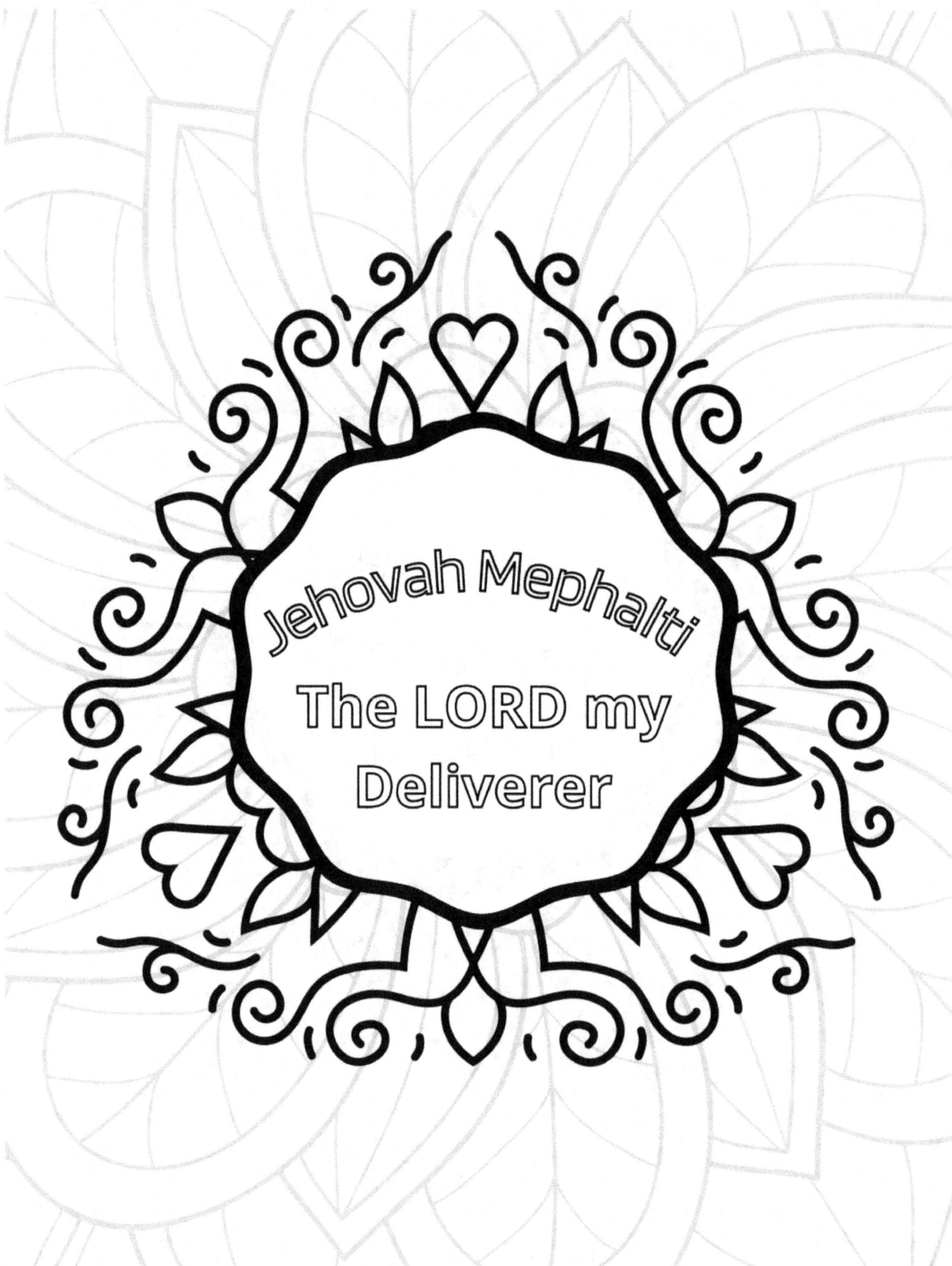

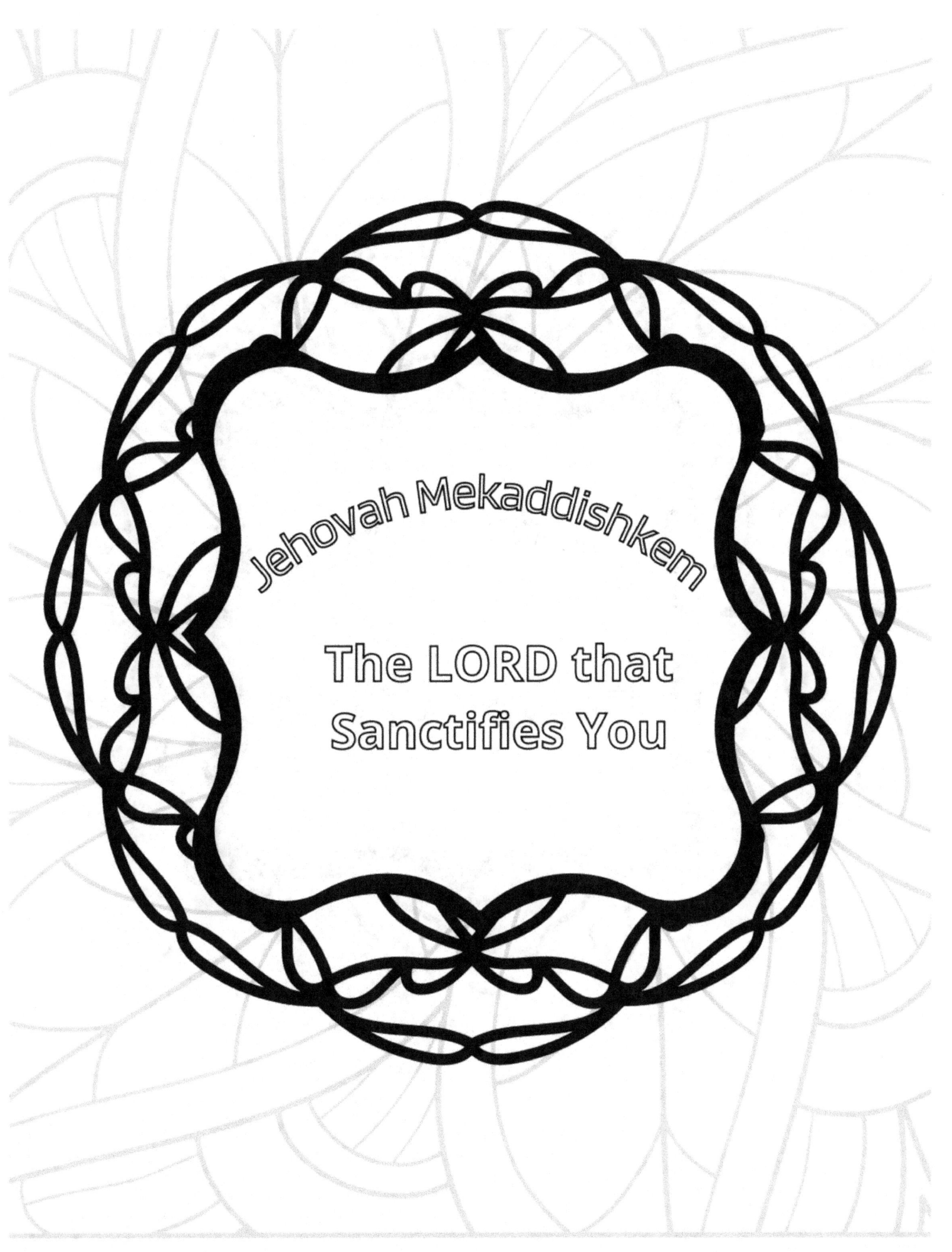

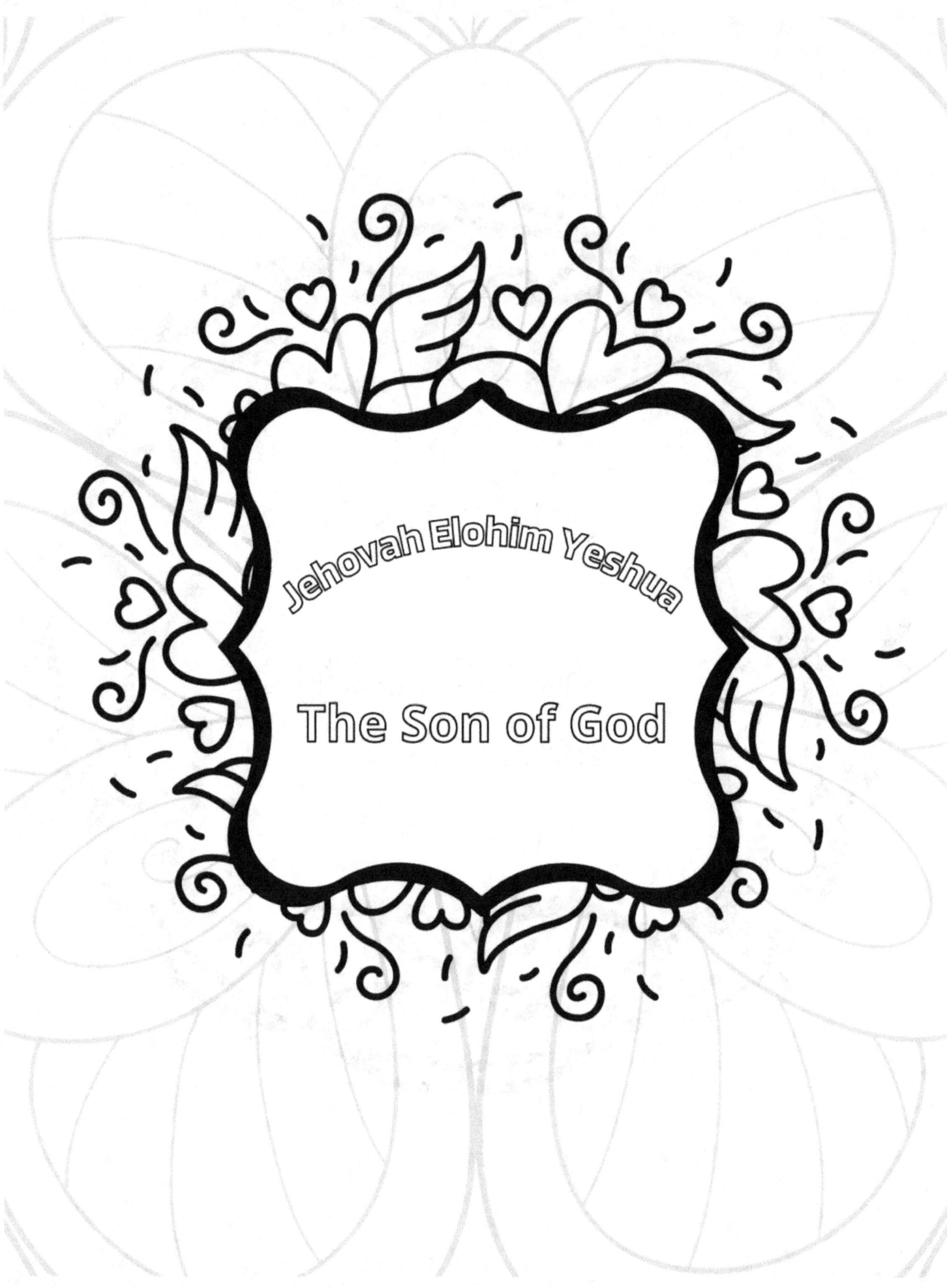

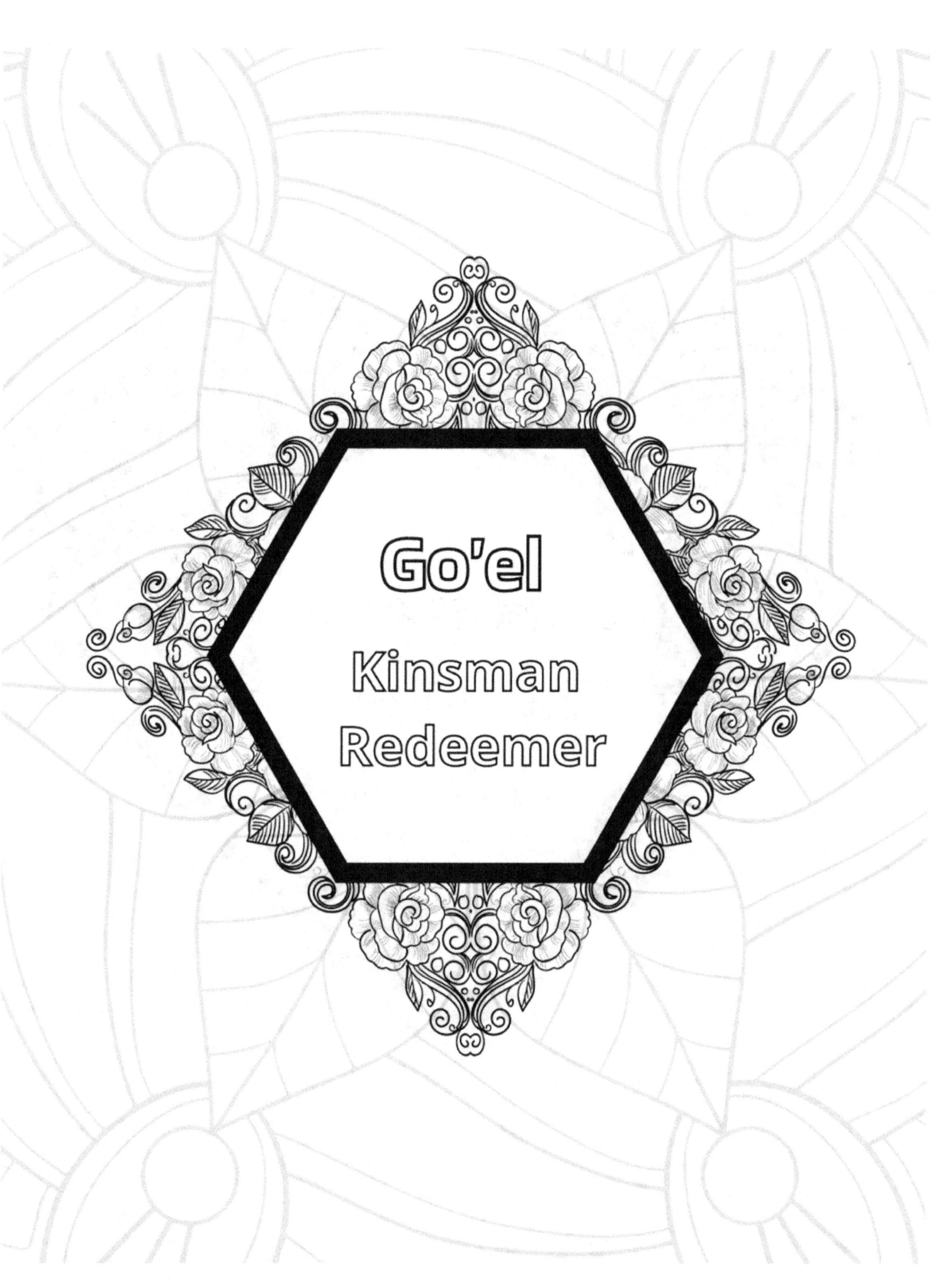

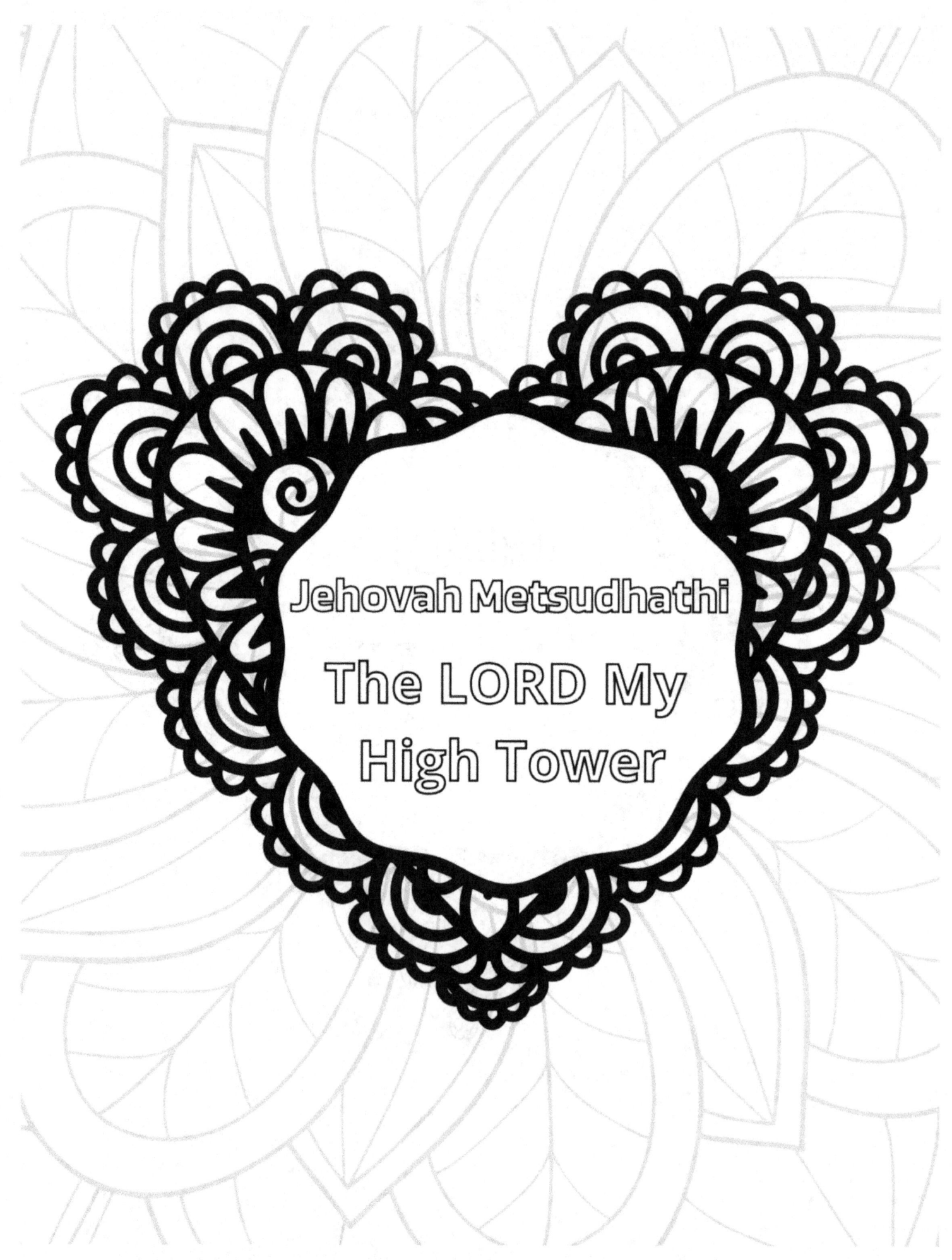

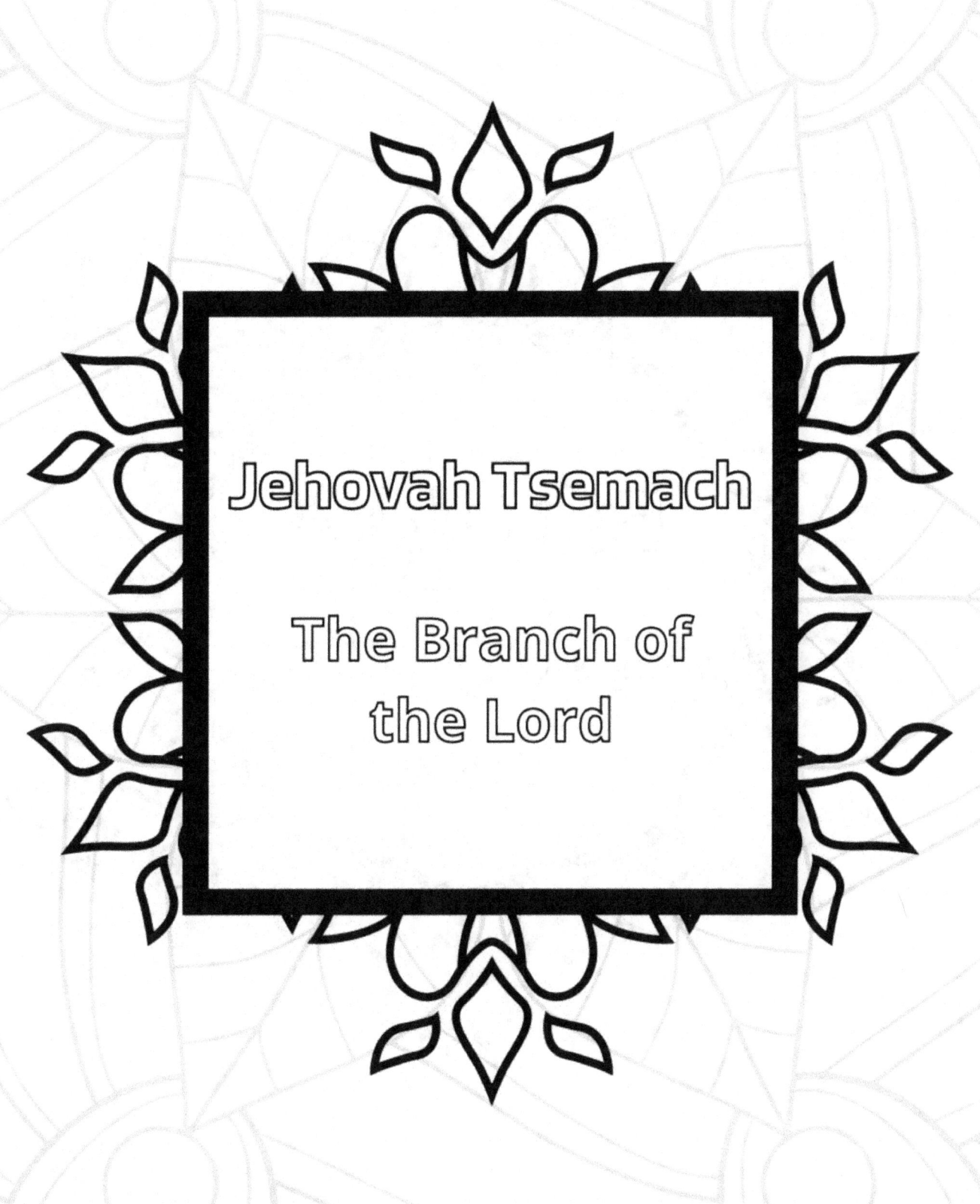

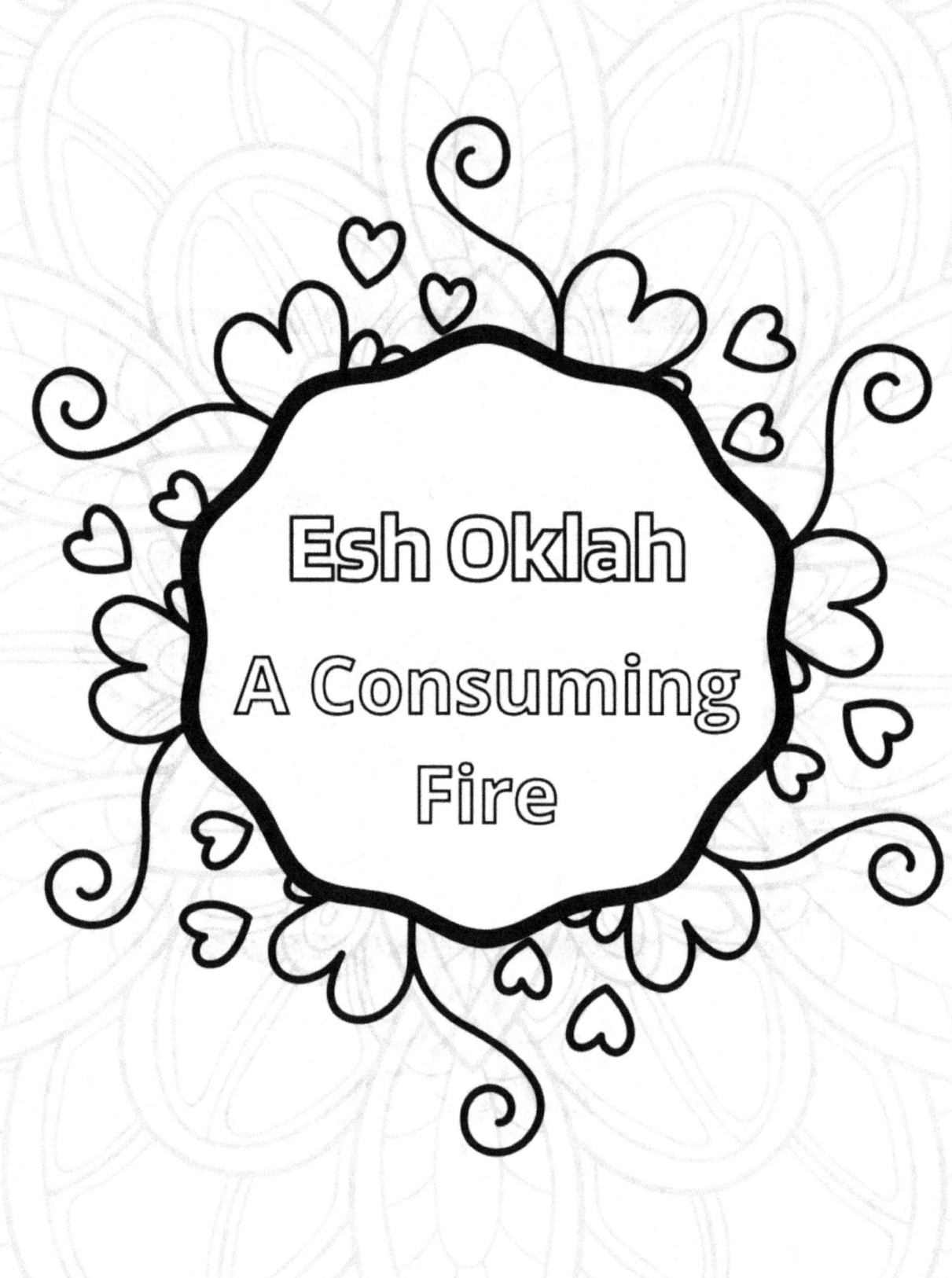

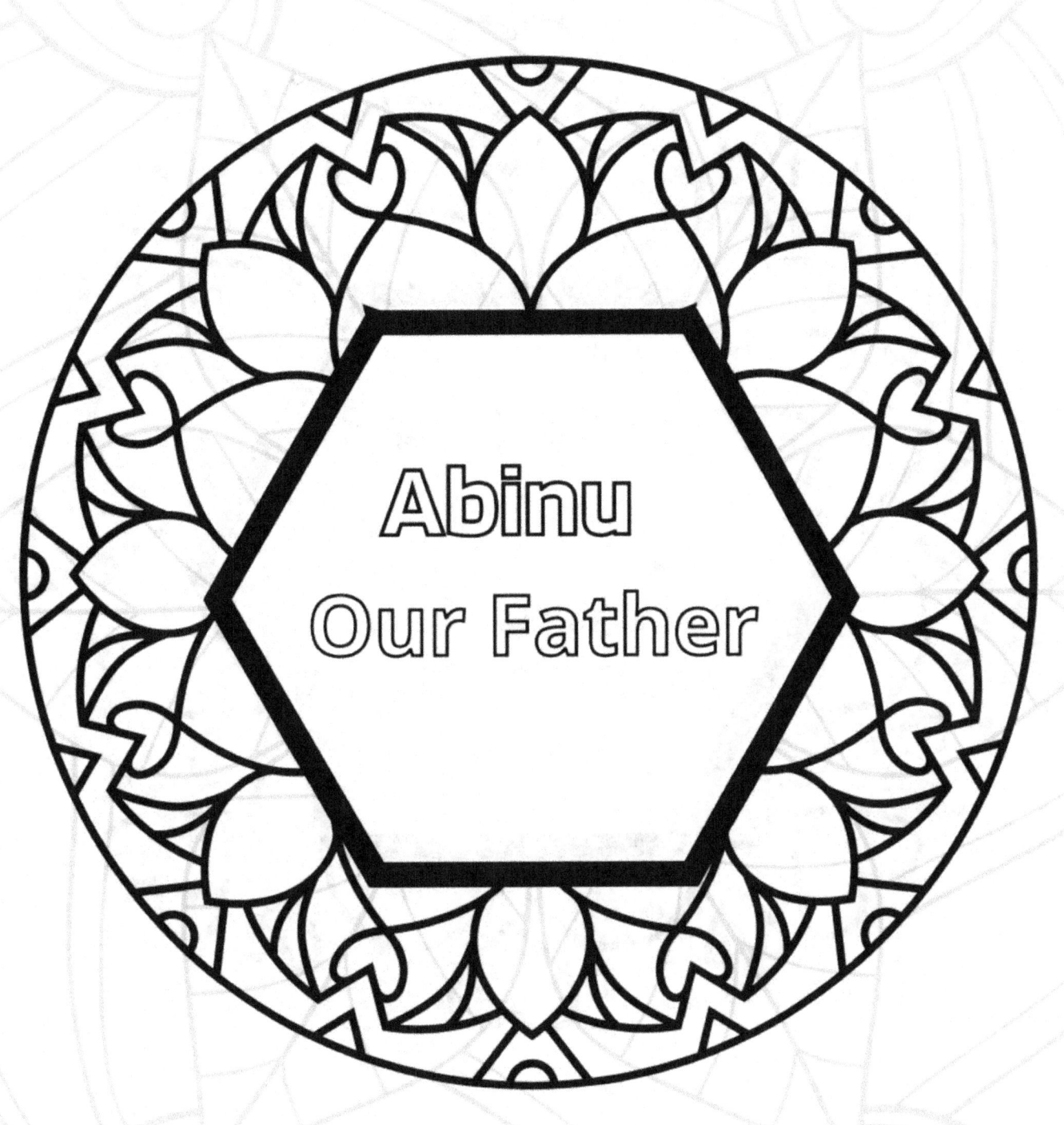

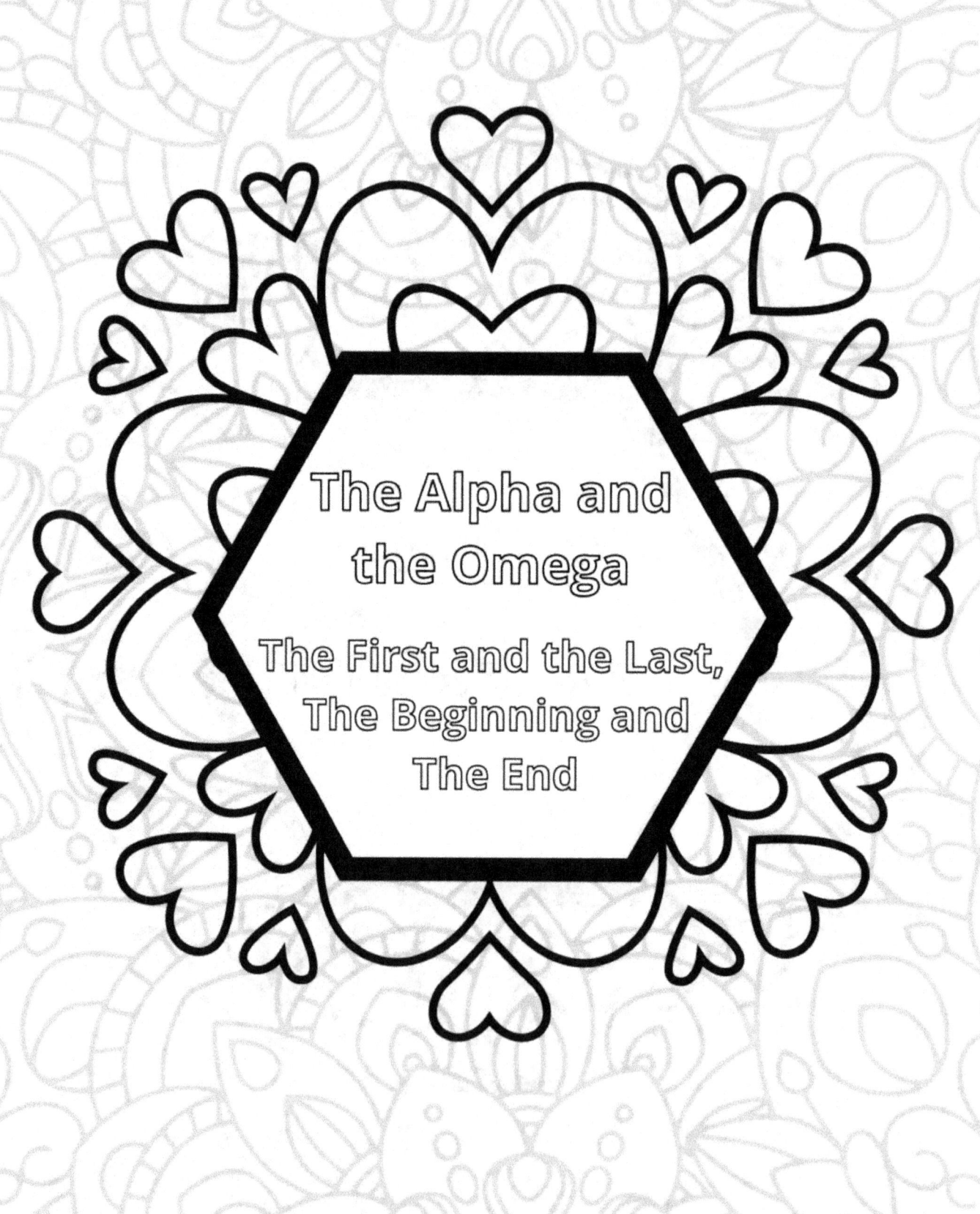

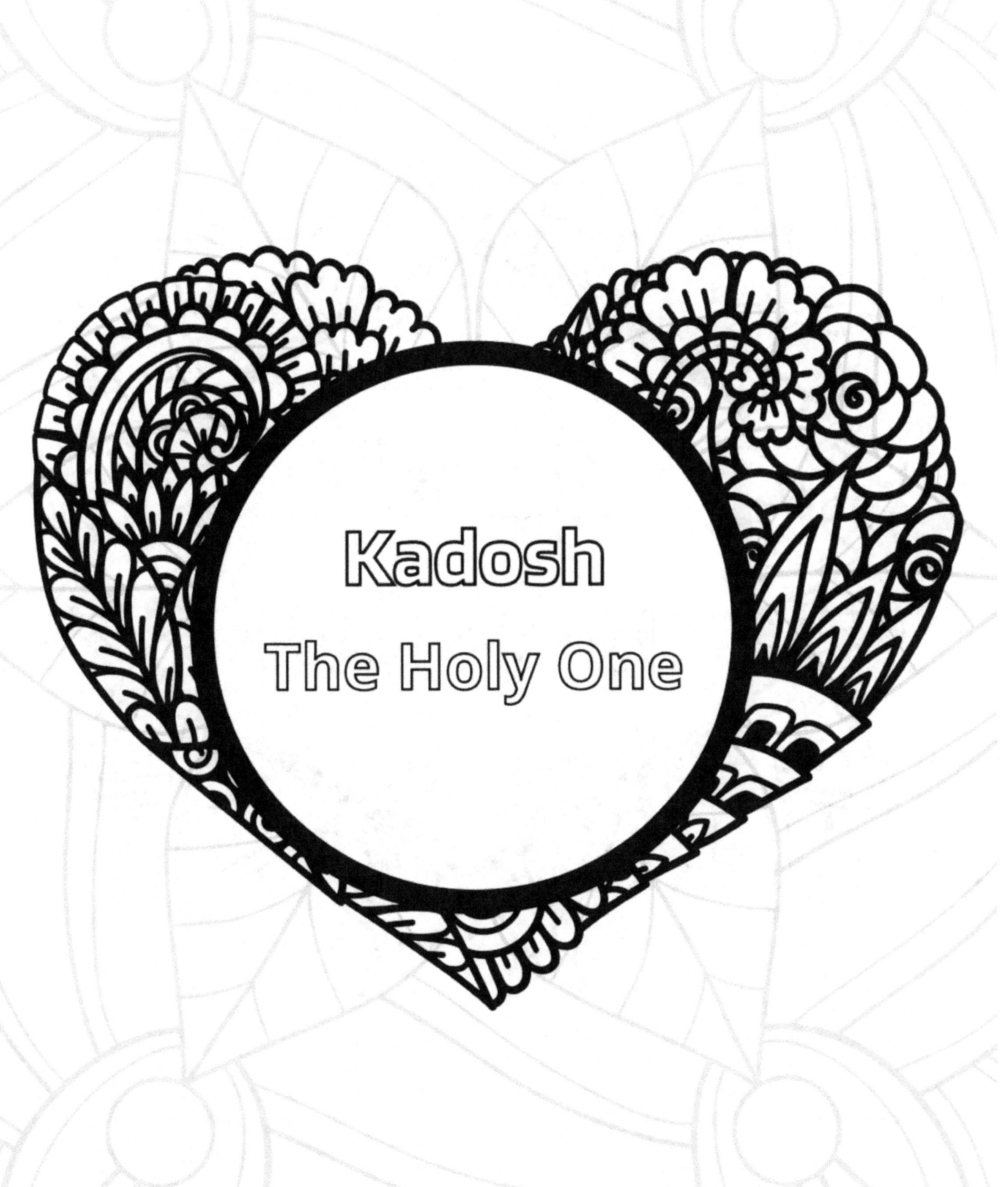

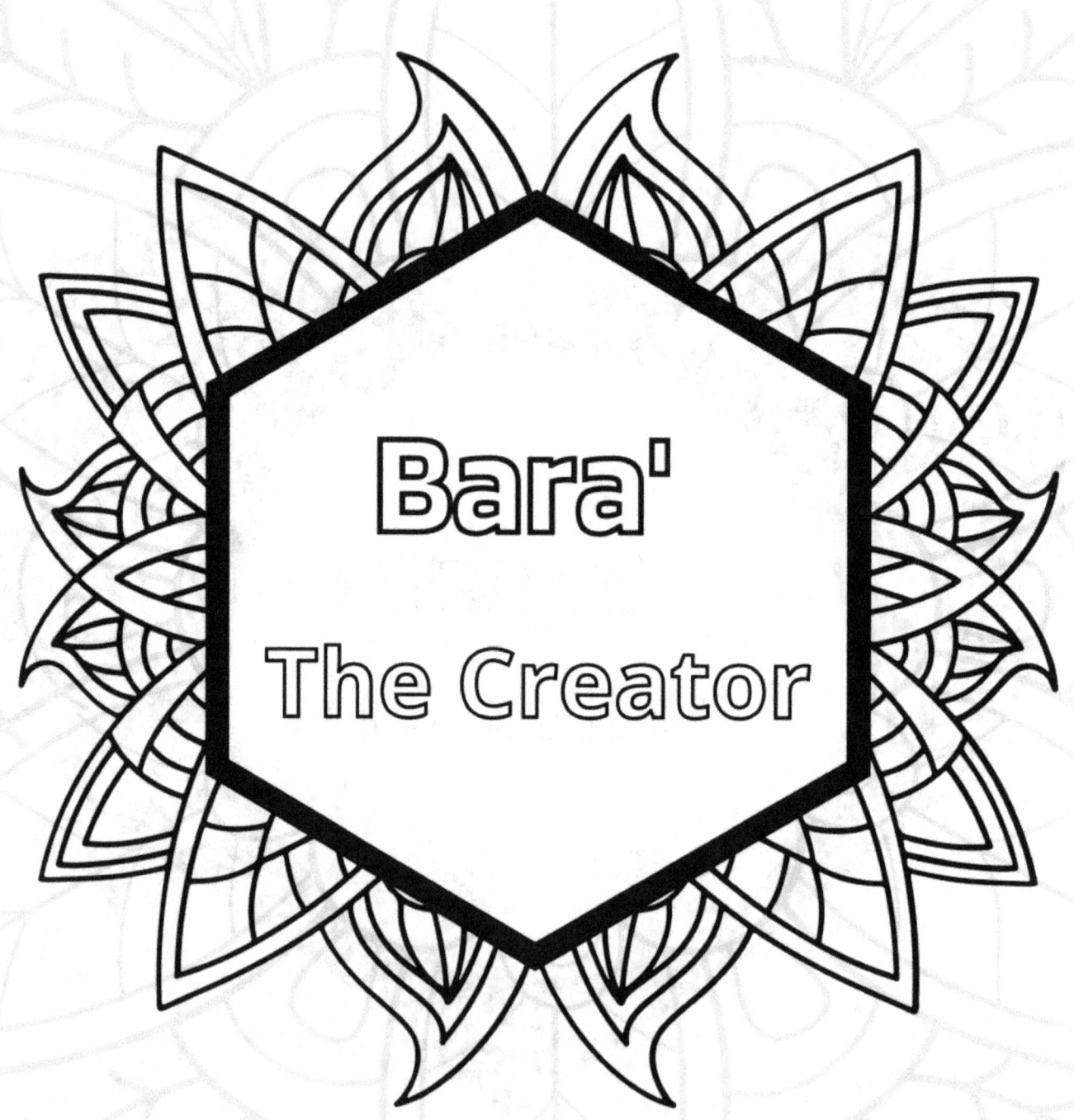

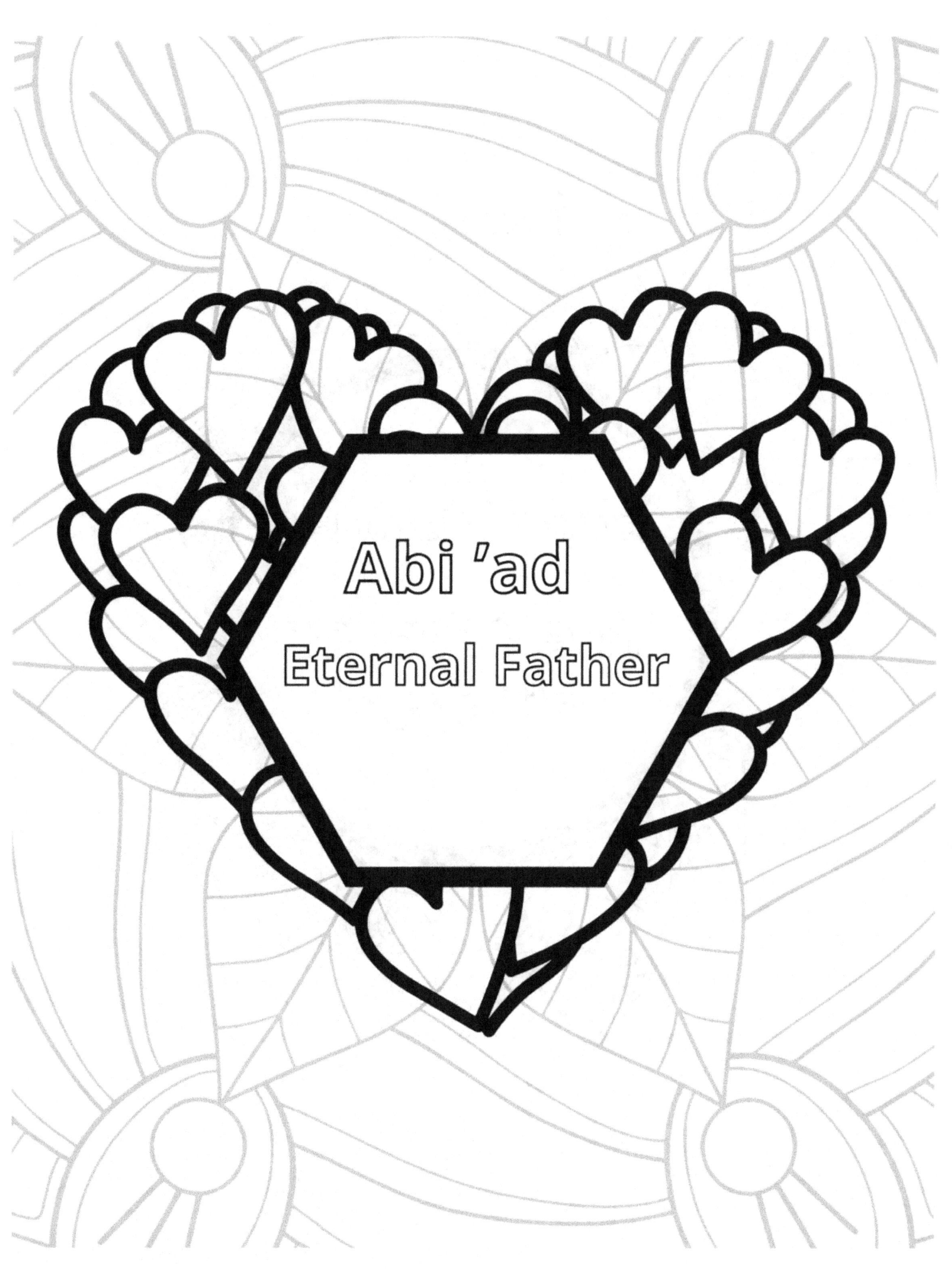

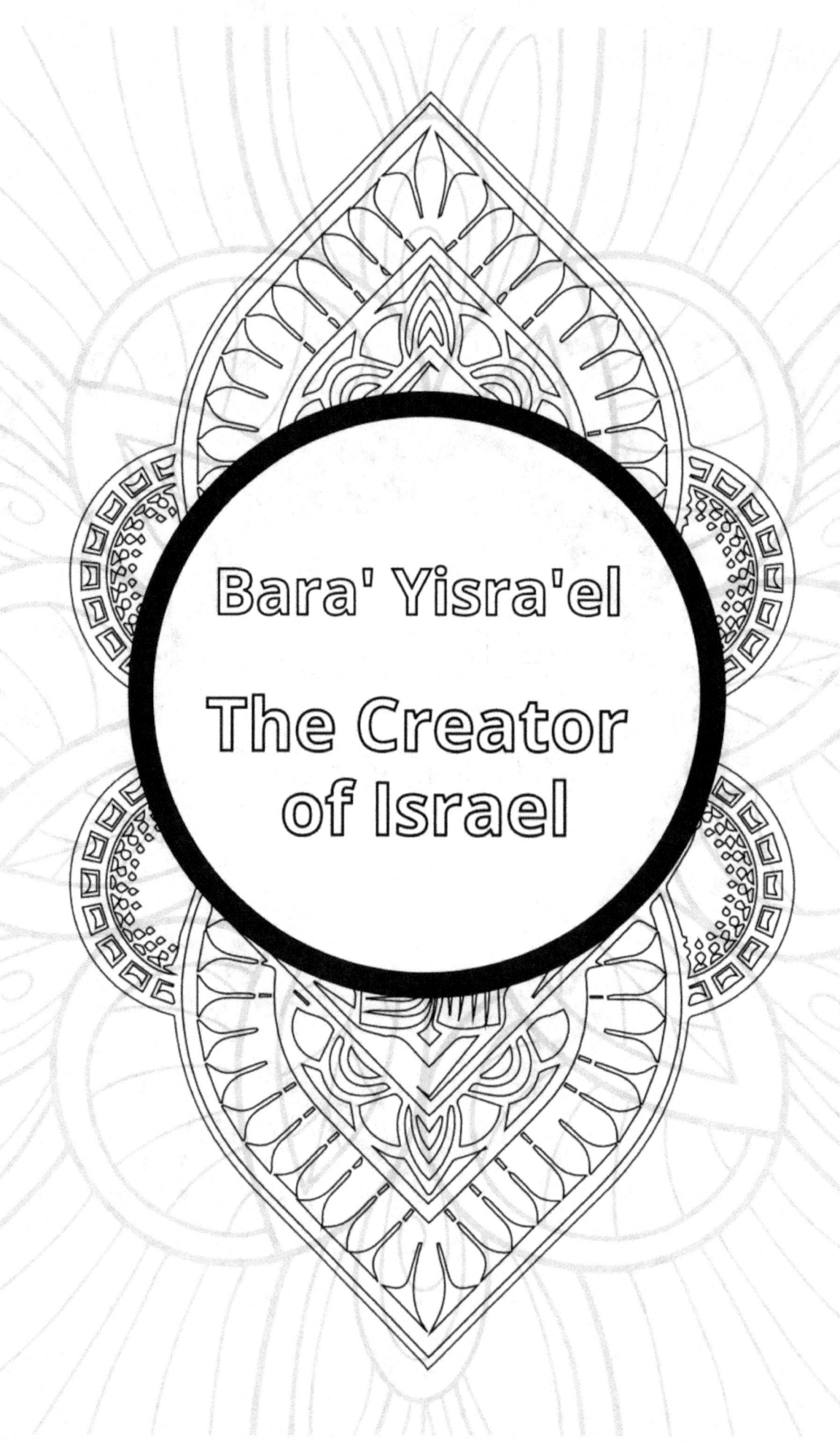

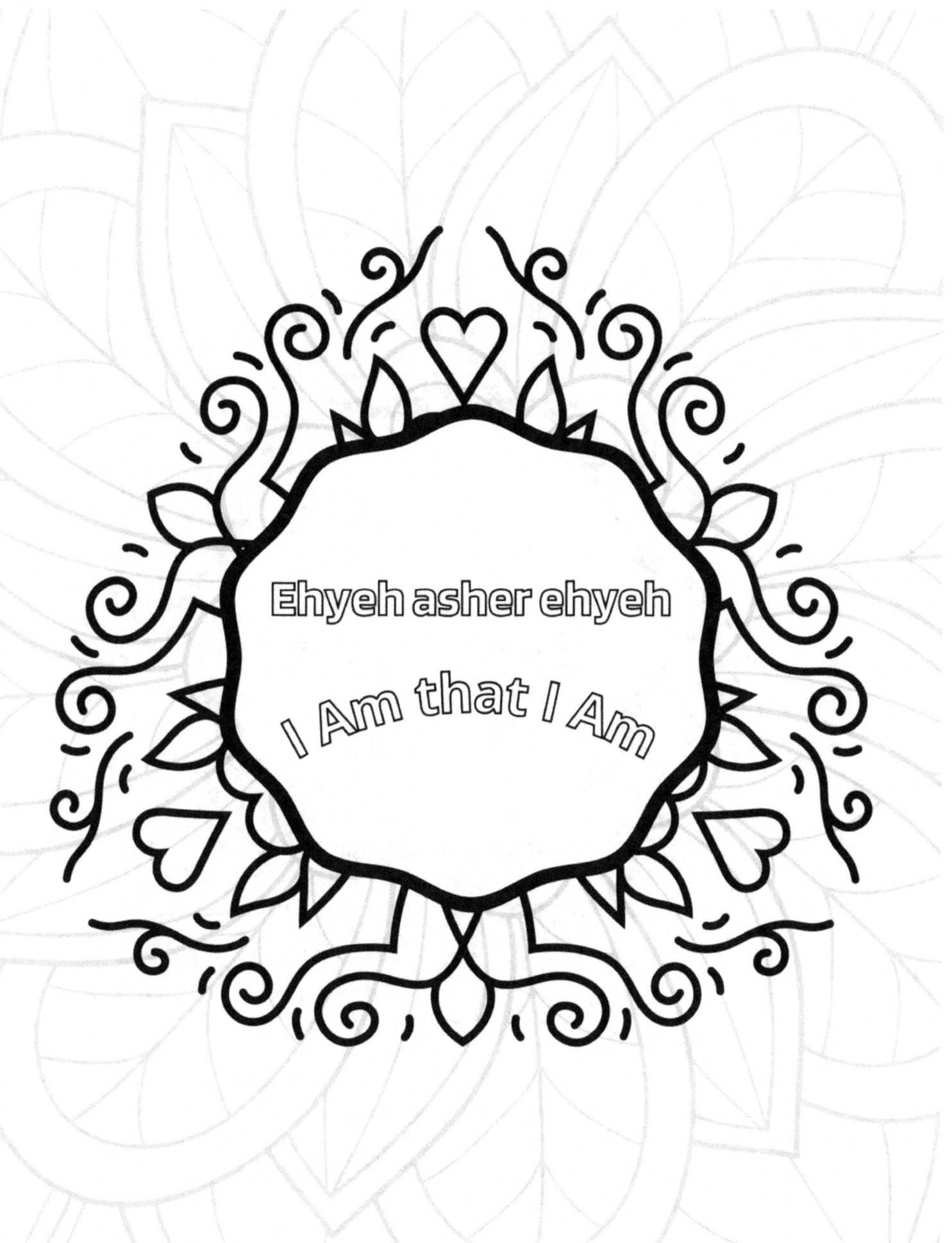

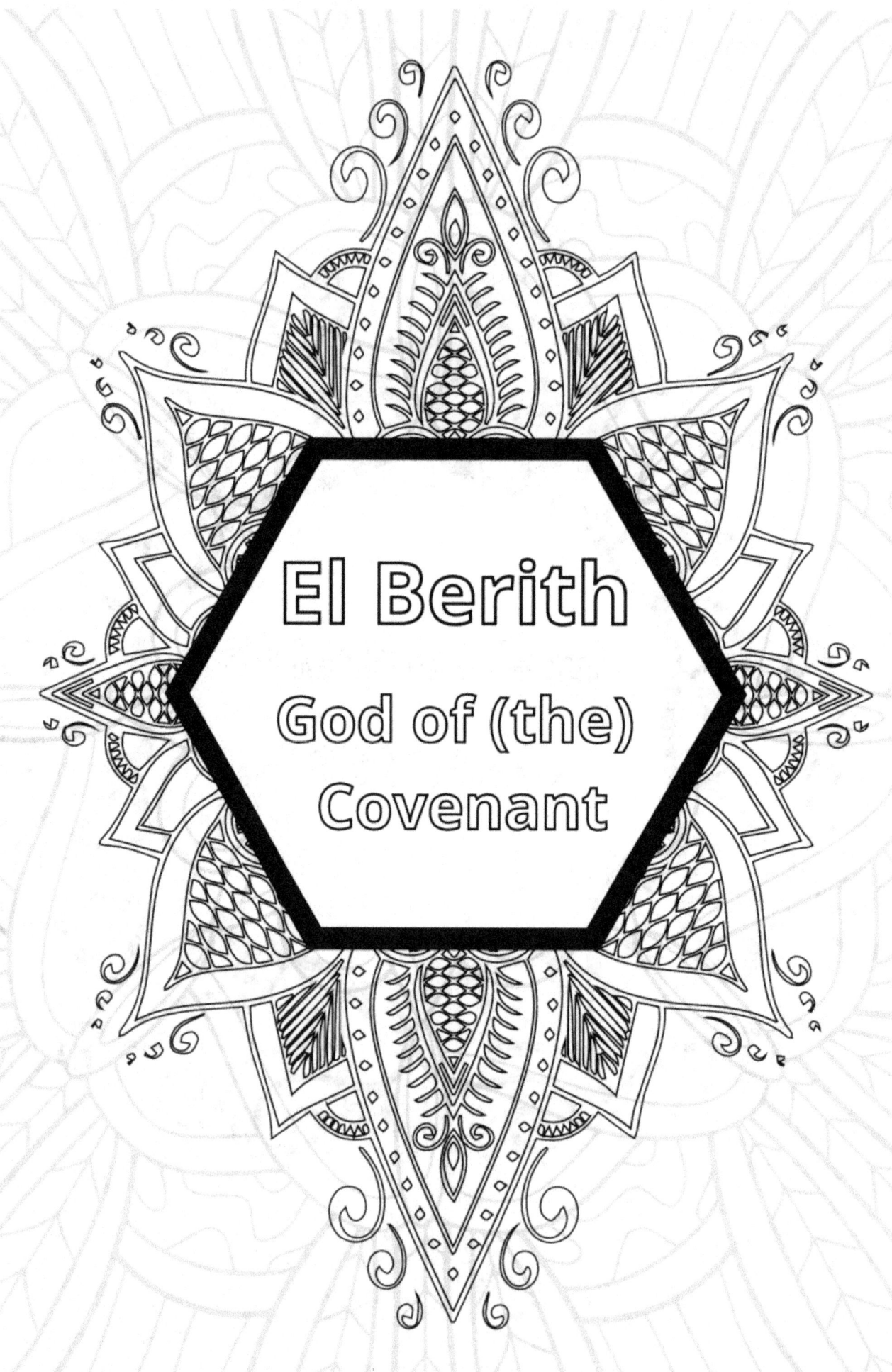

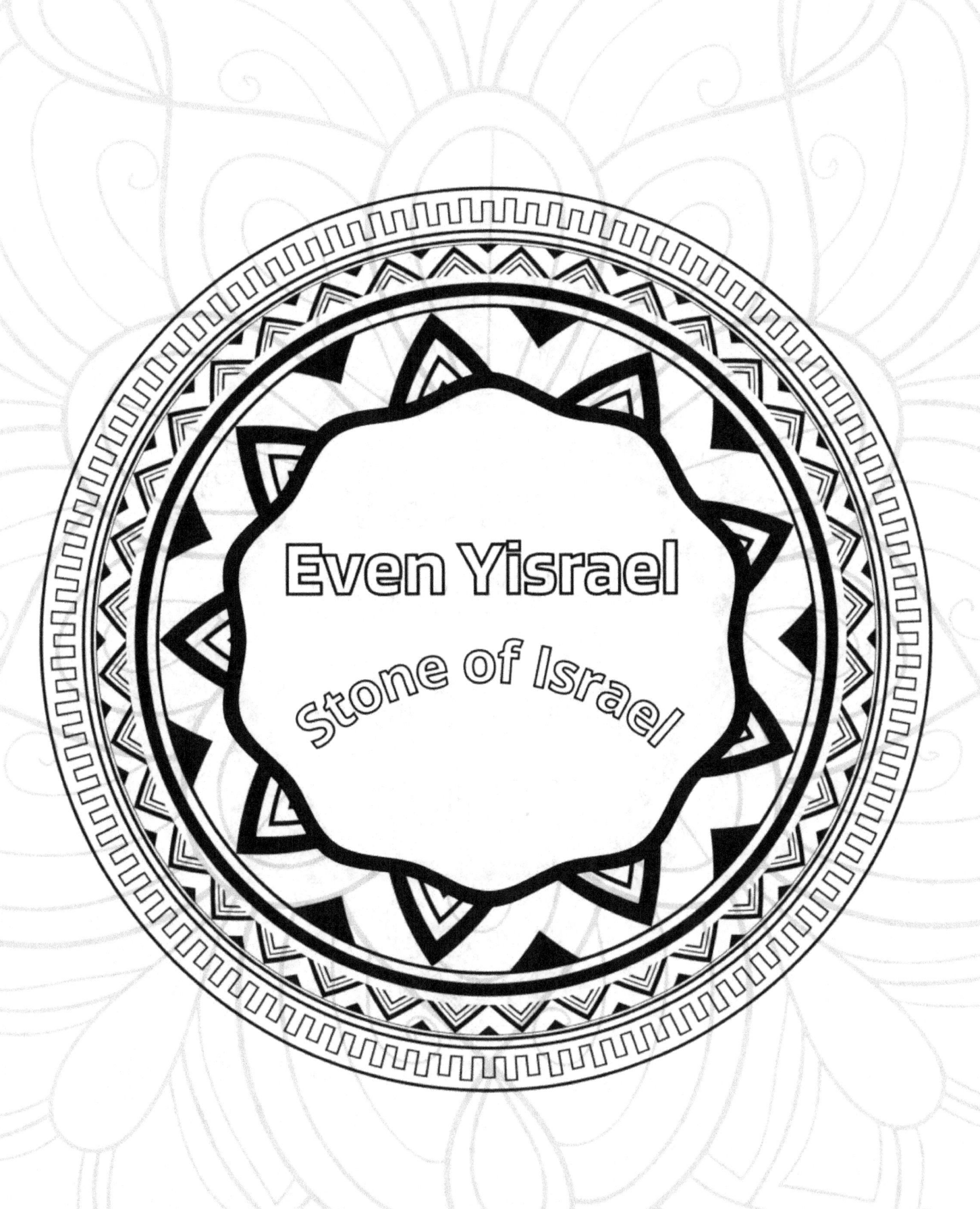

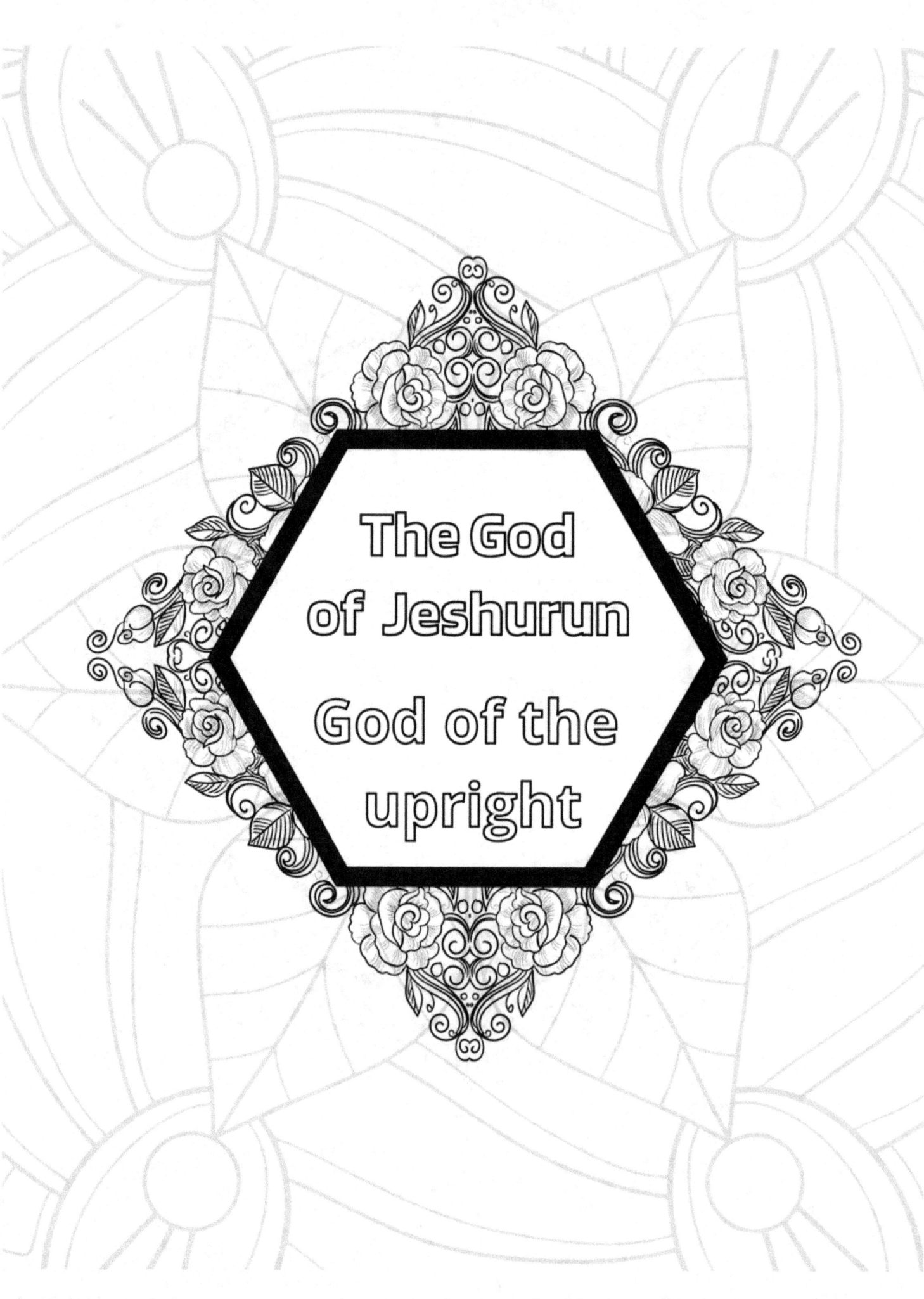

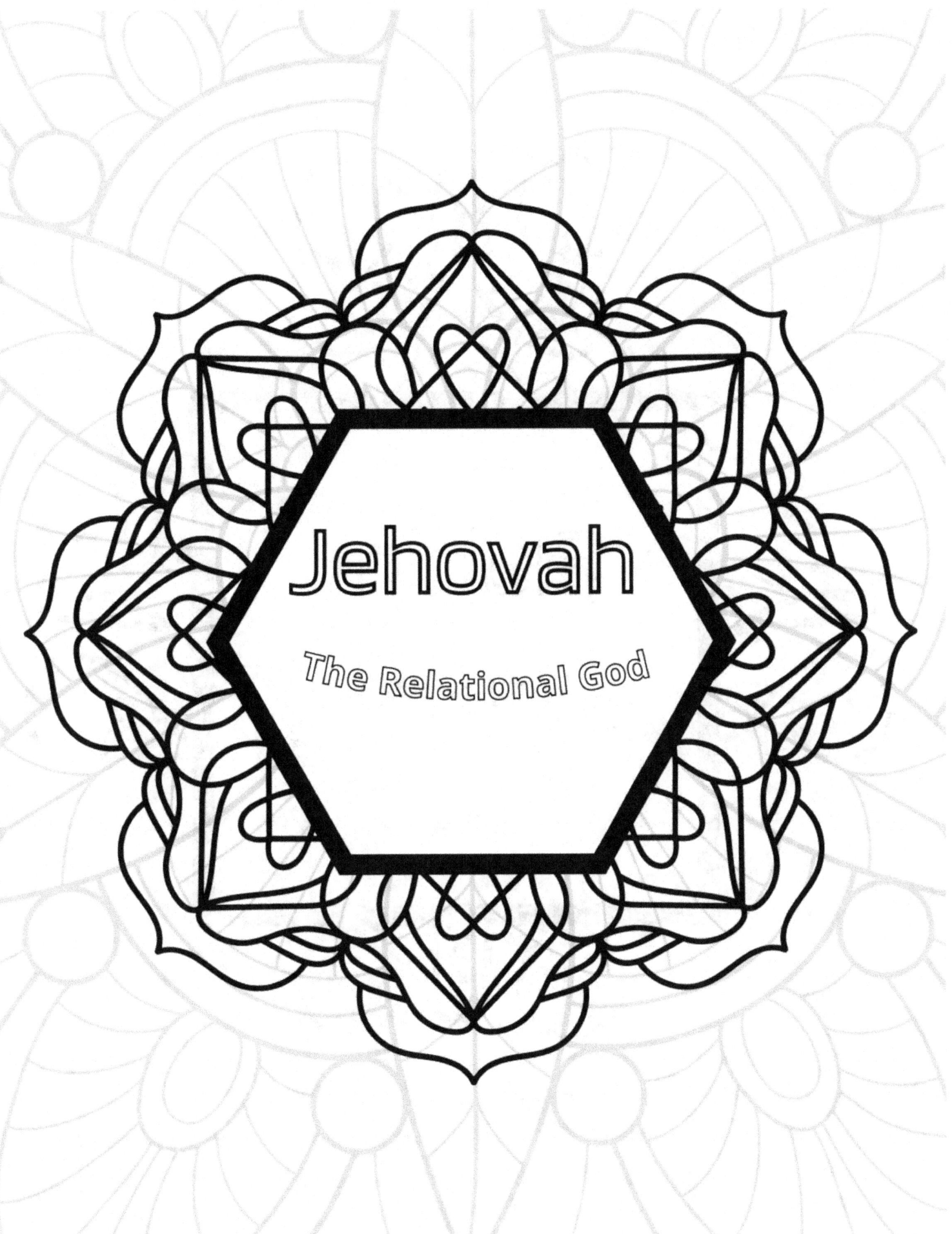

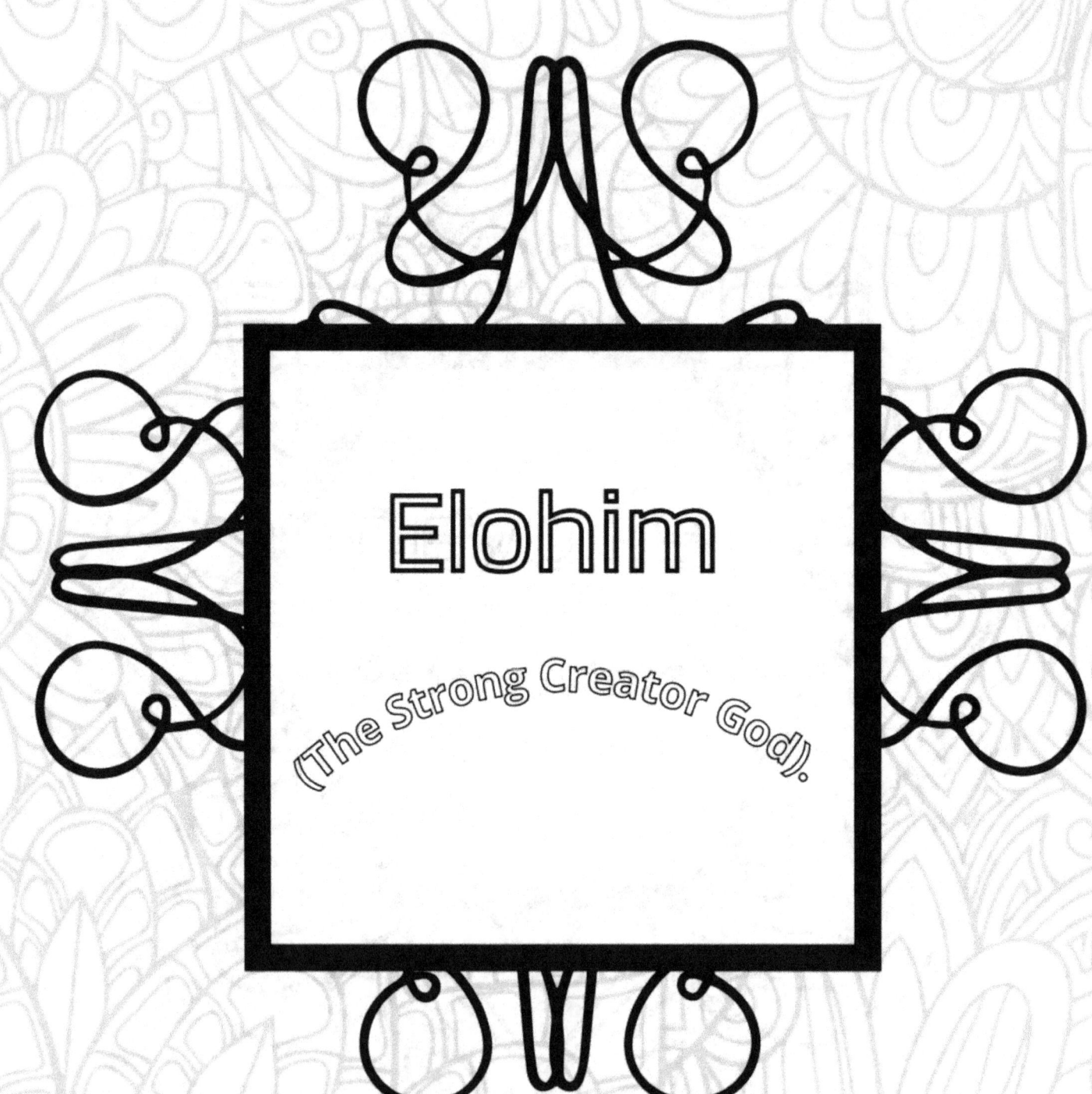

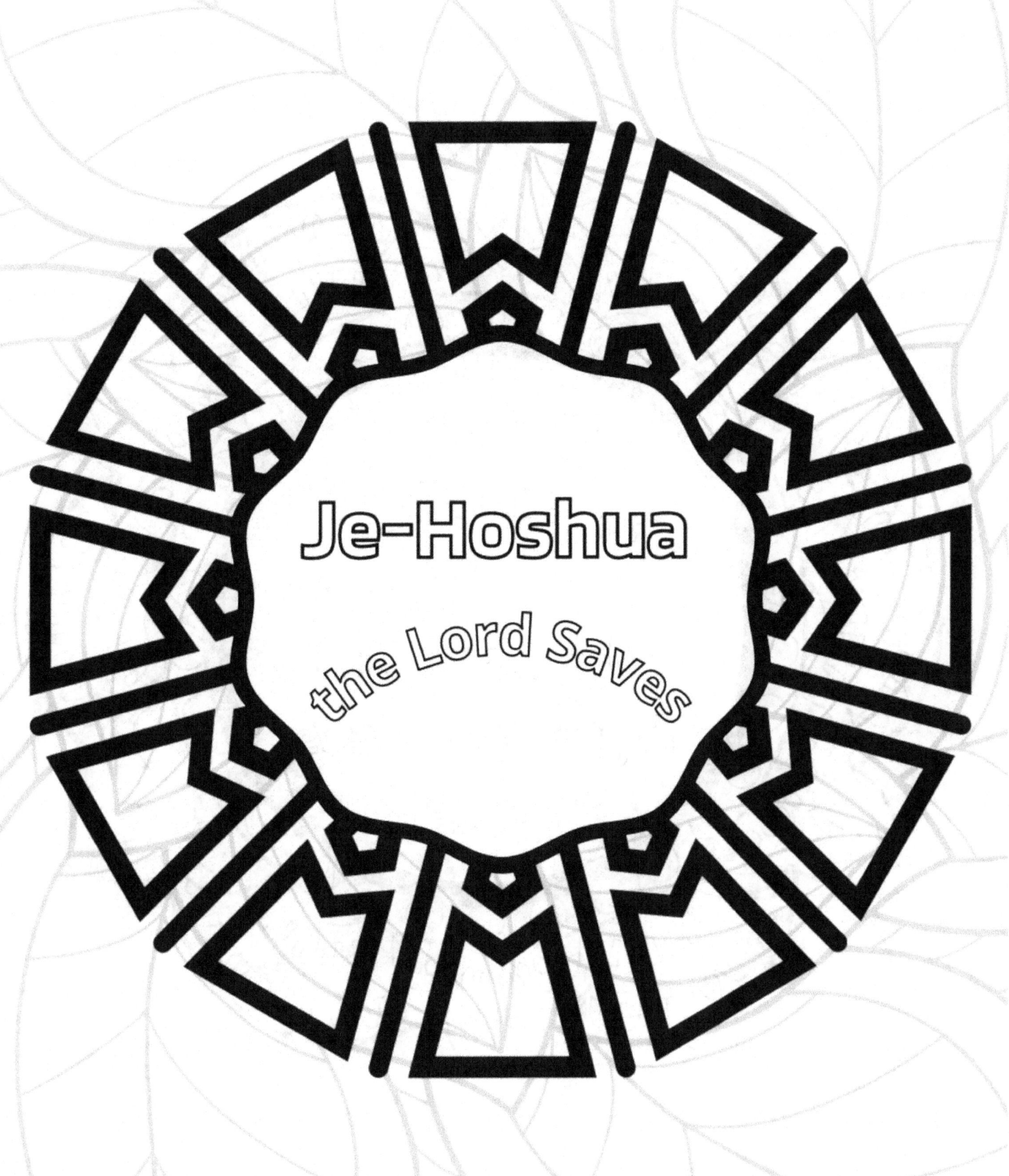

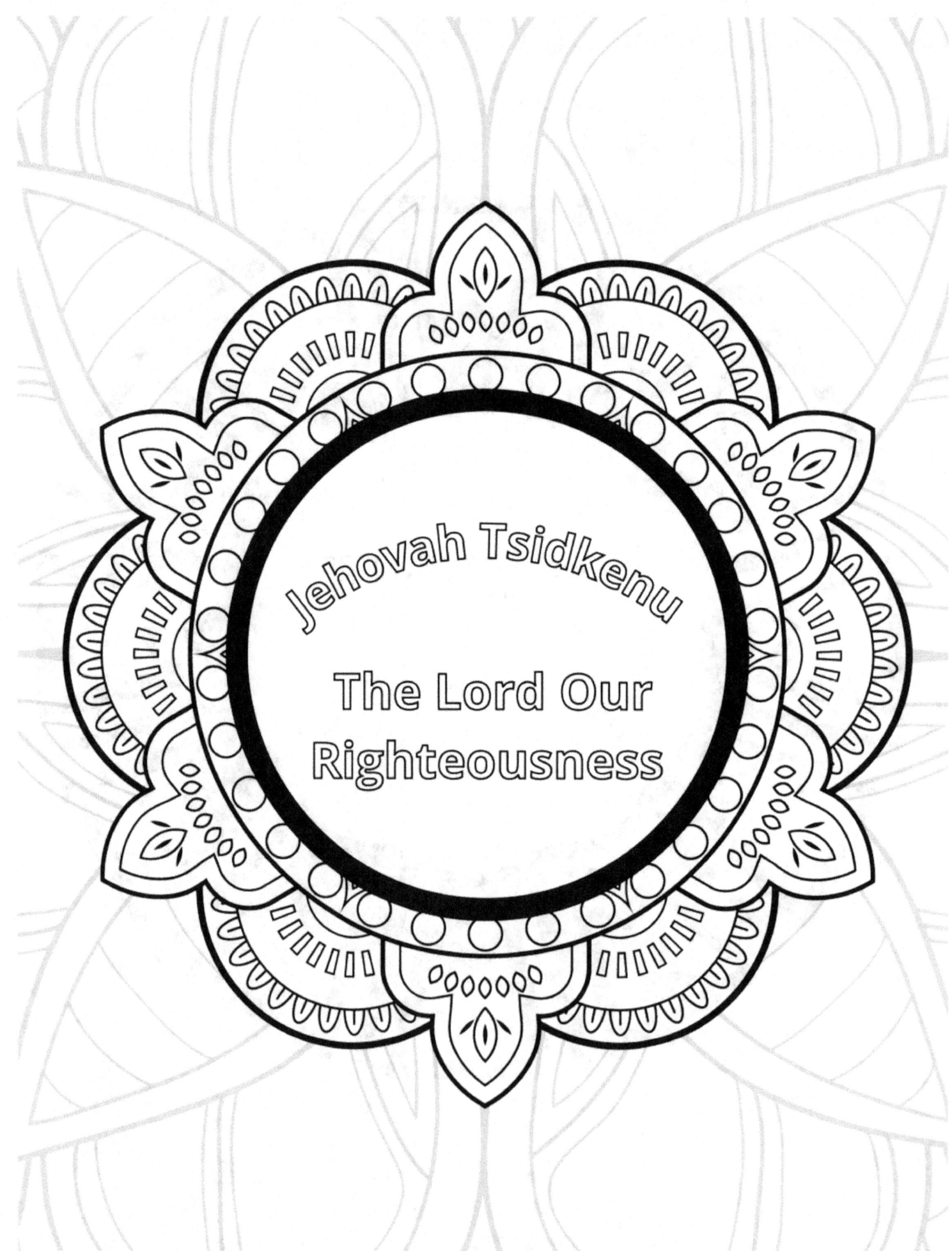

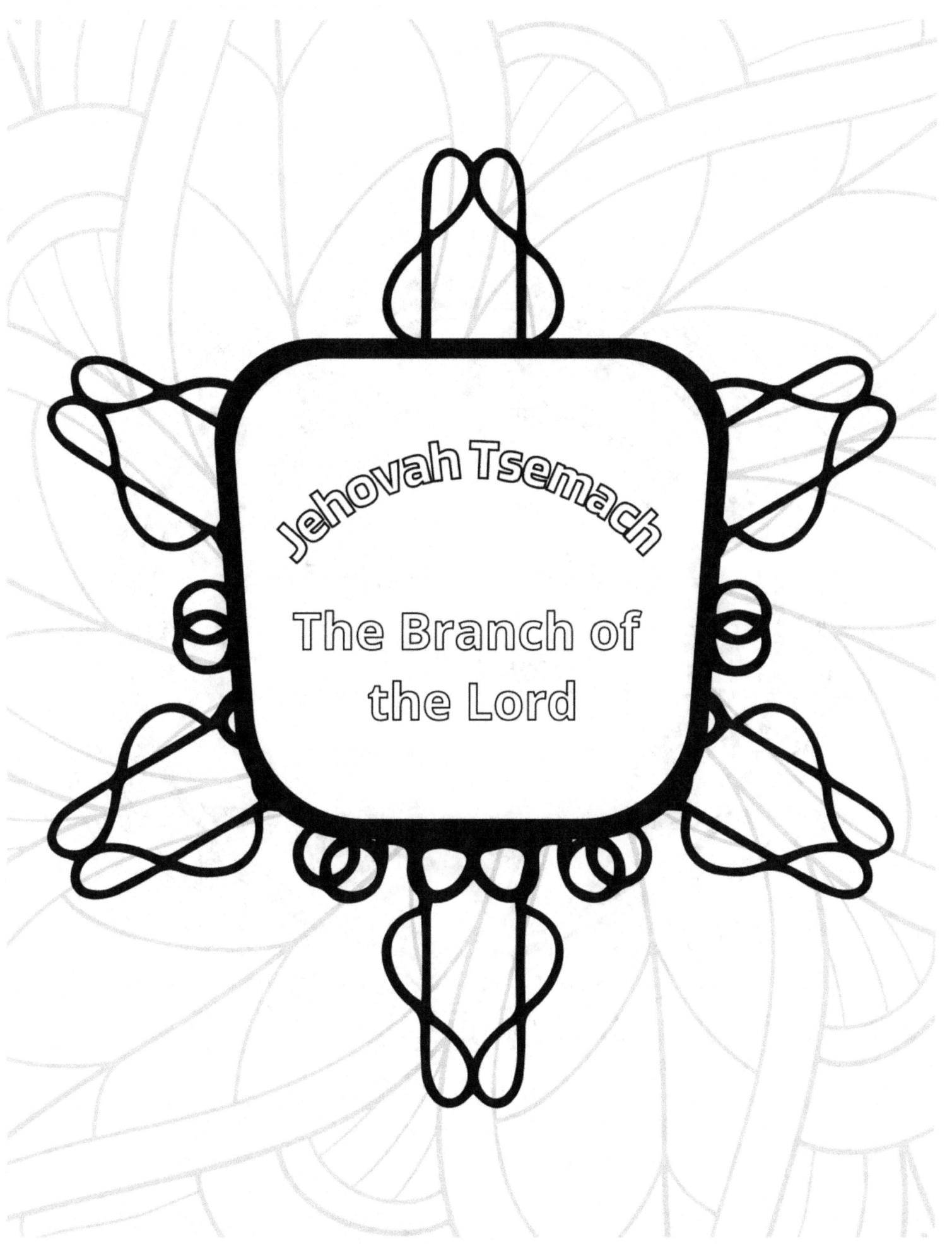

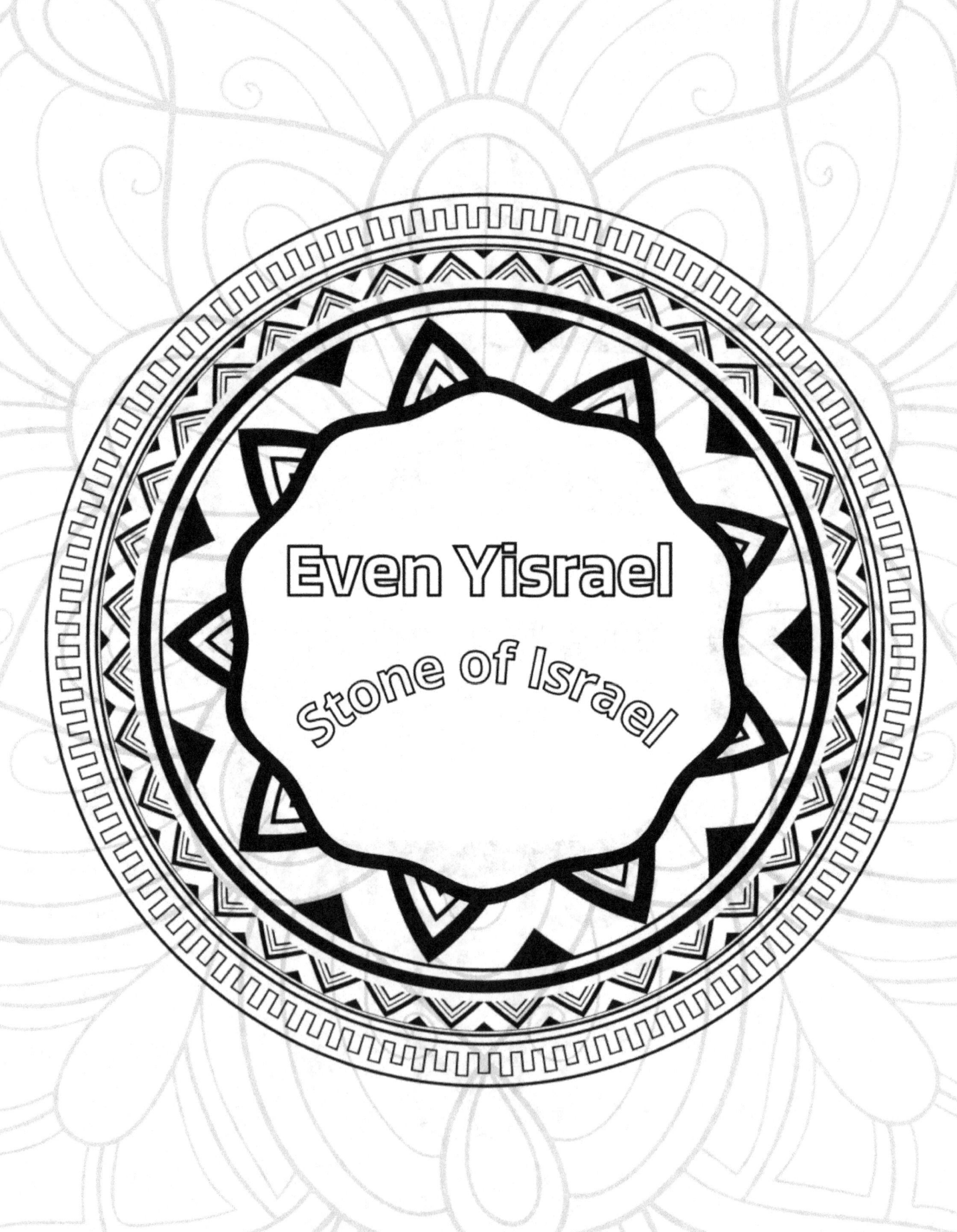

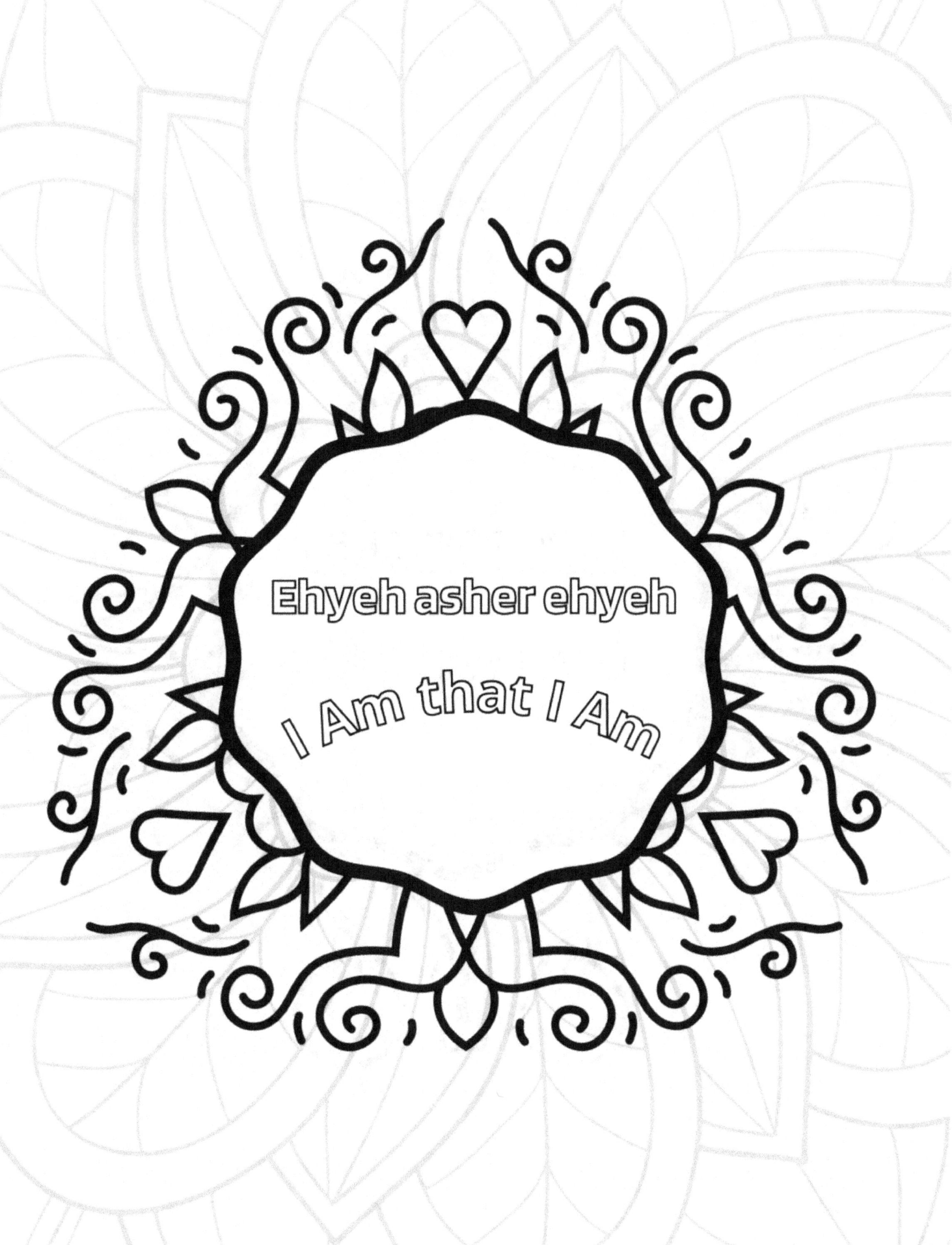

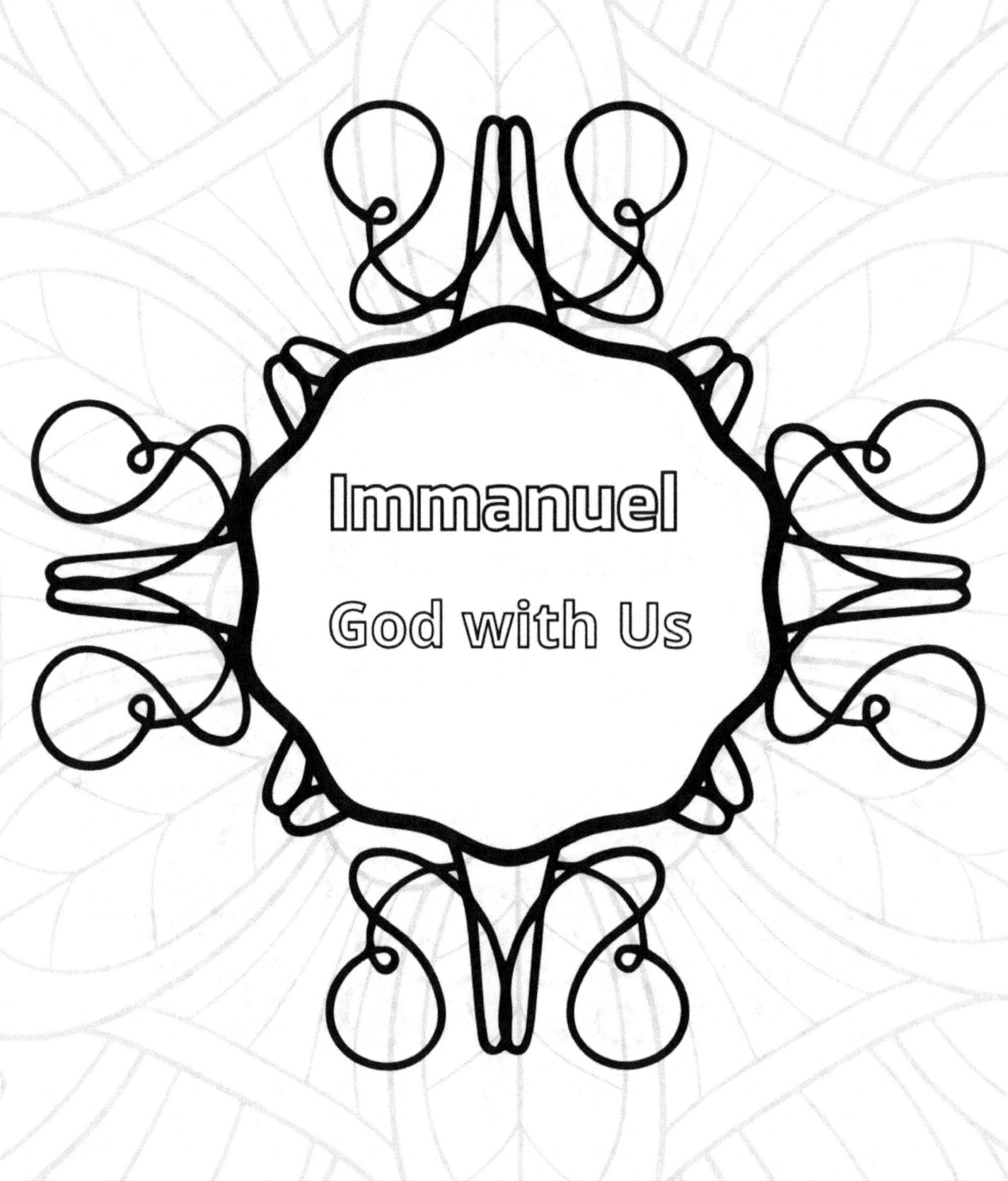

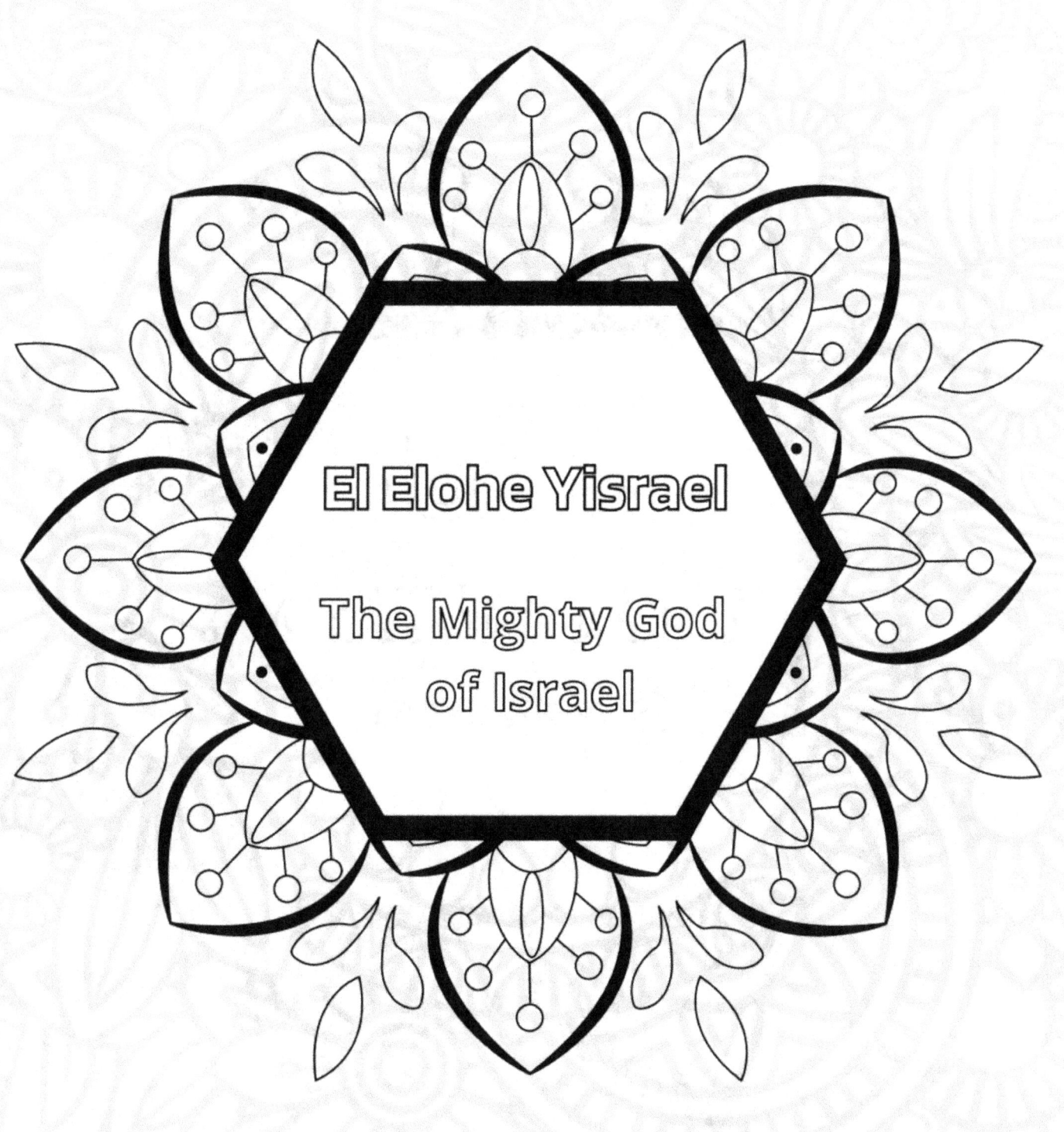

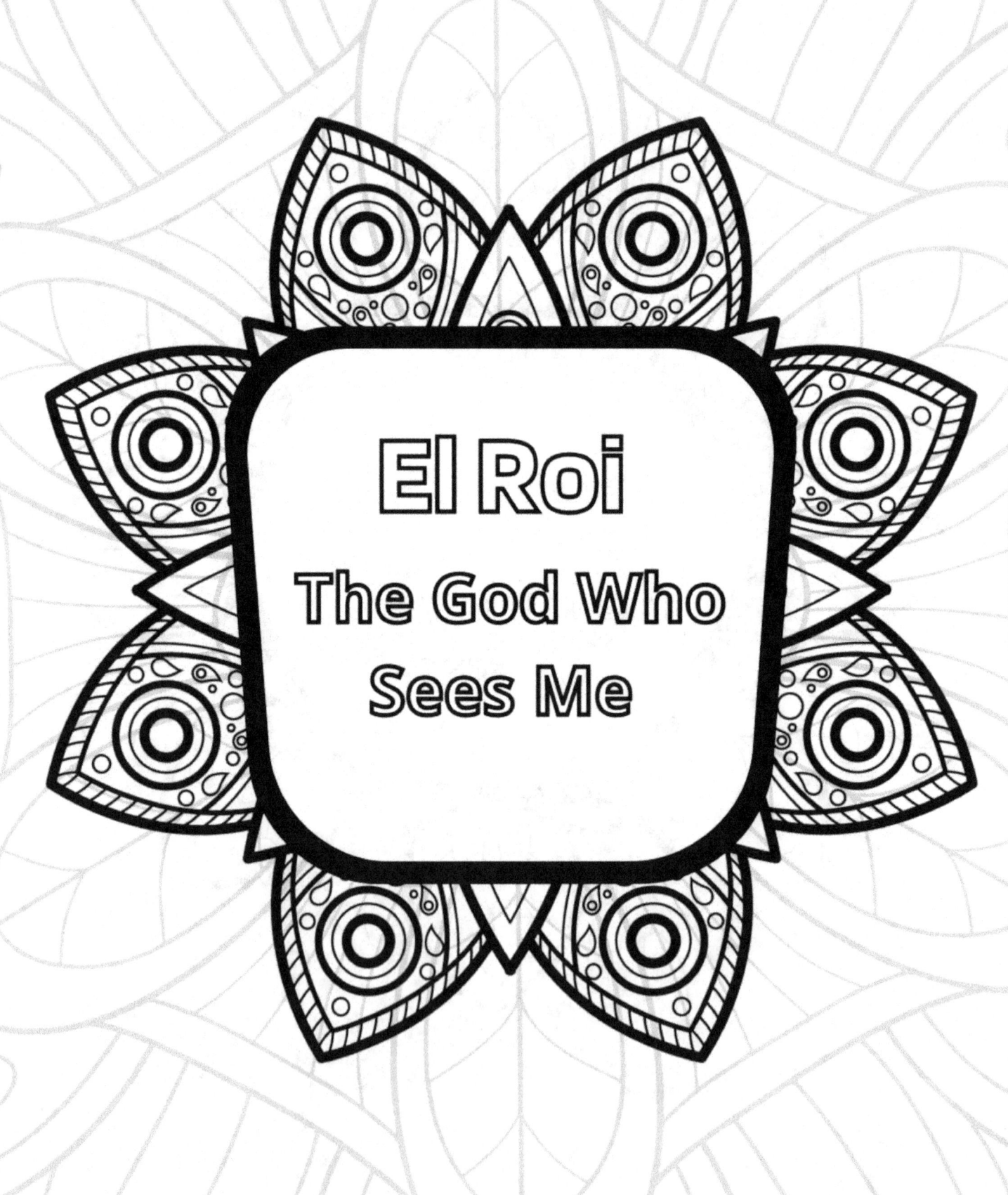

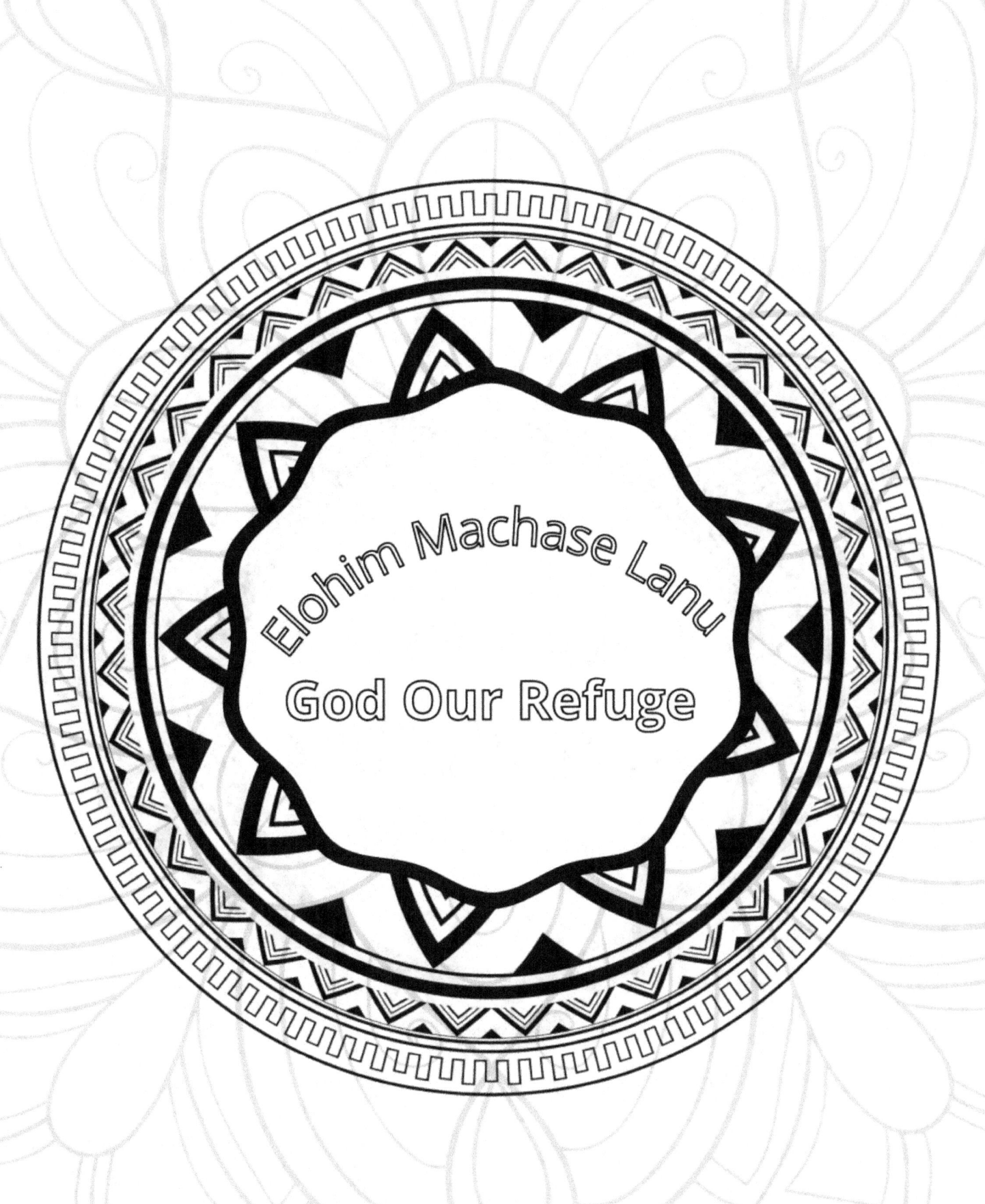

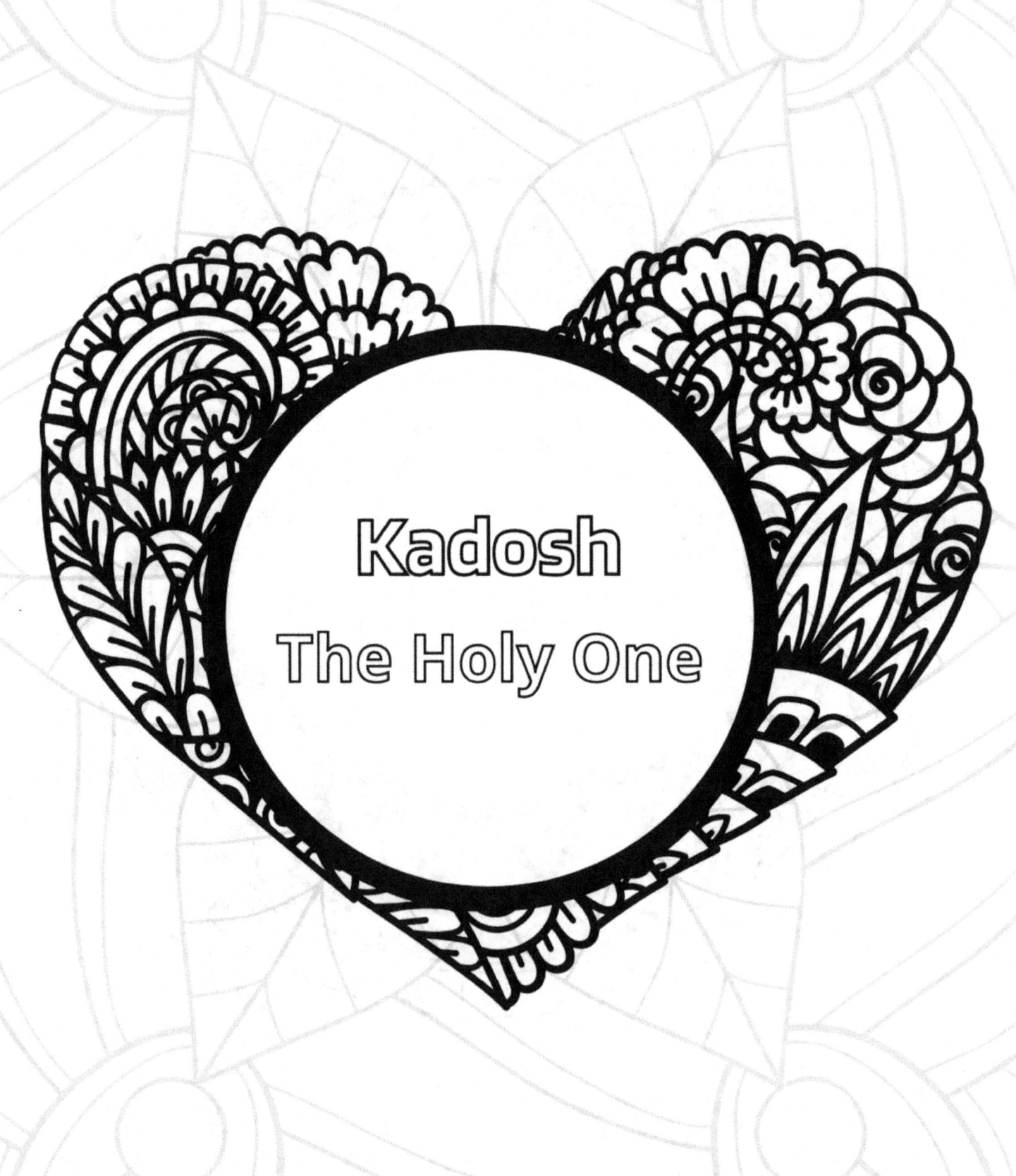

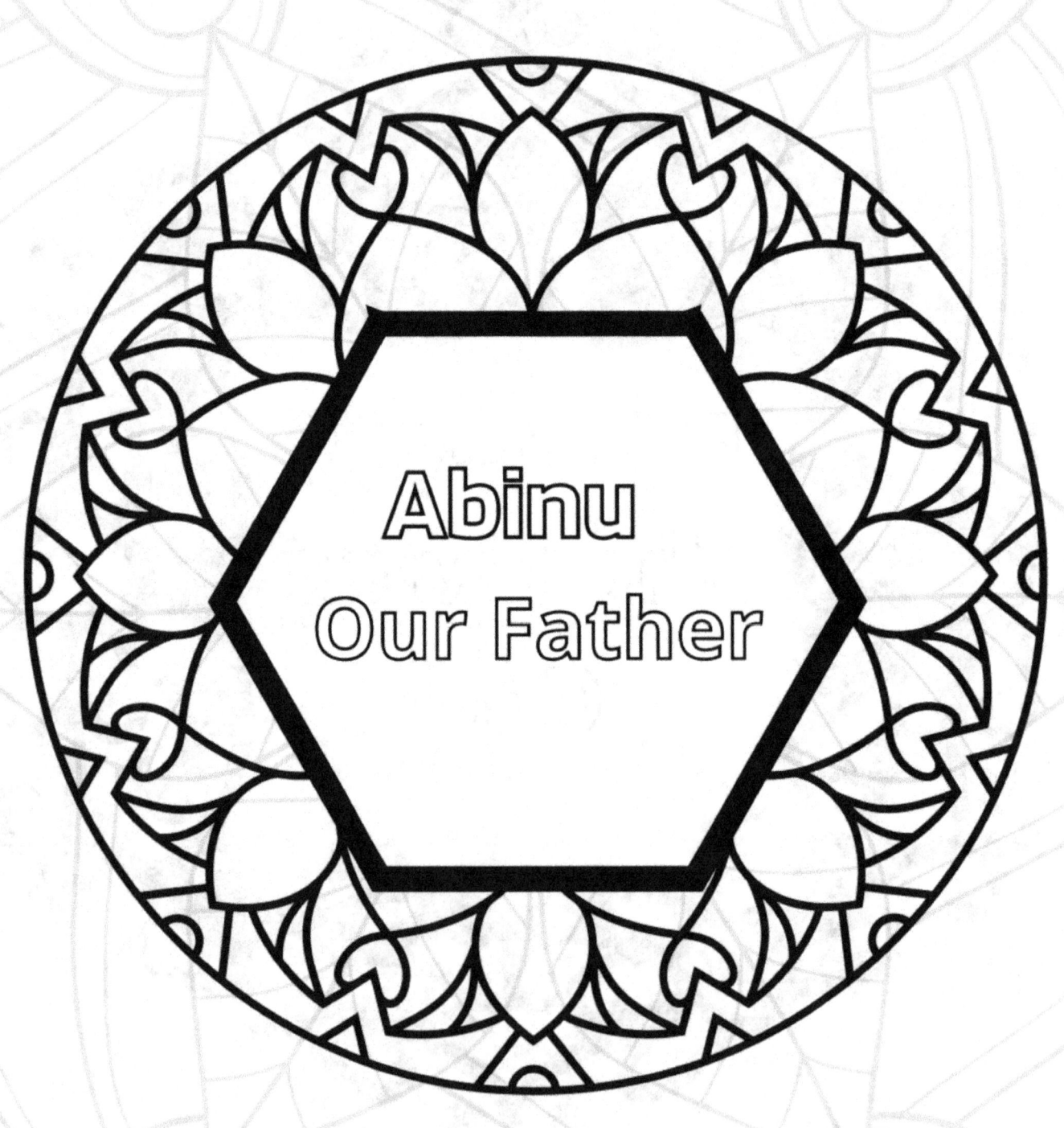

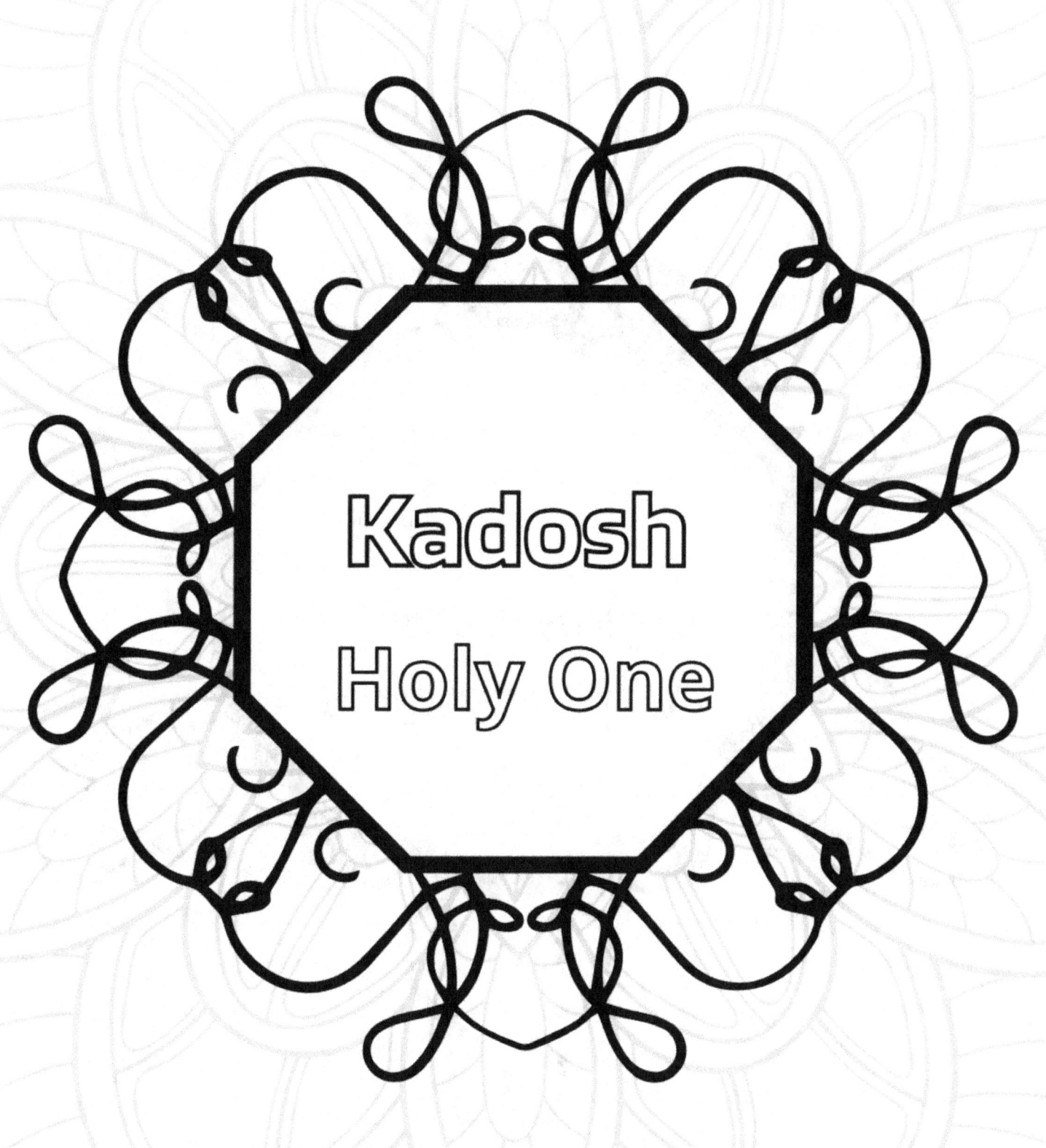

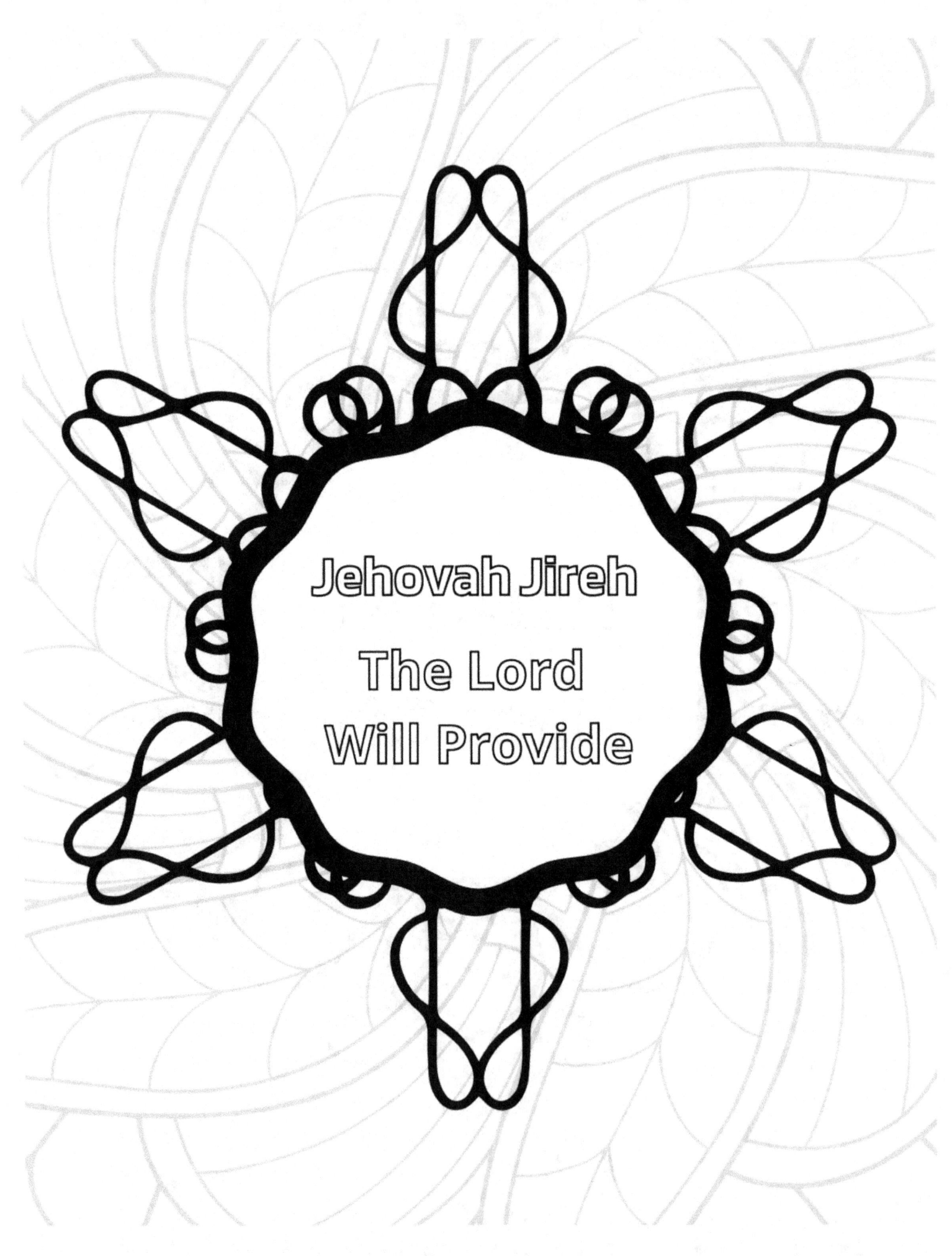

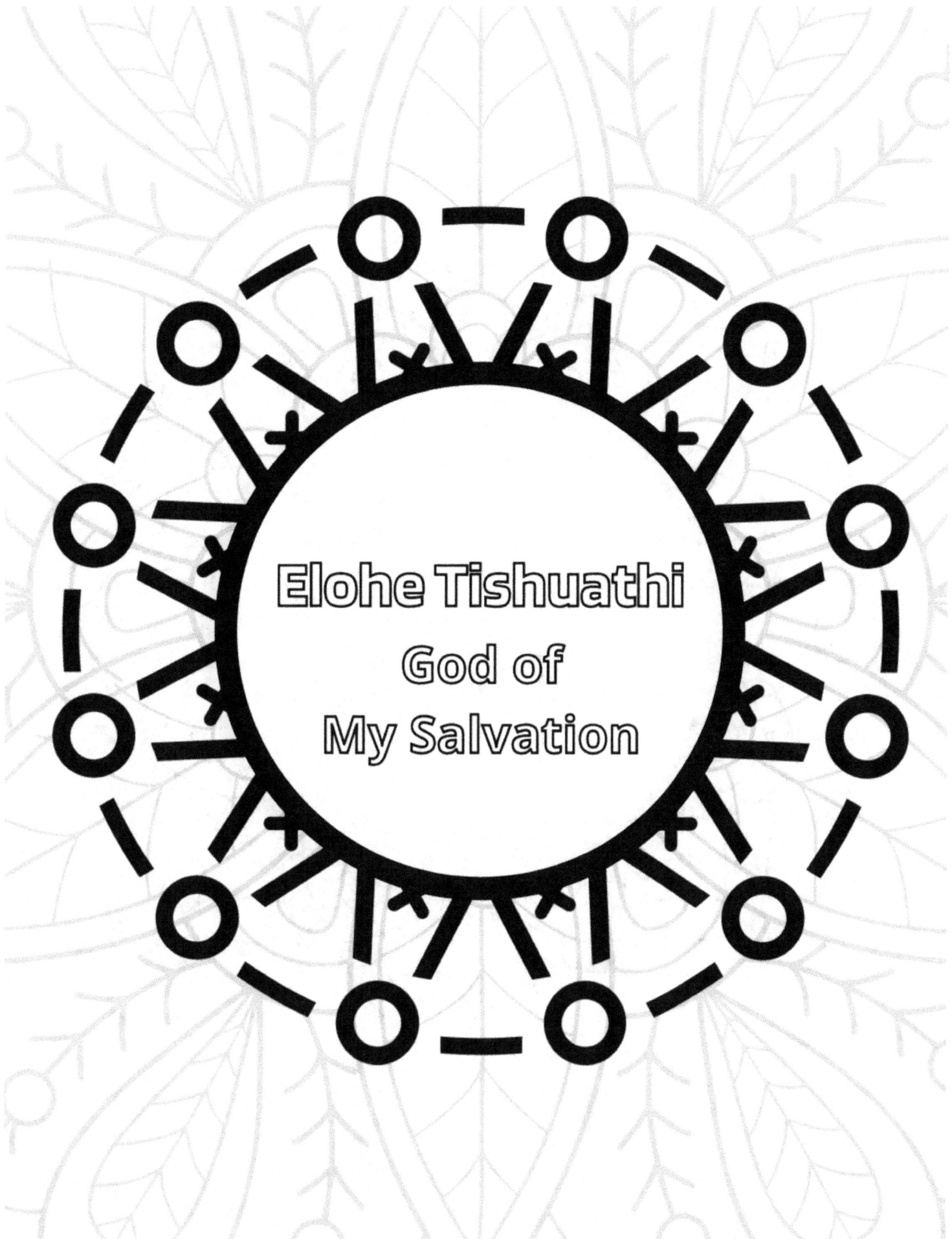

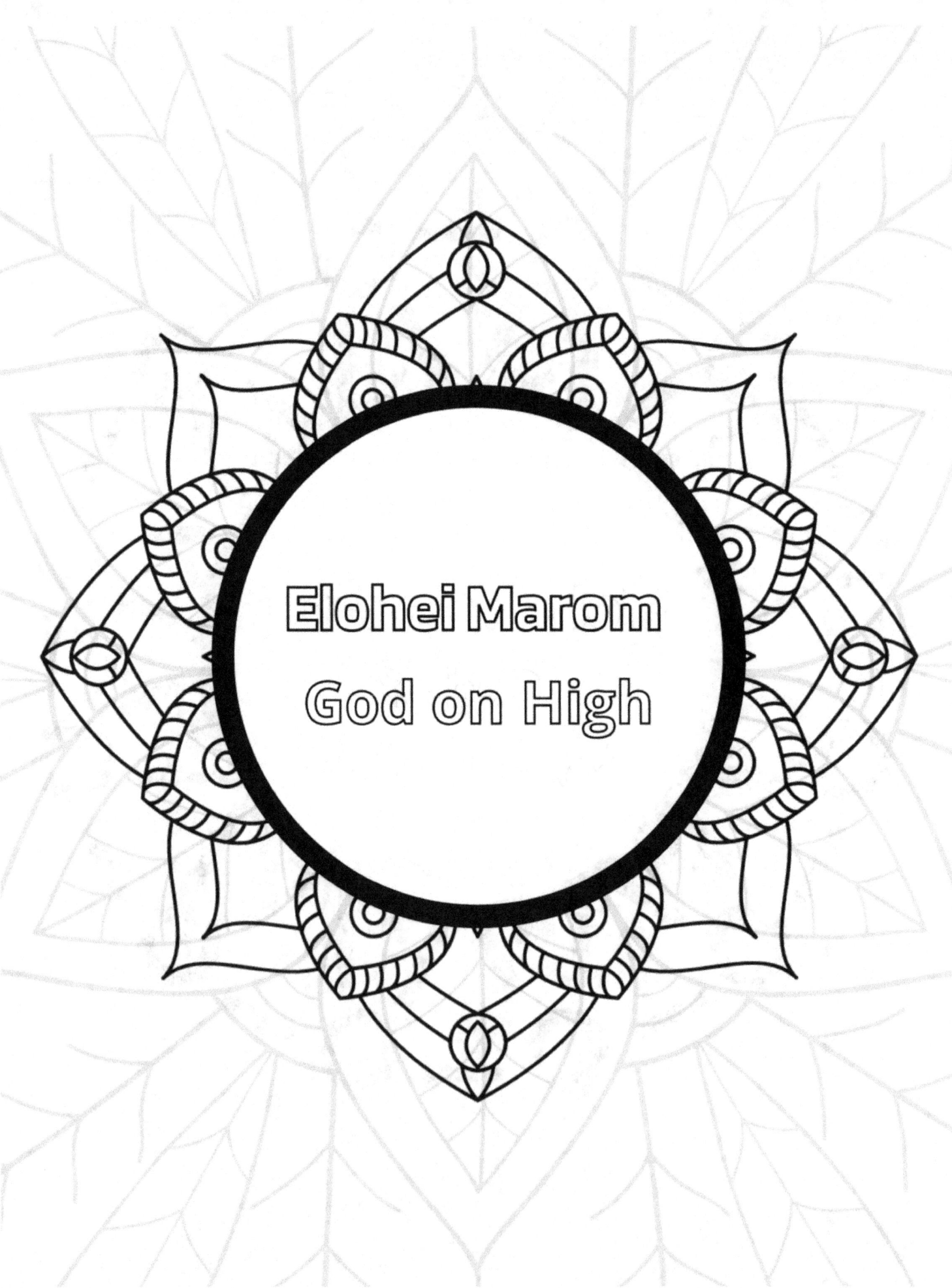

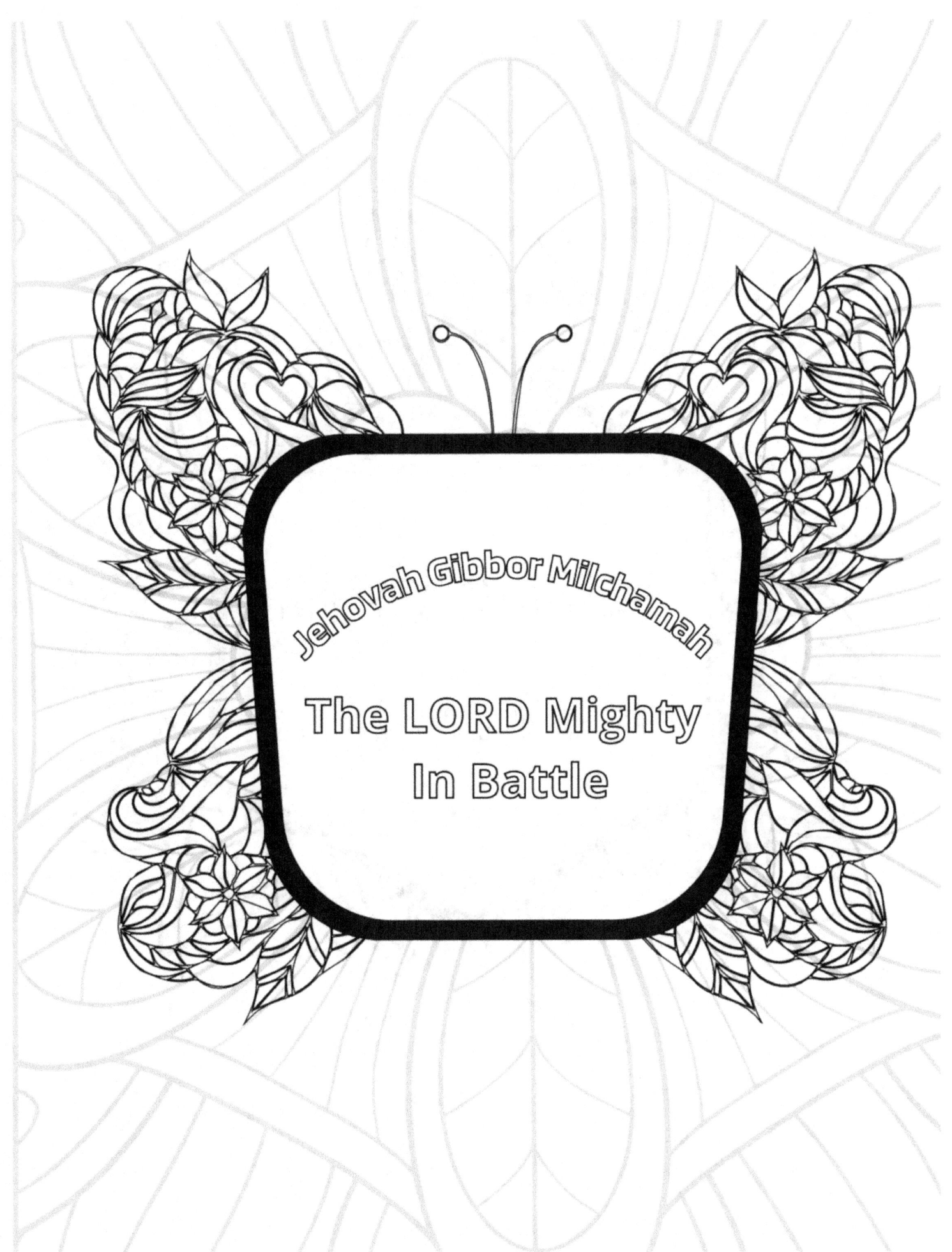

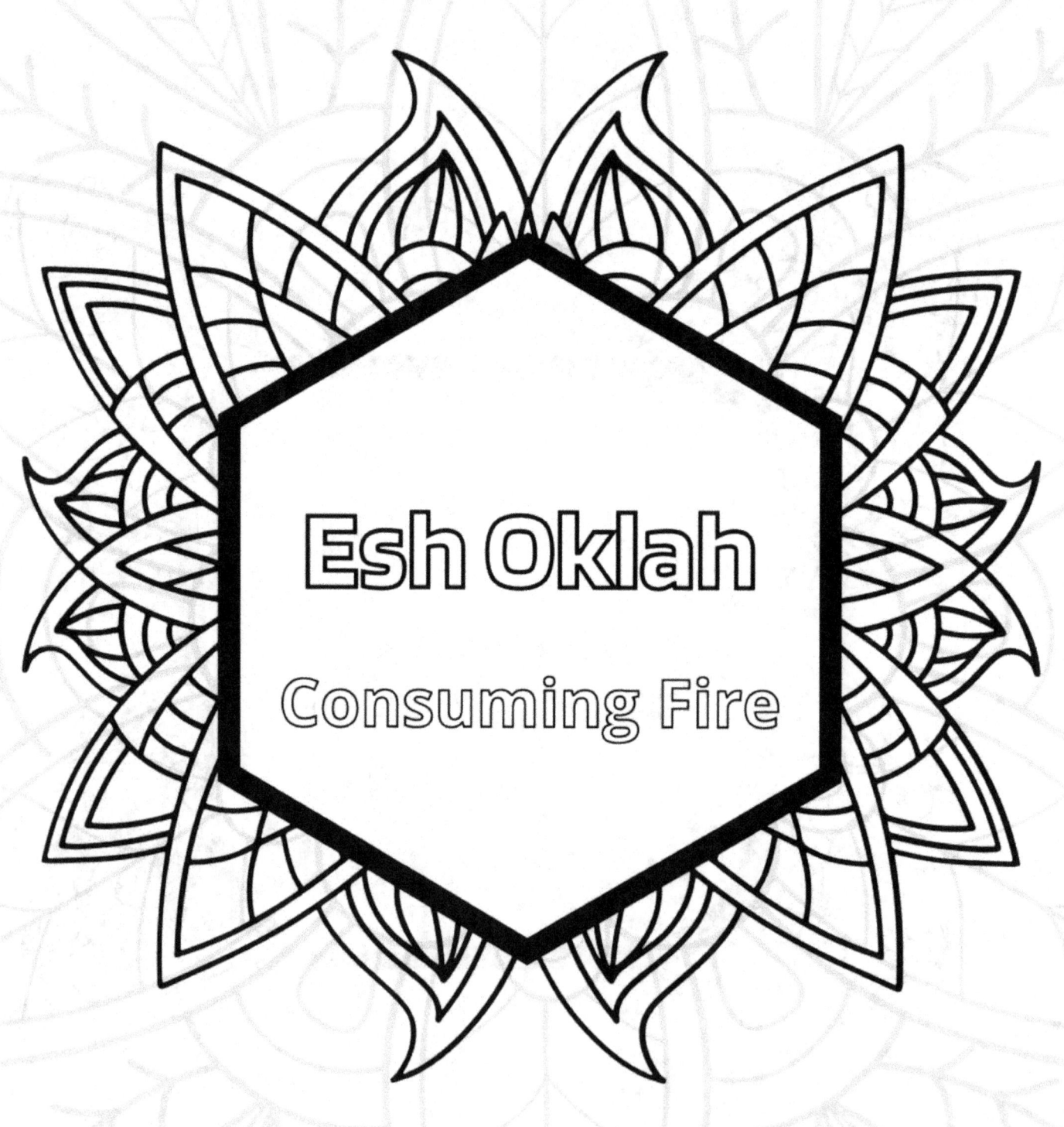

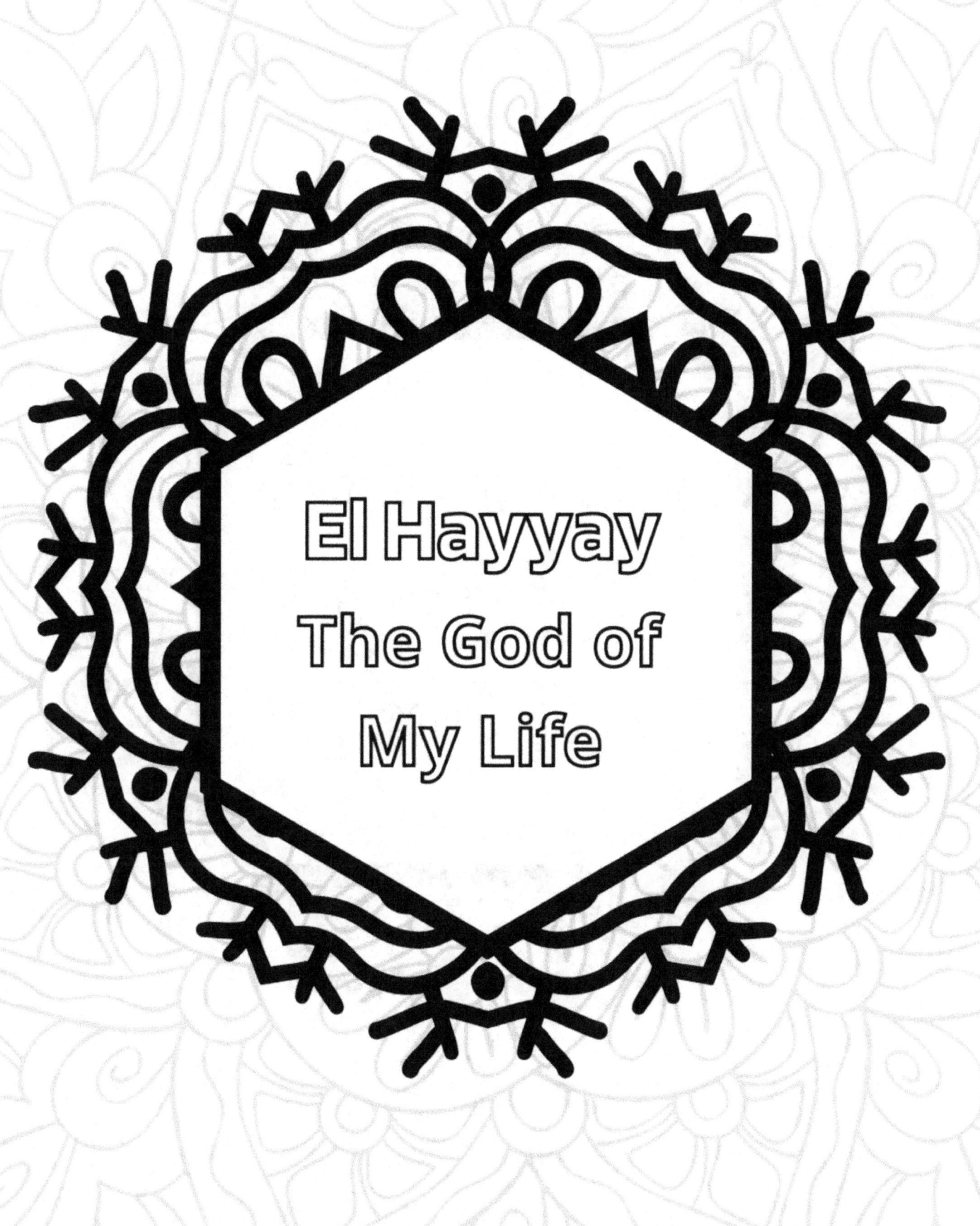

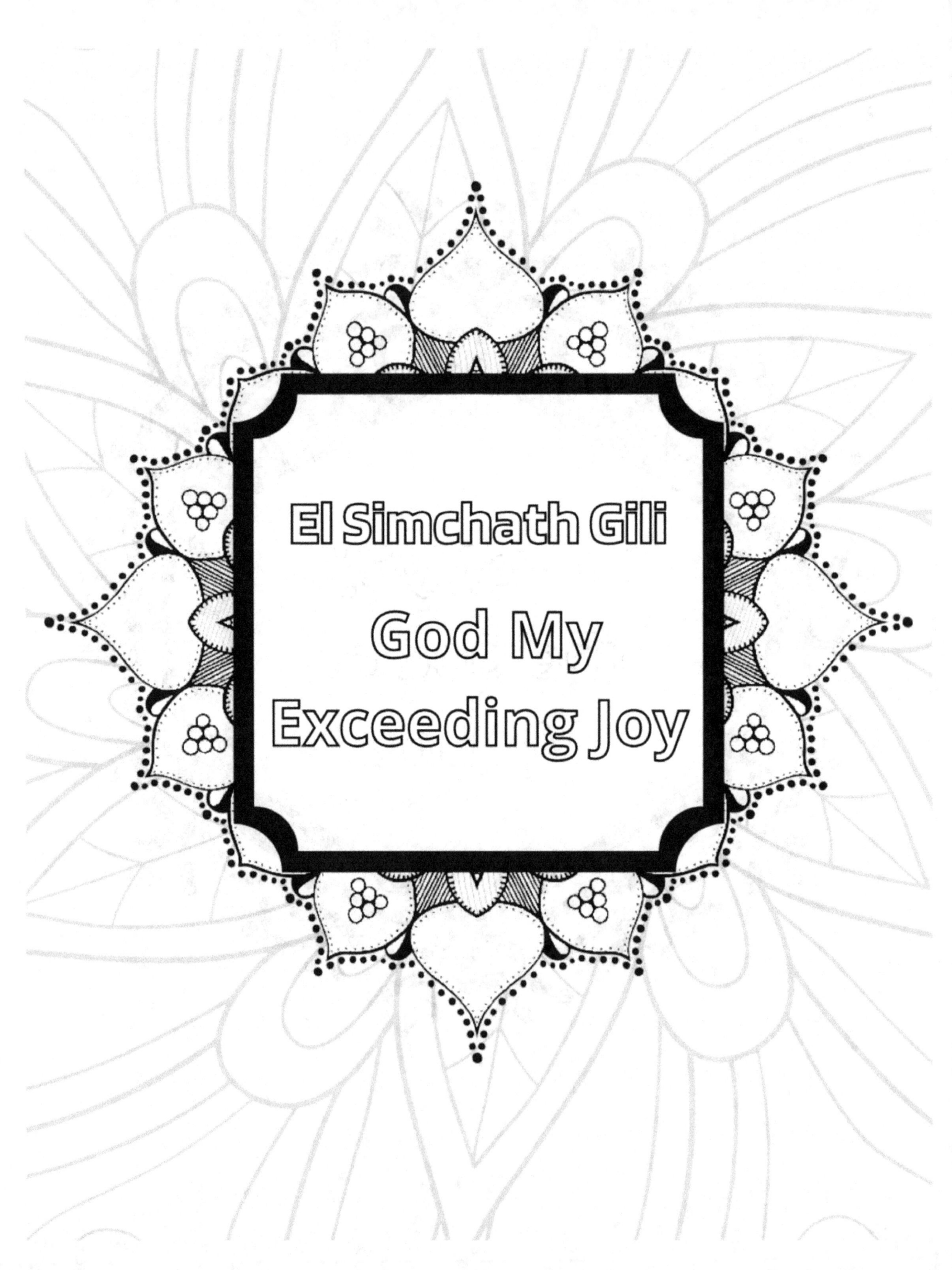

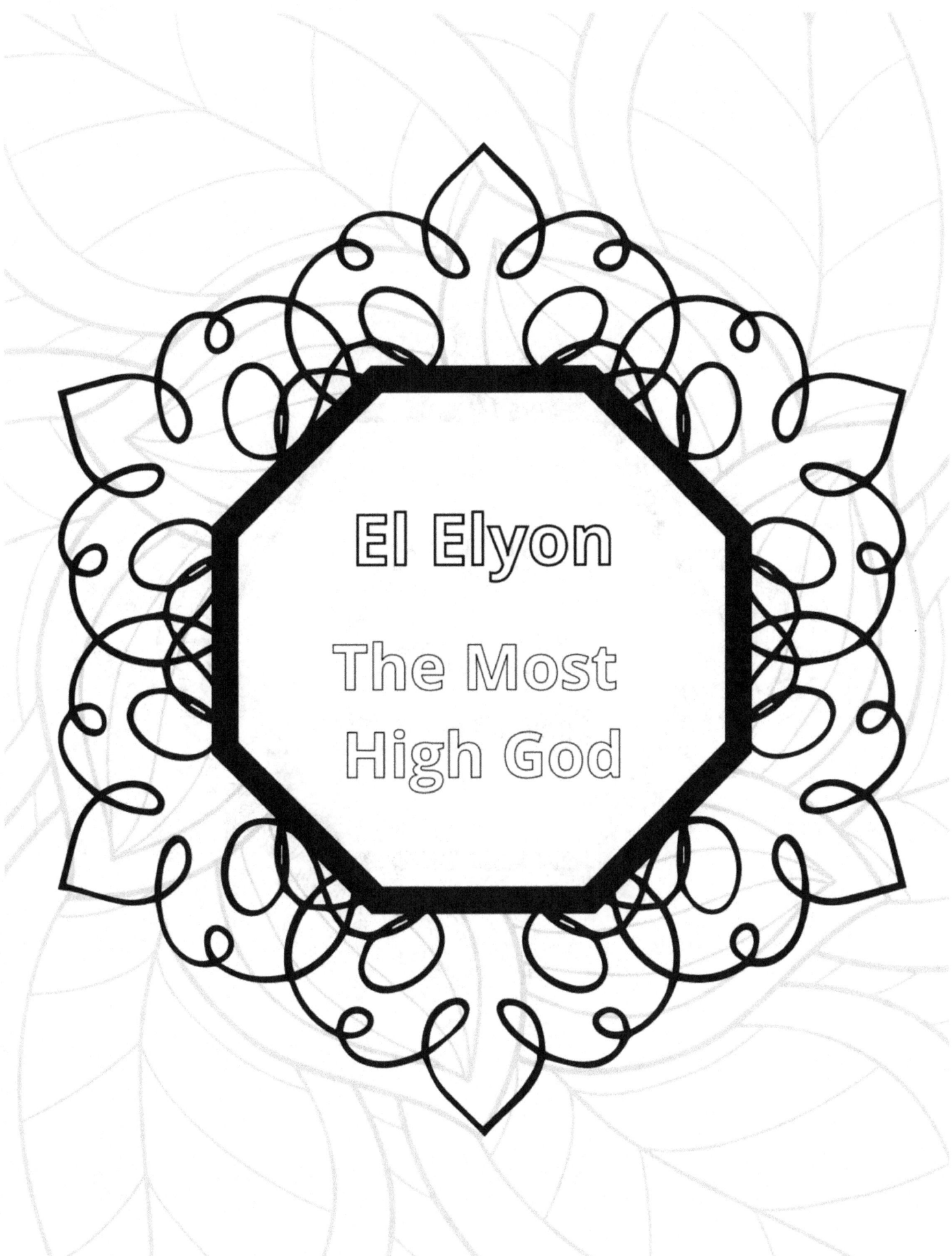

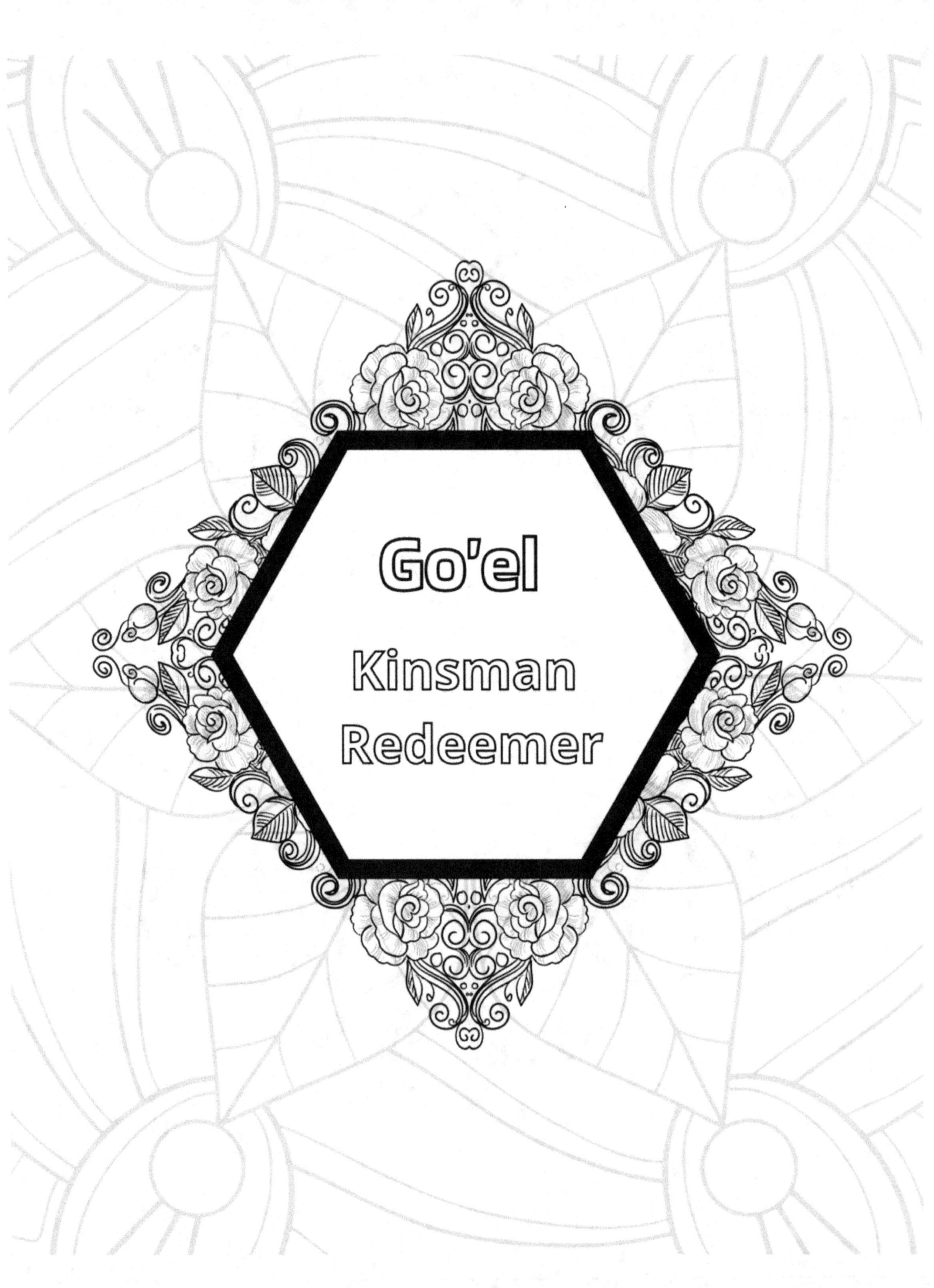

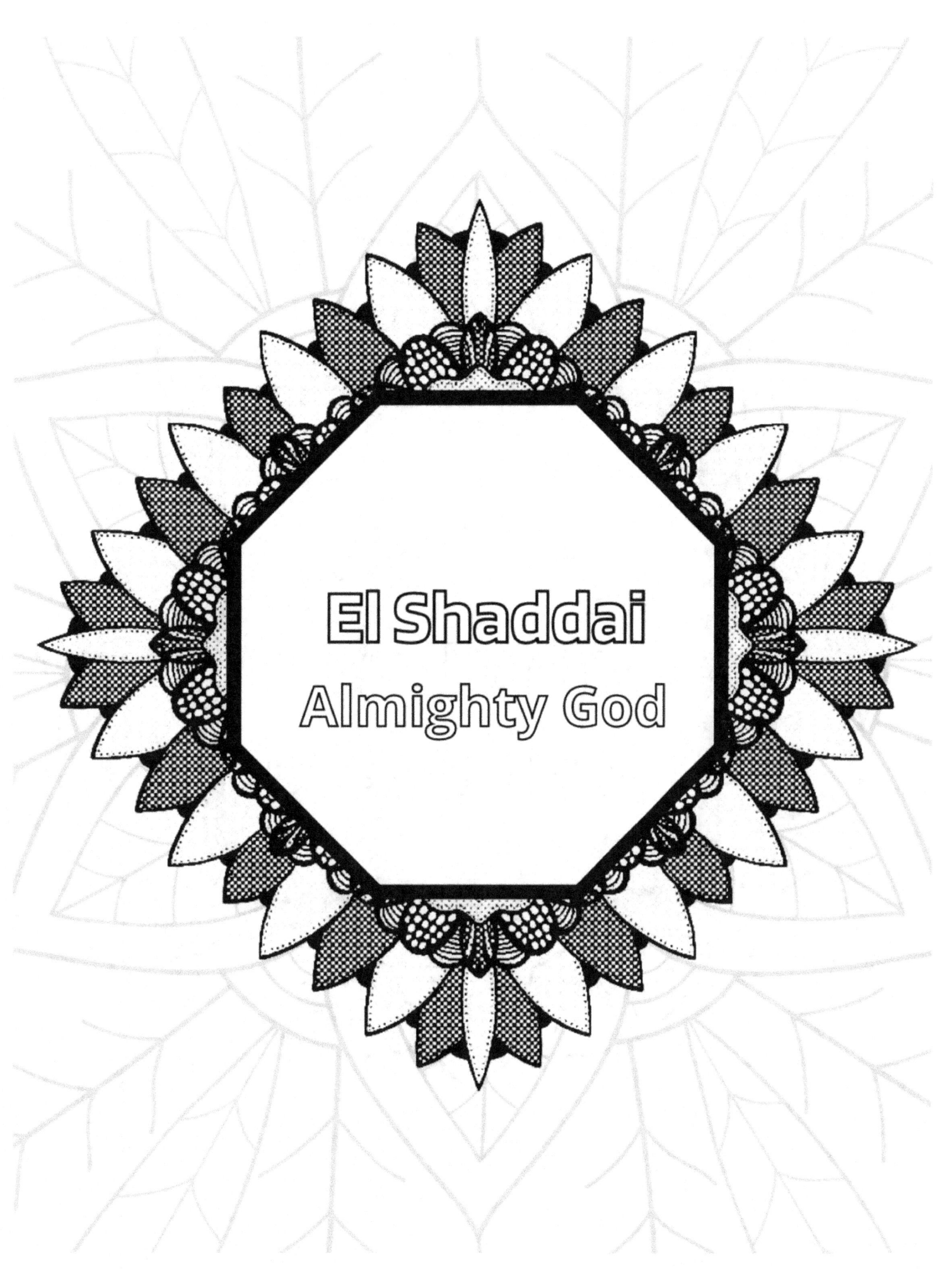

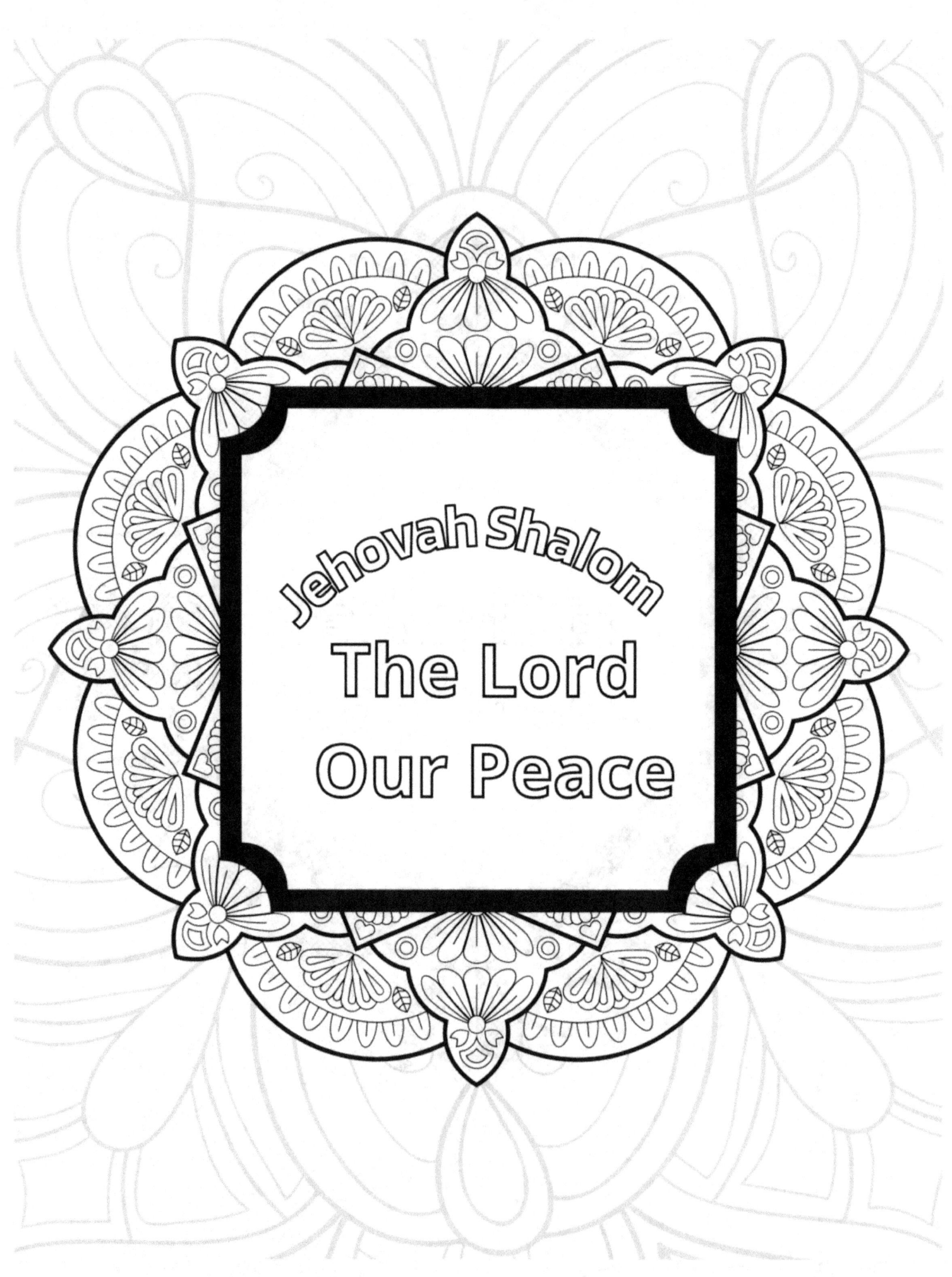

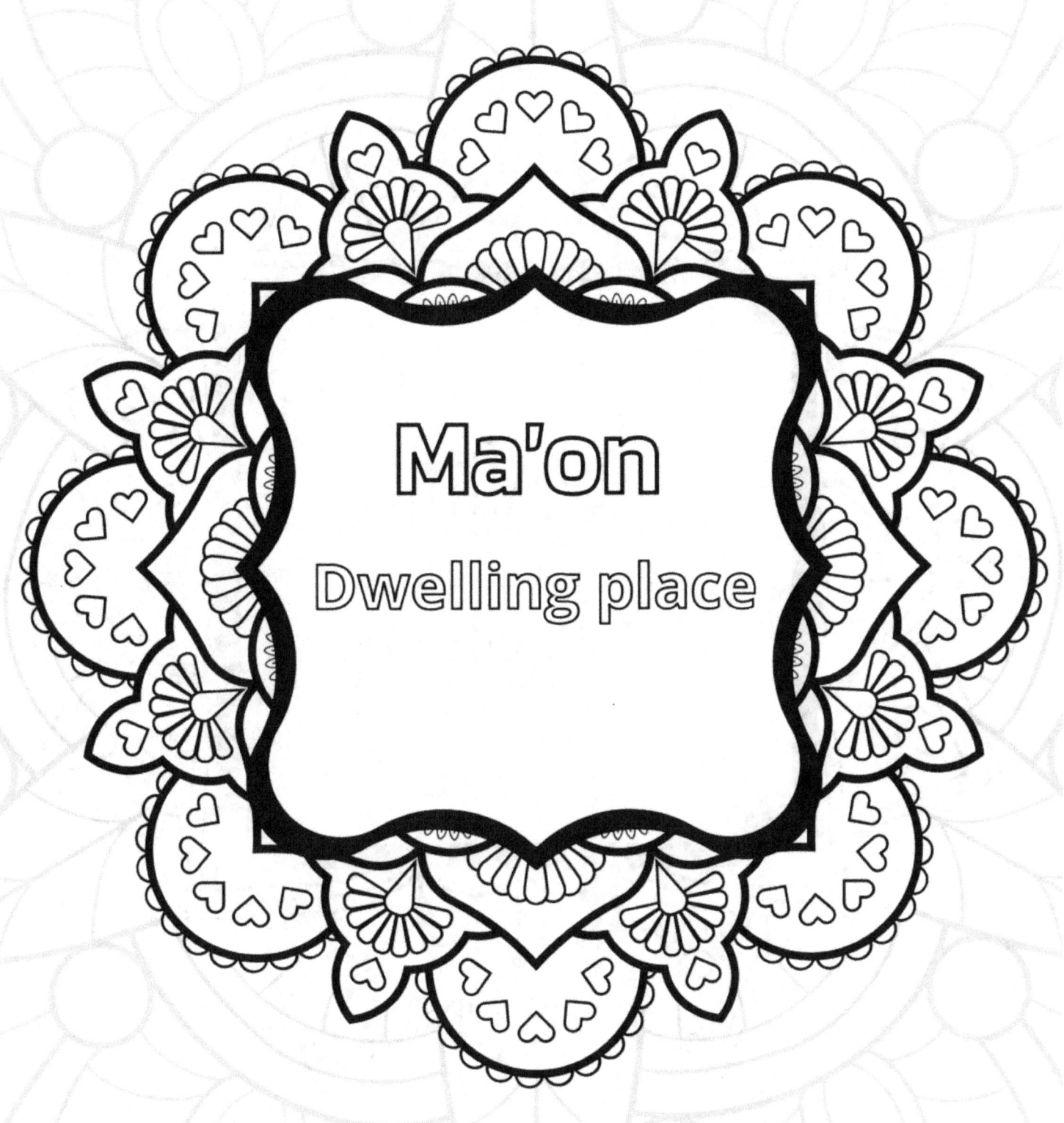

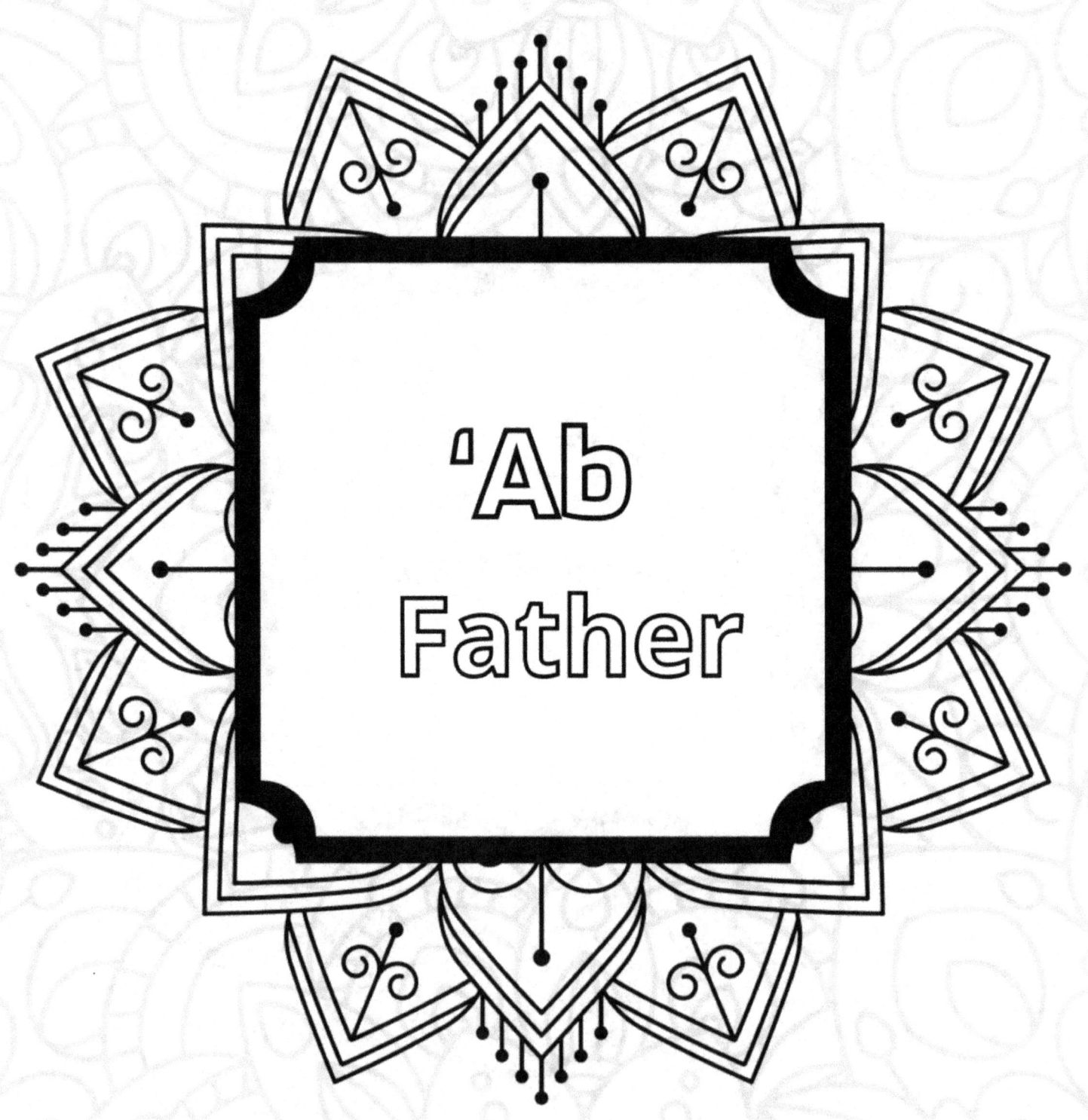

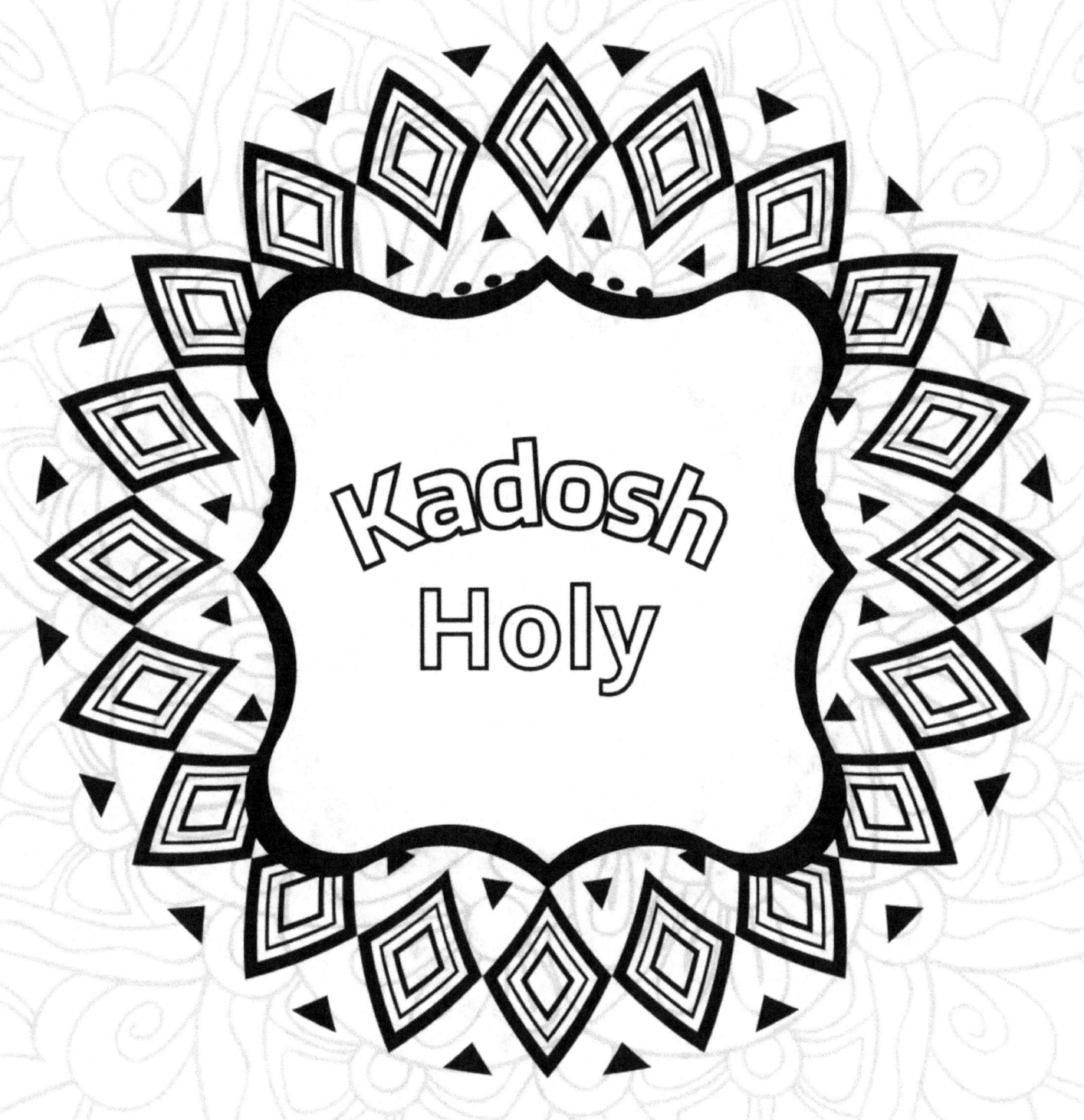

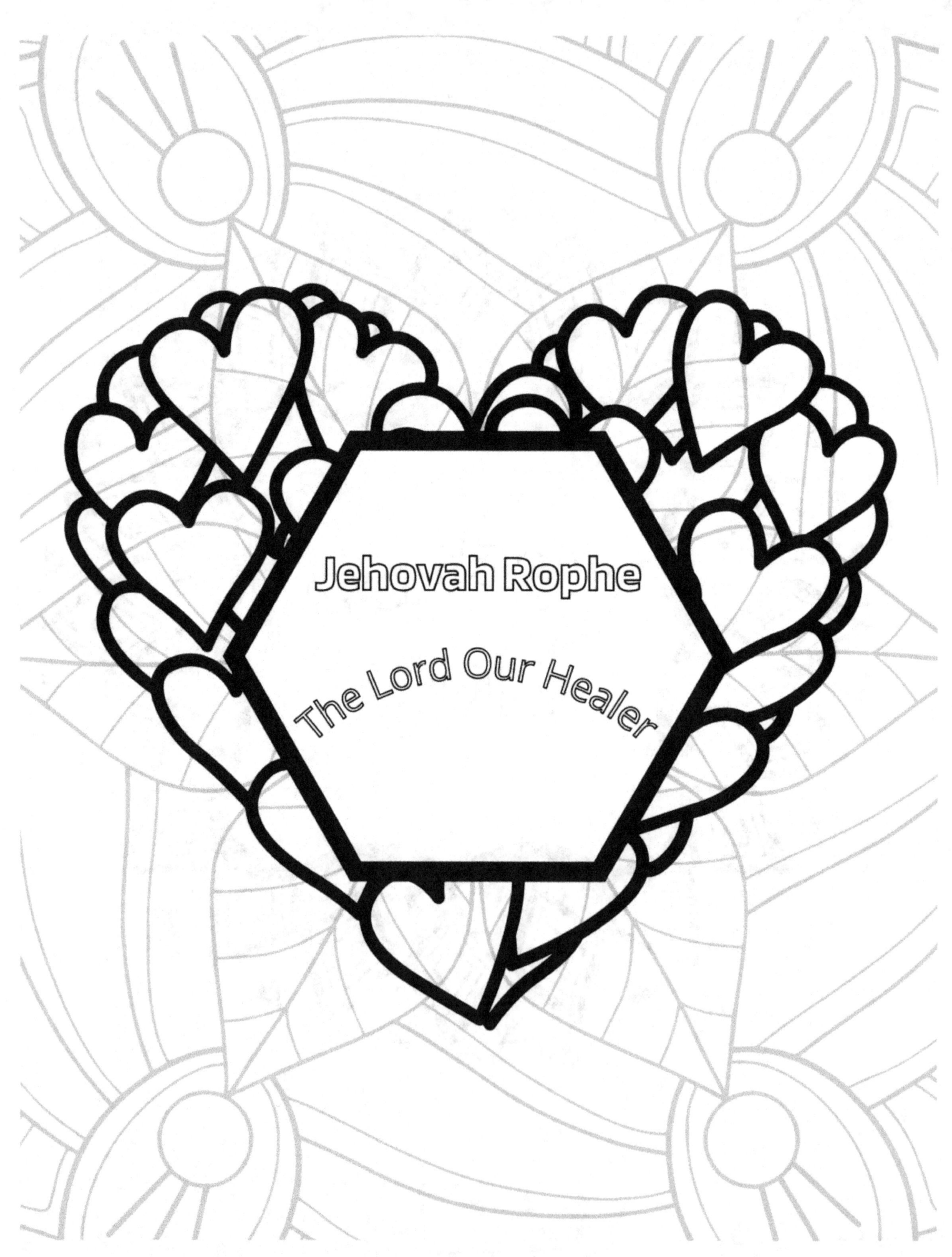

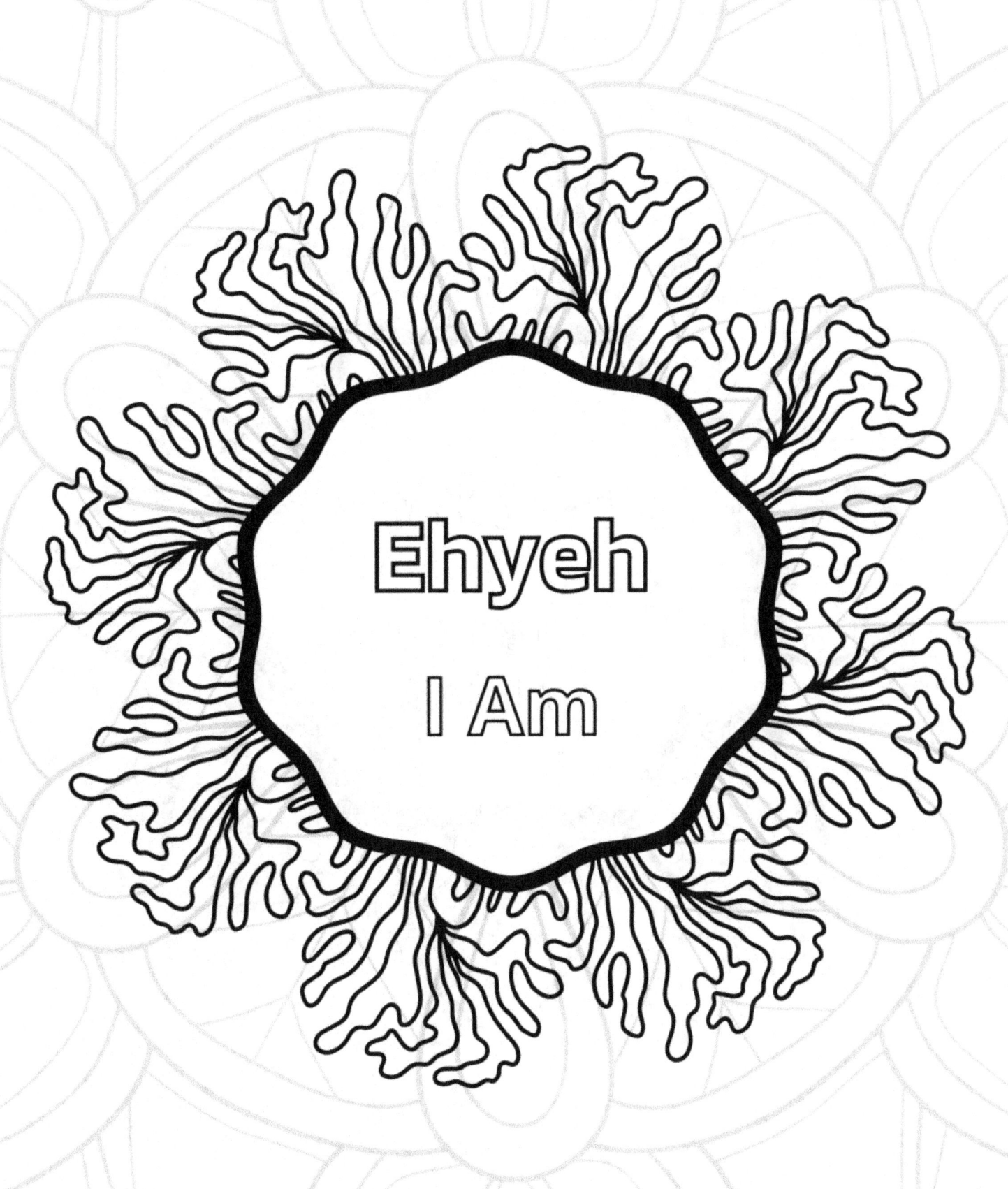

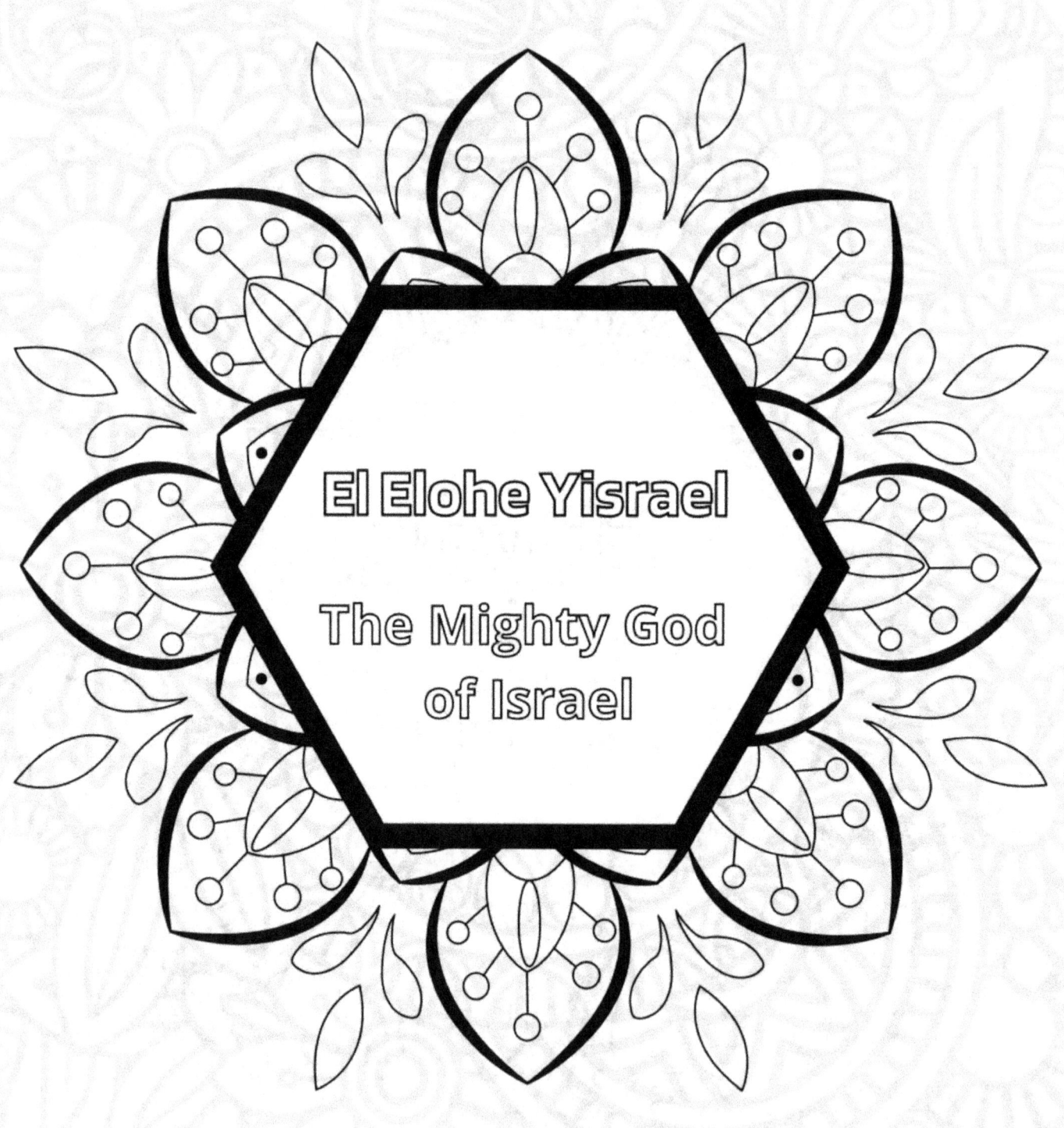

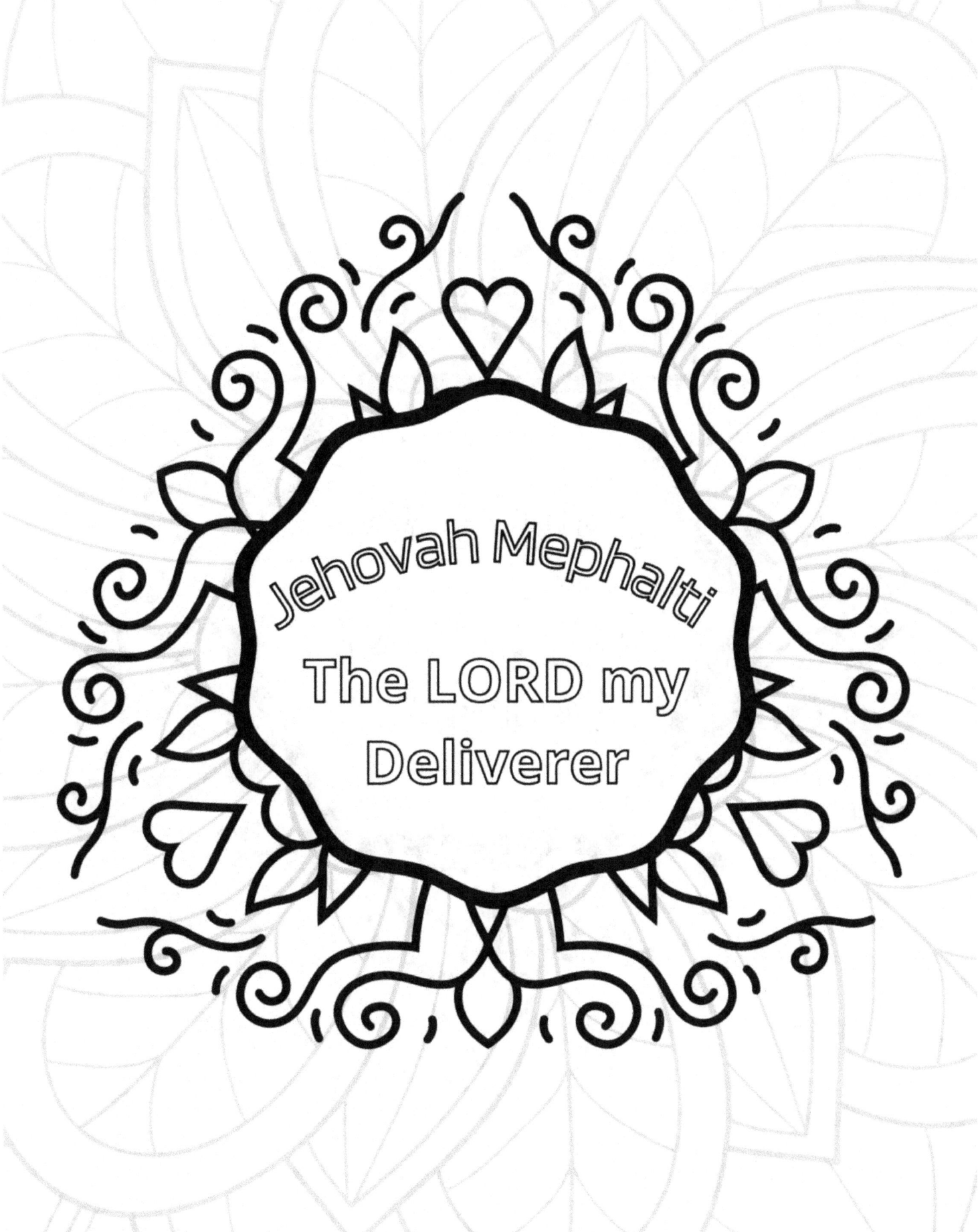

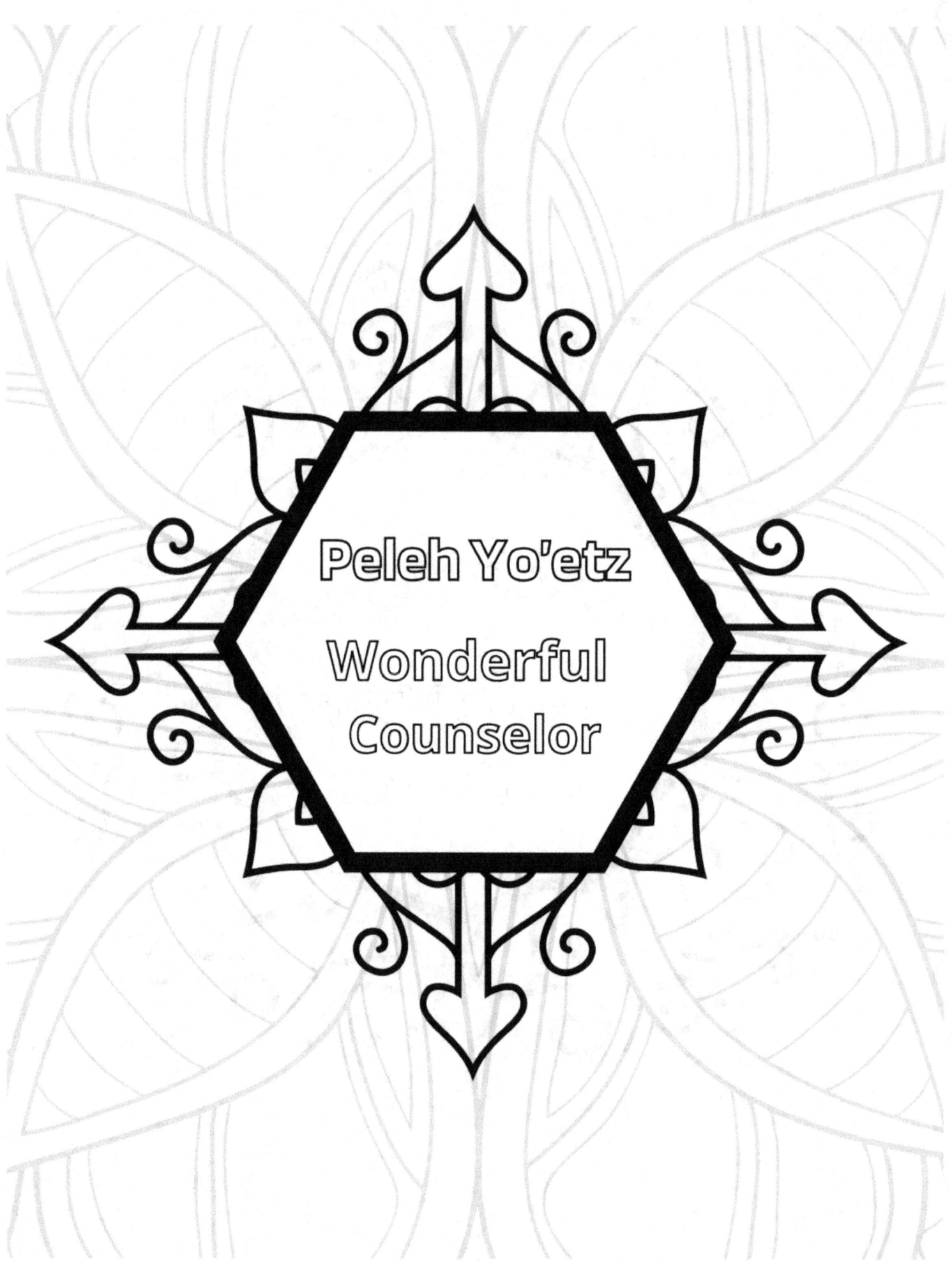

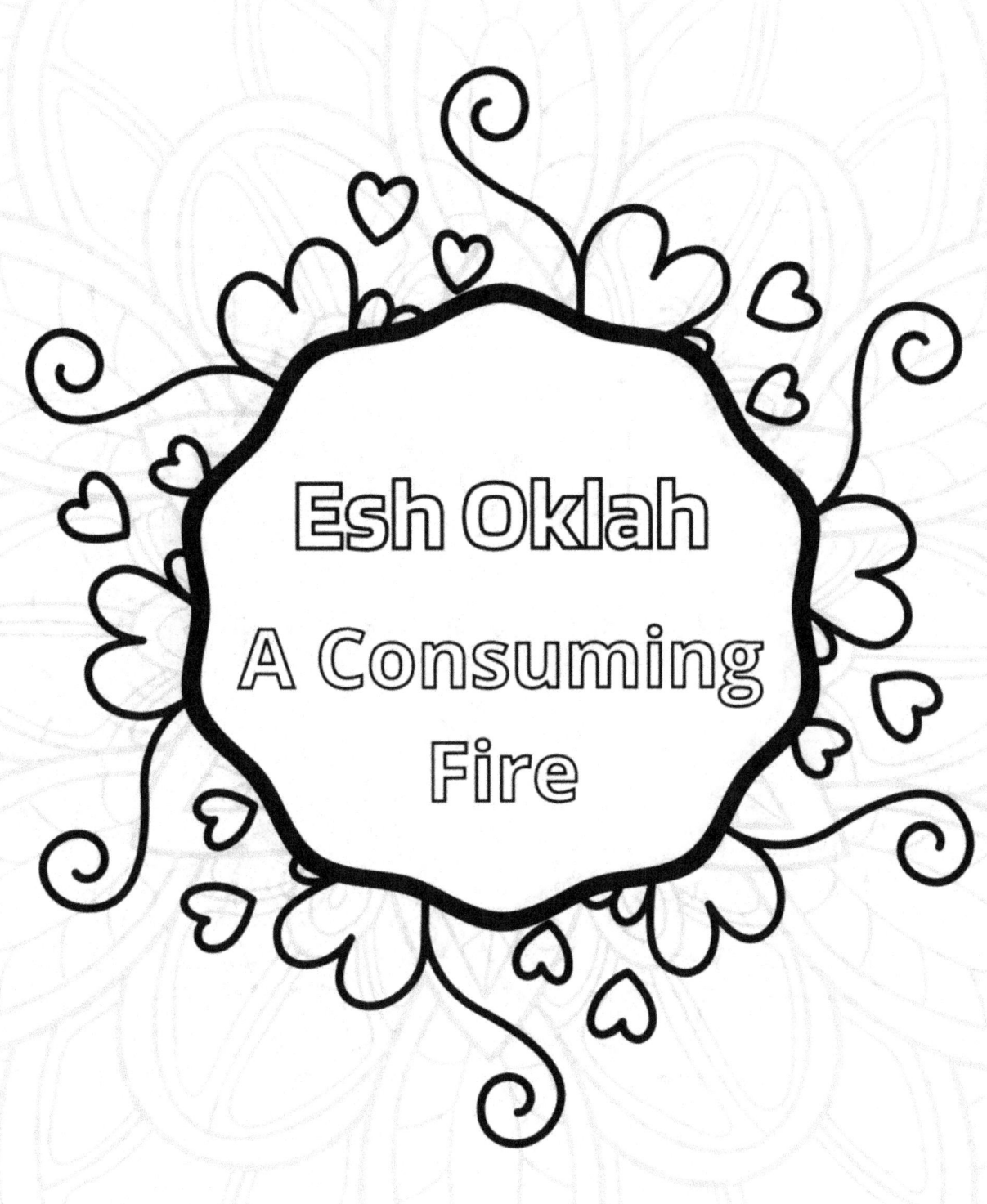

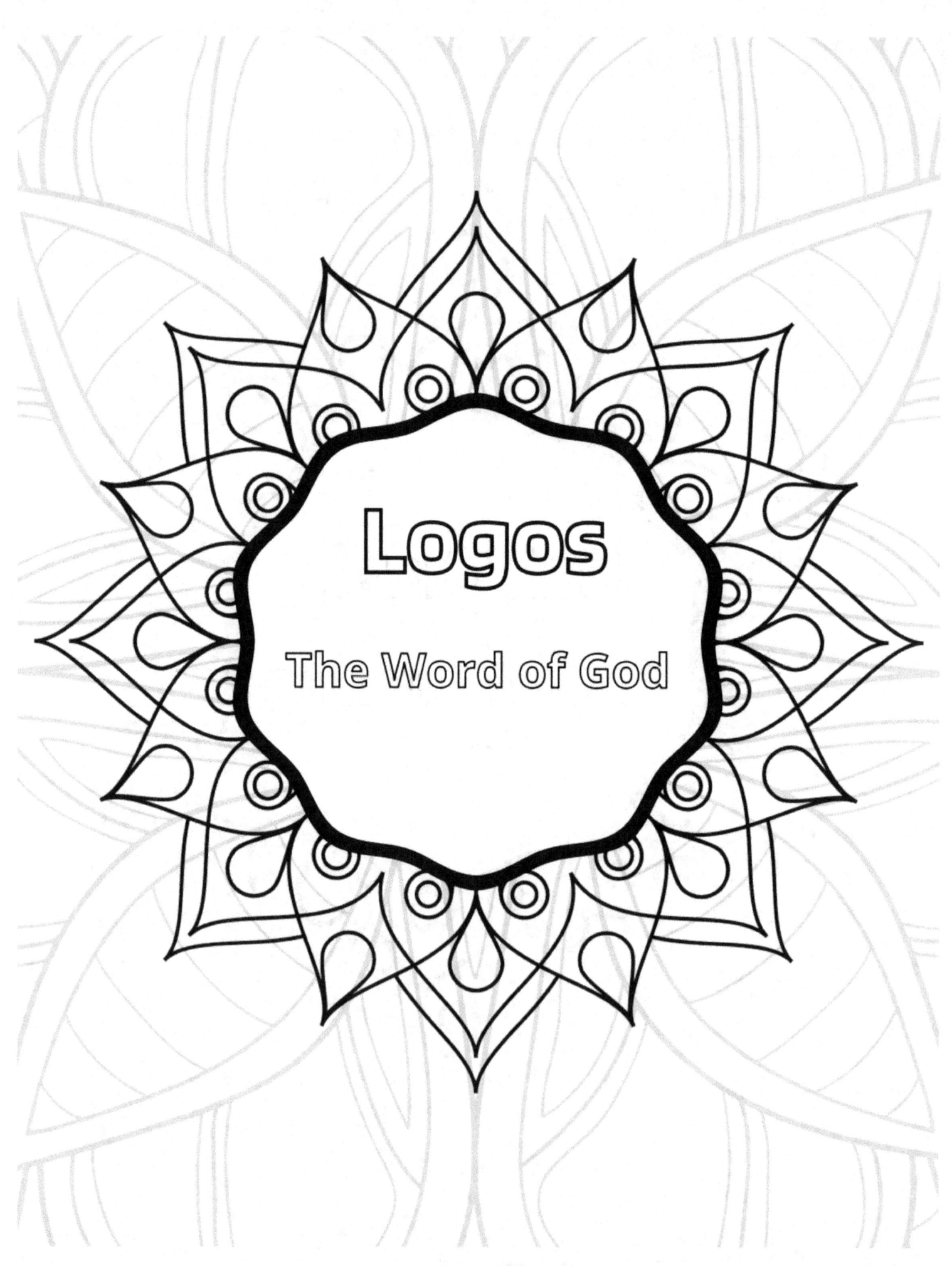

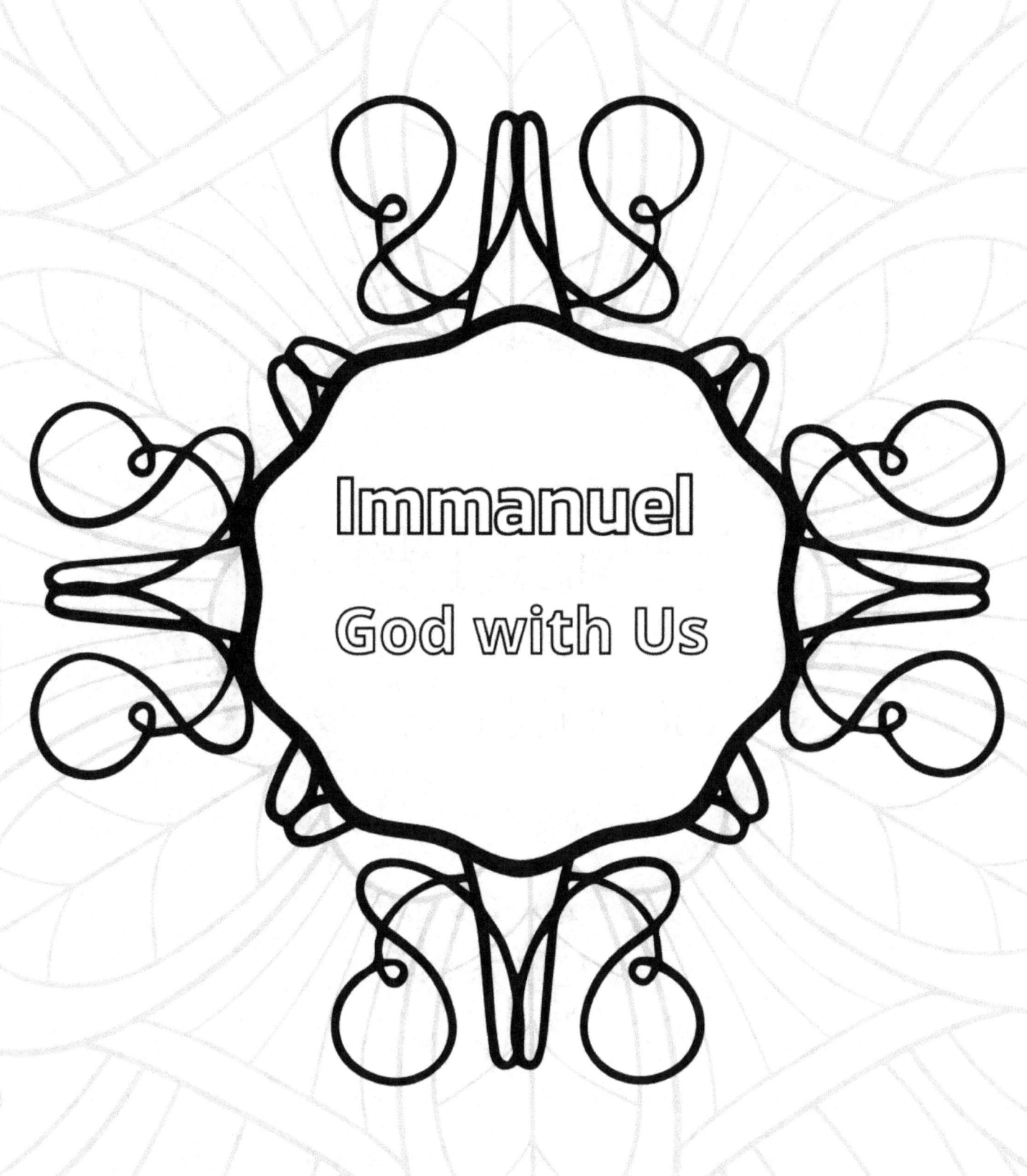

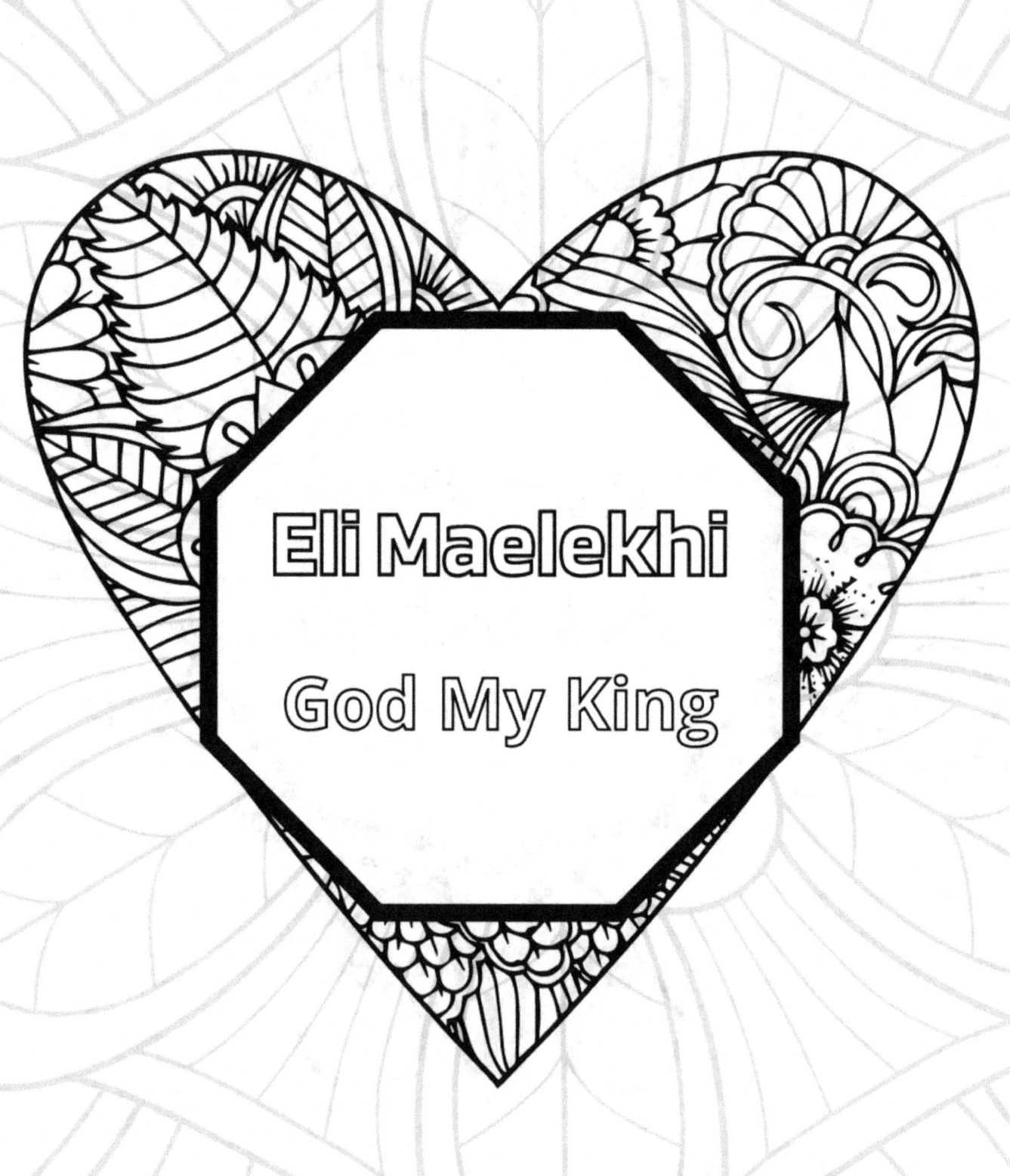

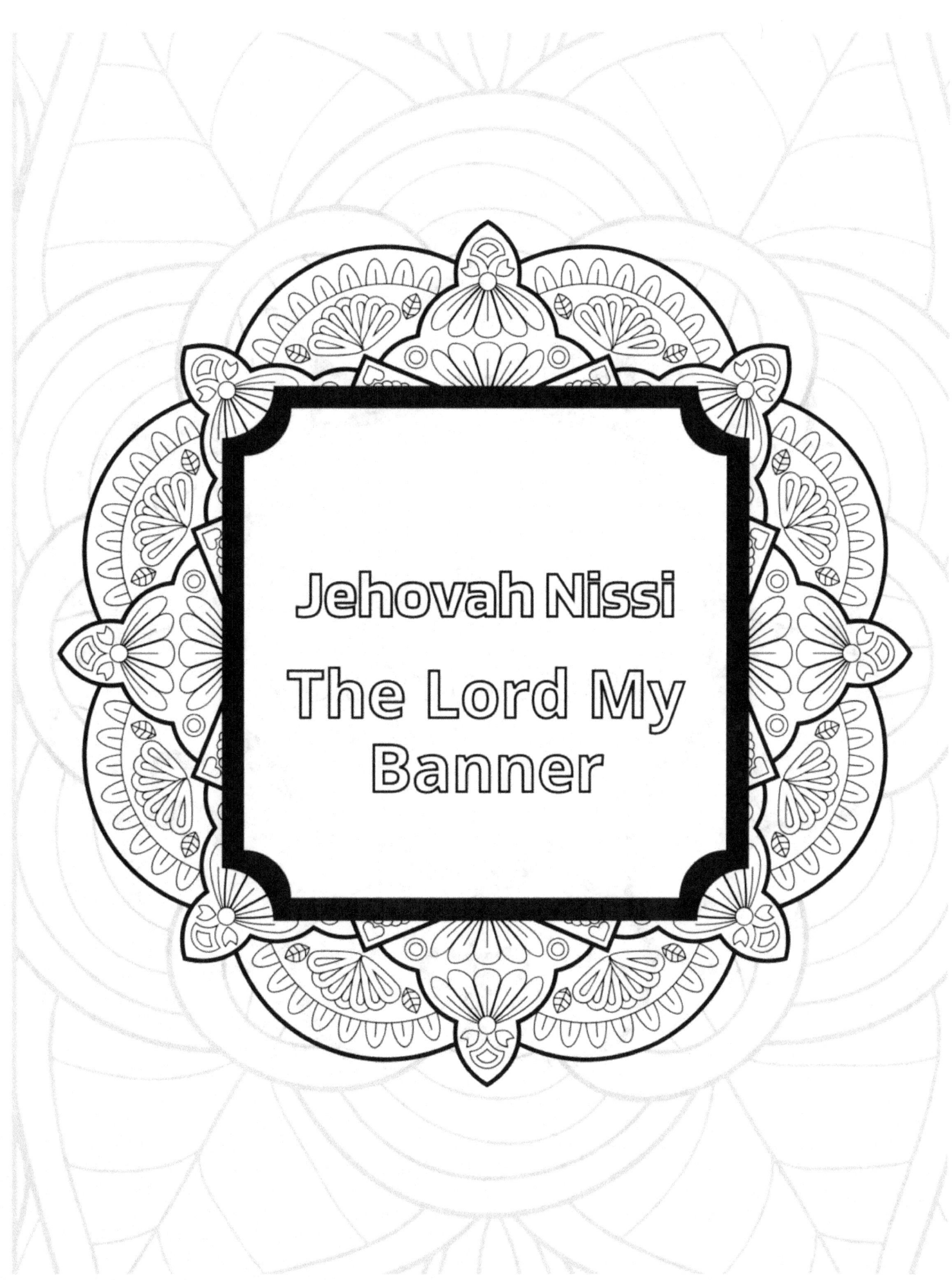

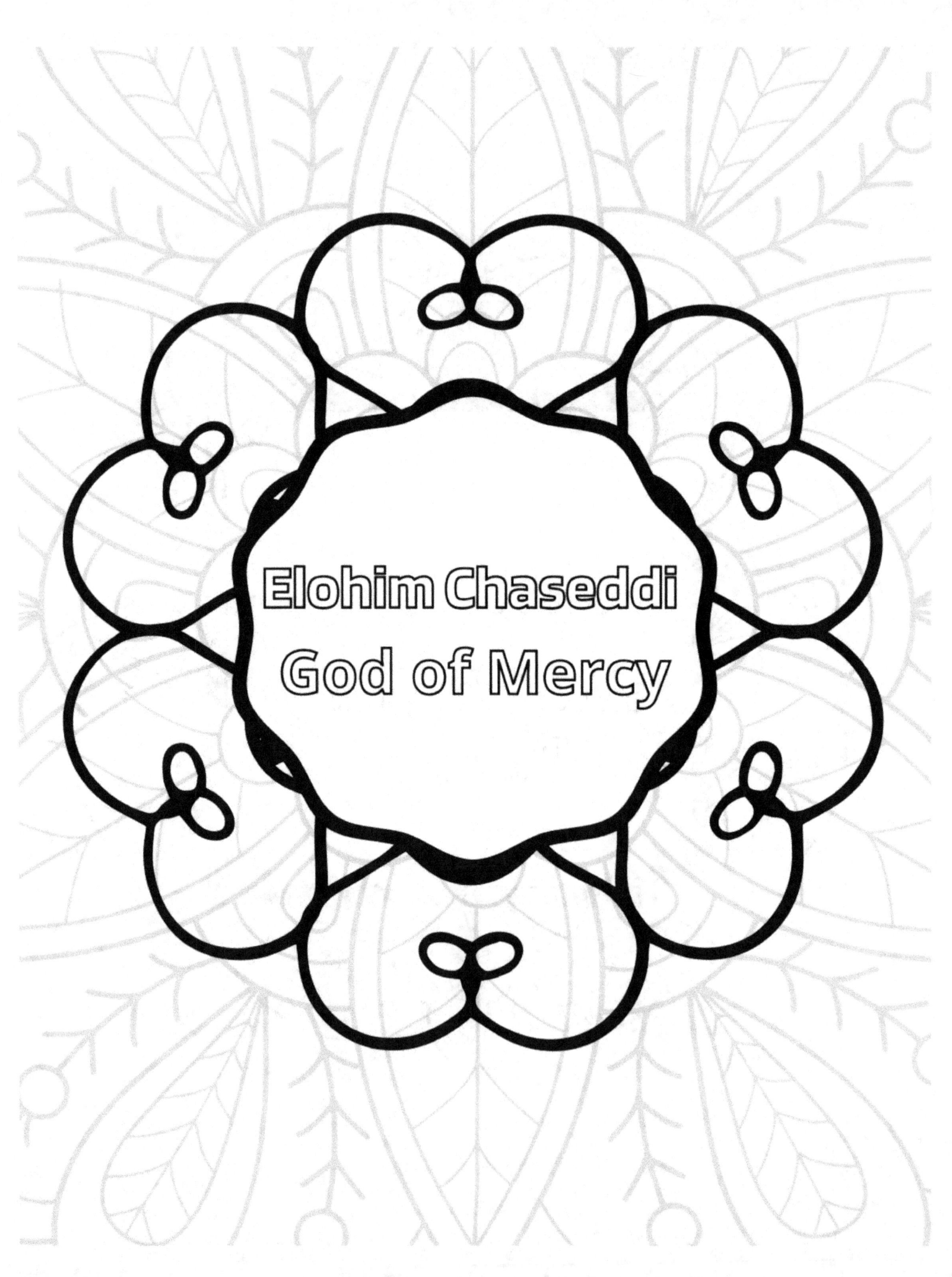

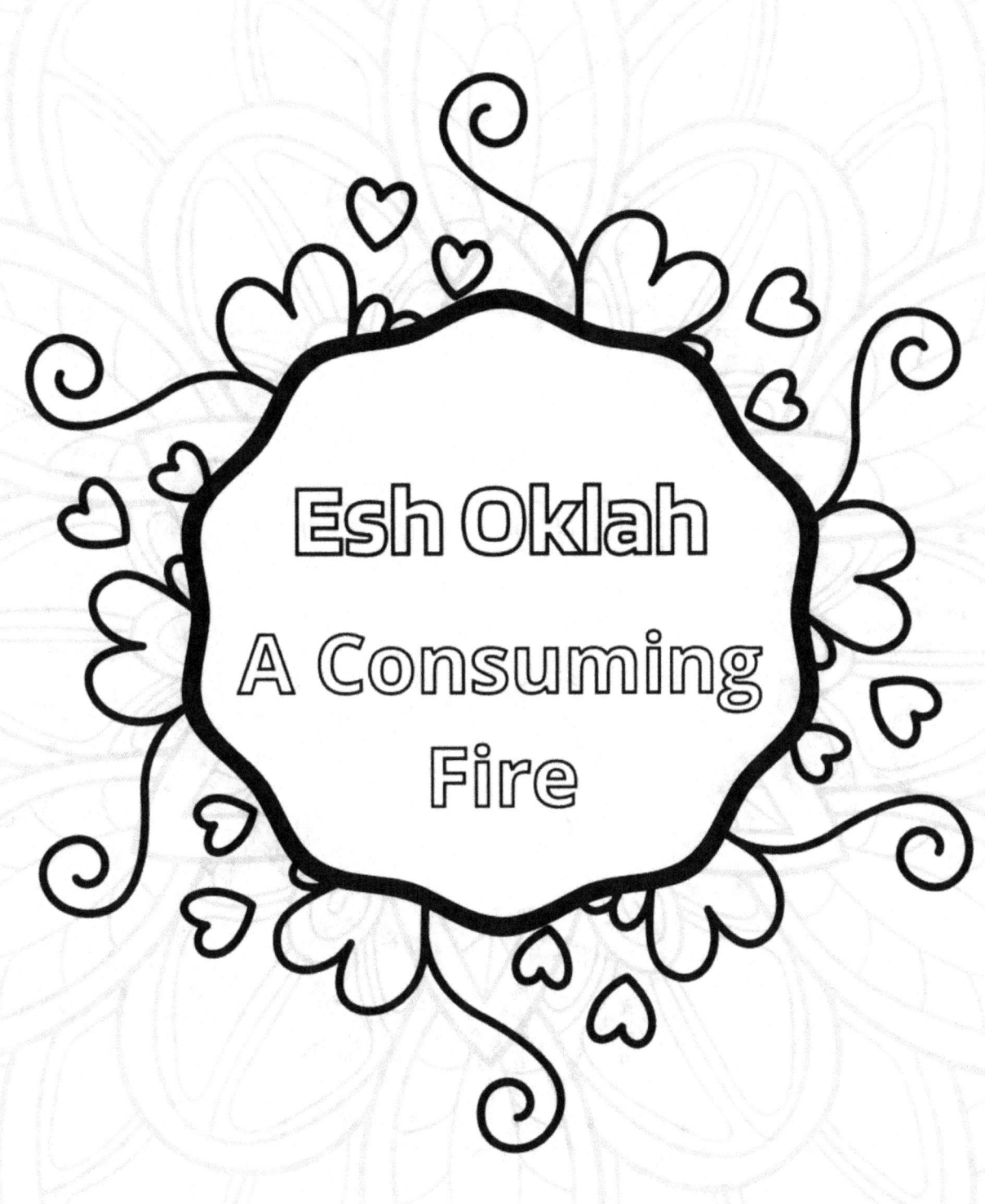

Immanuel

God with Us

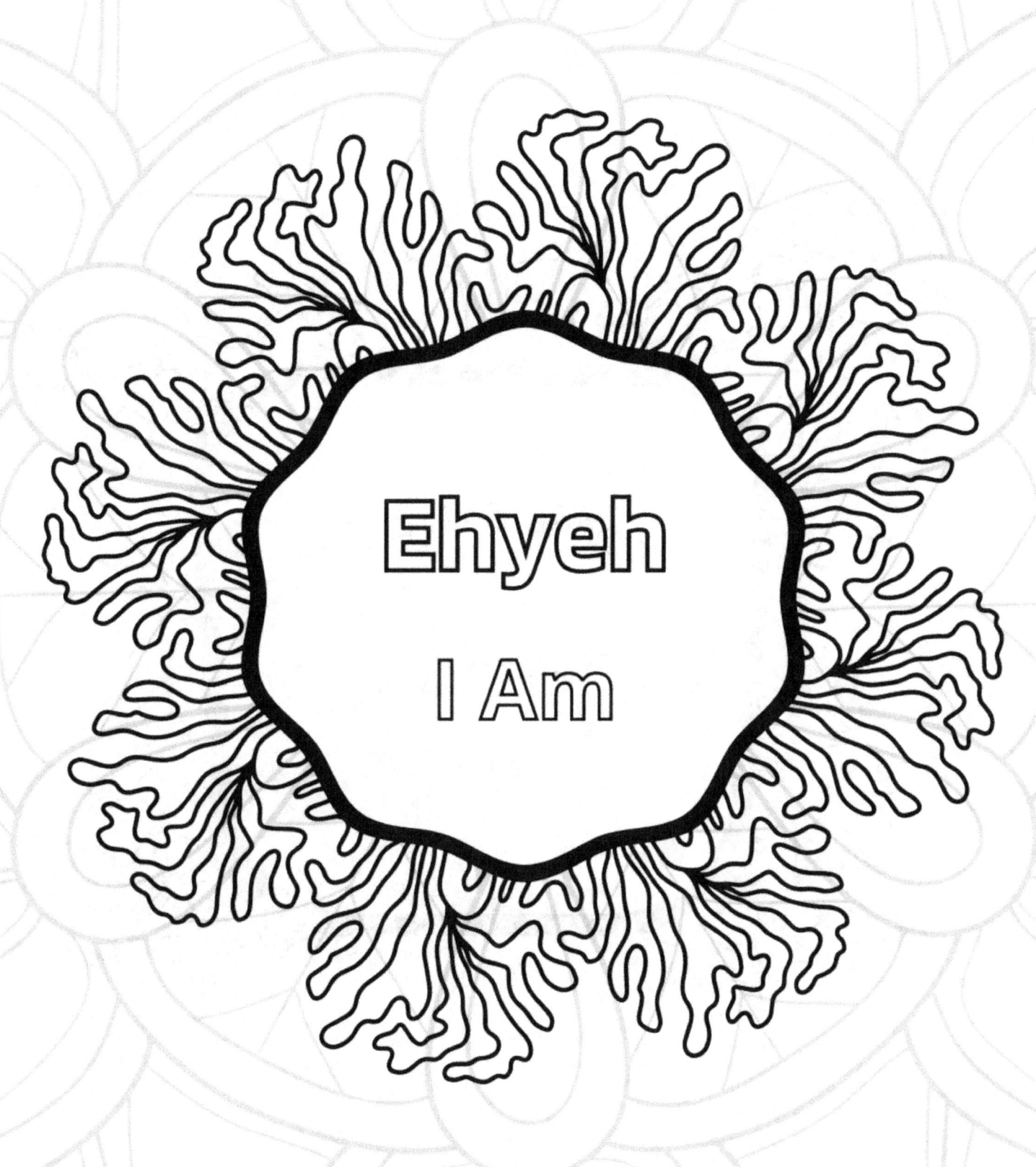

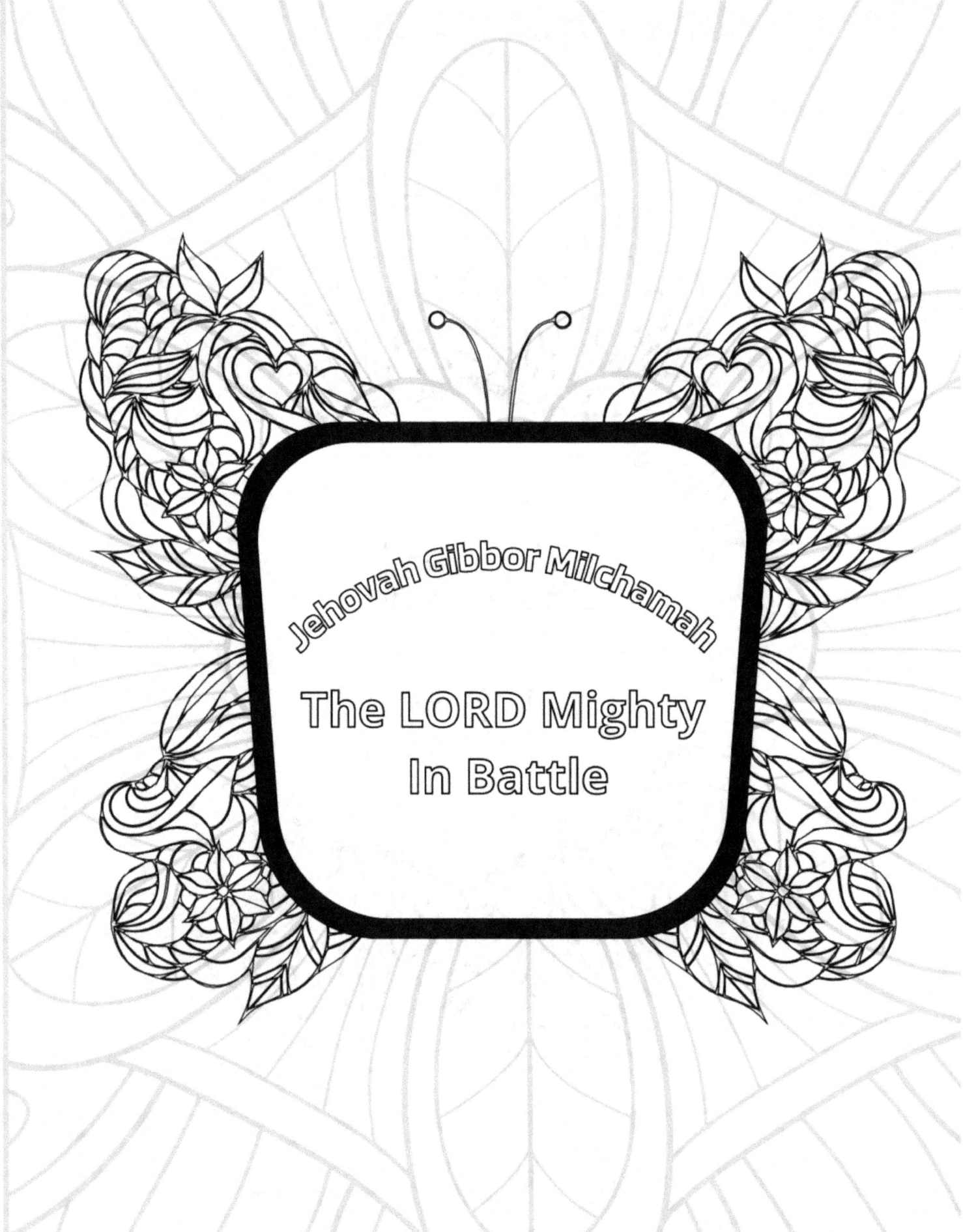

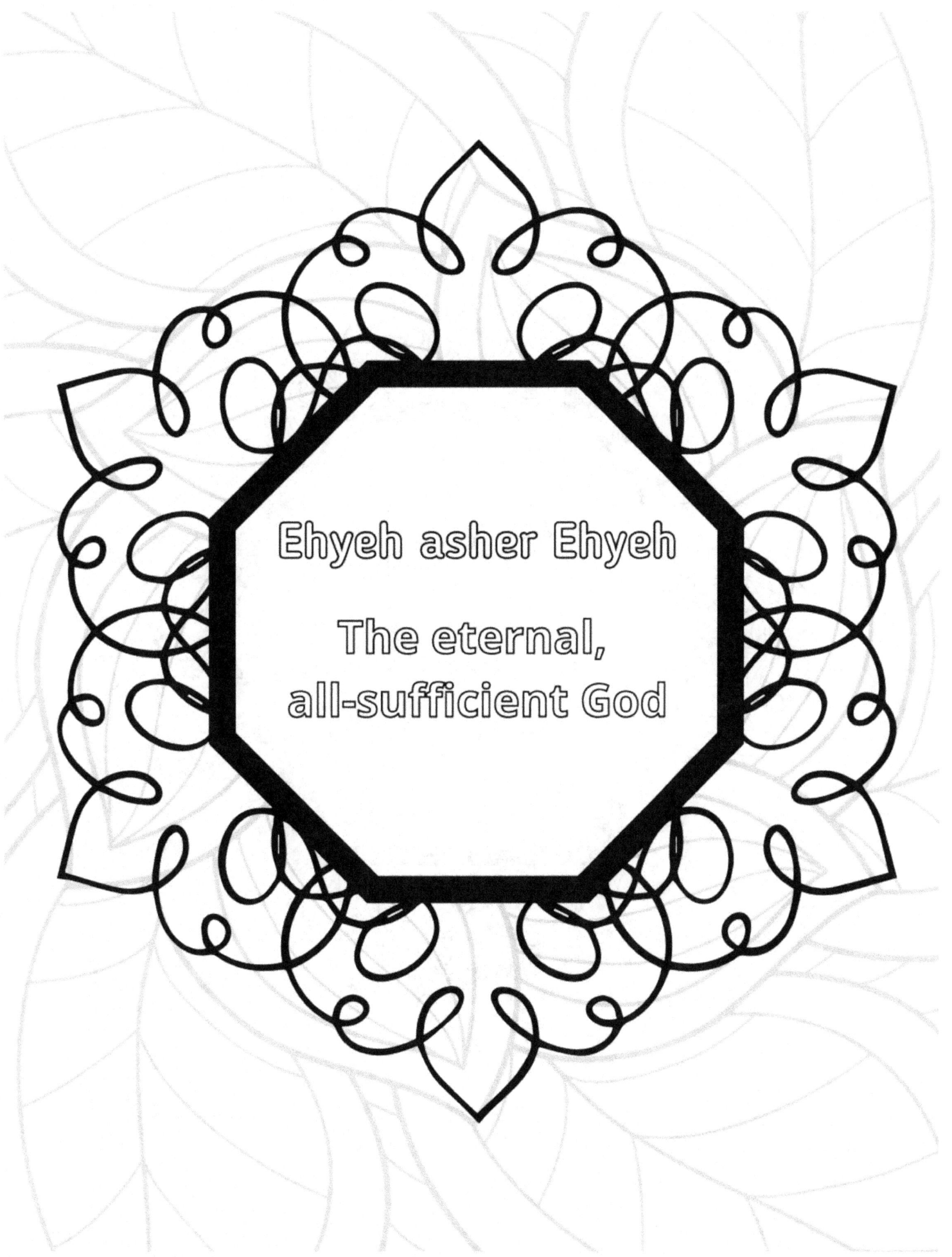

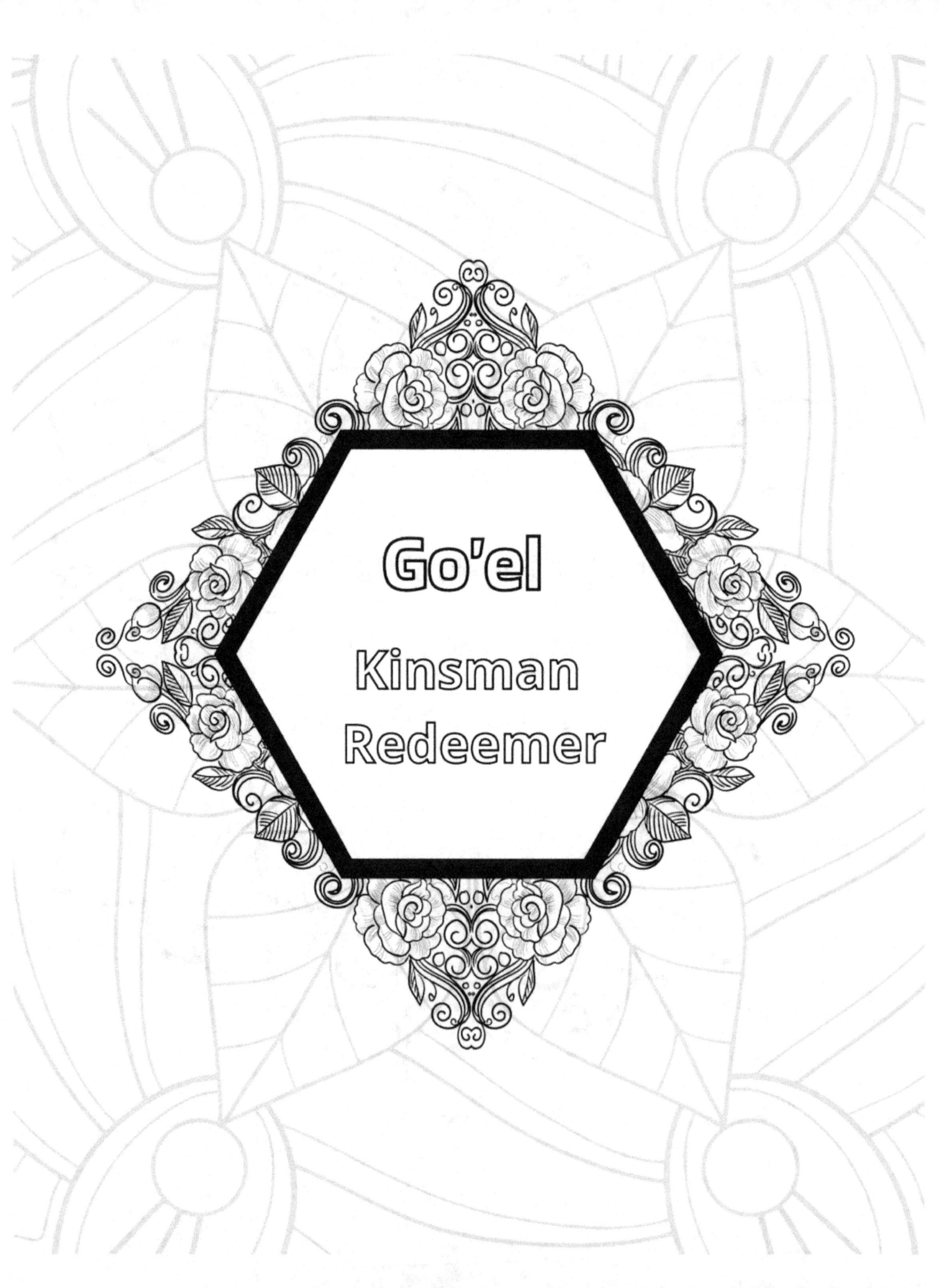

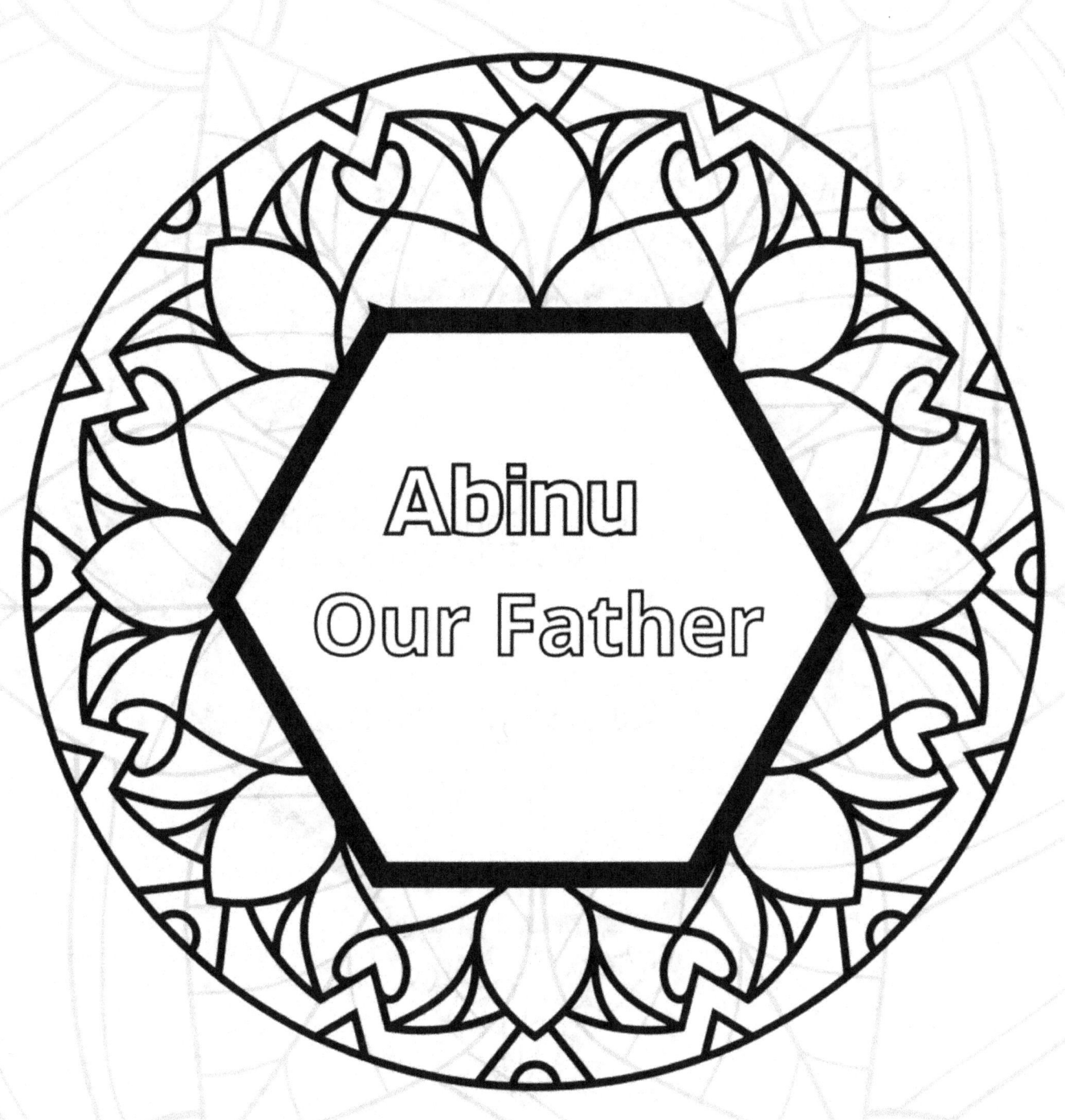

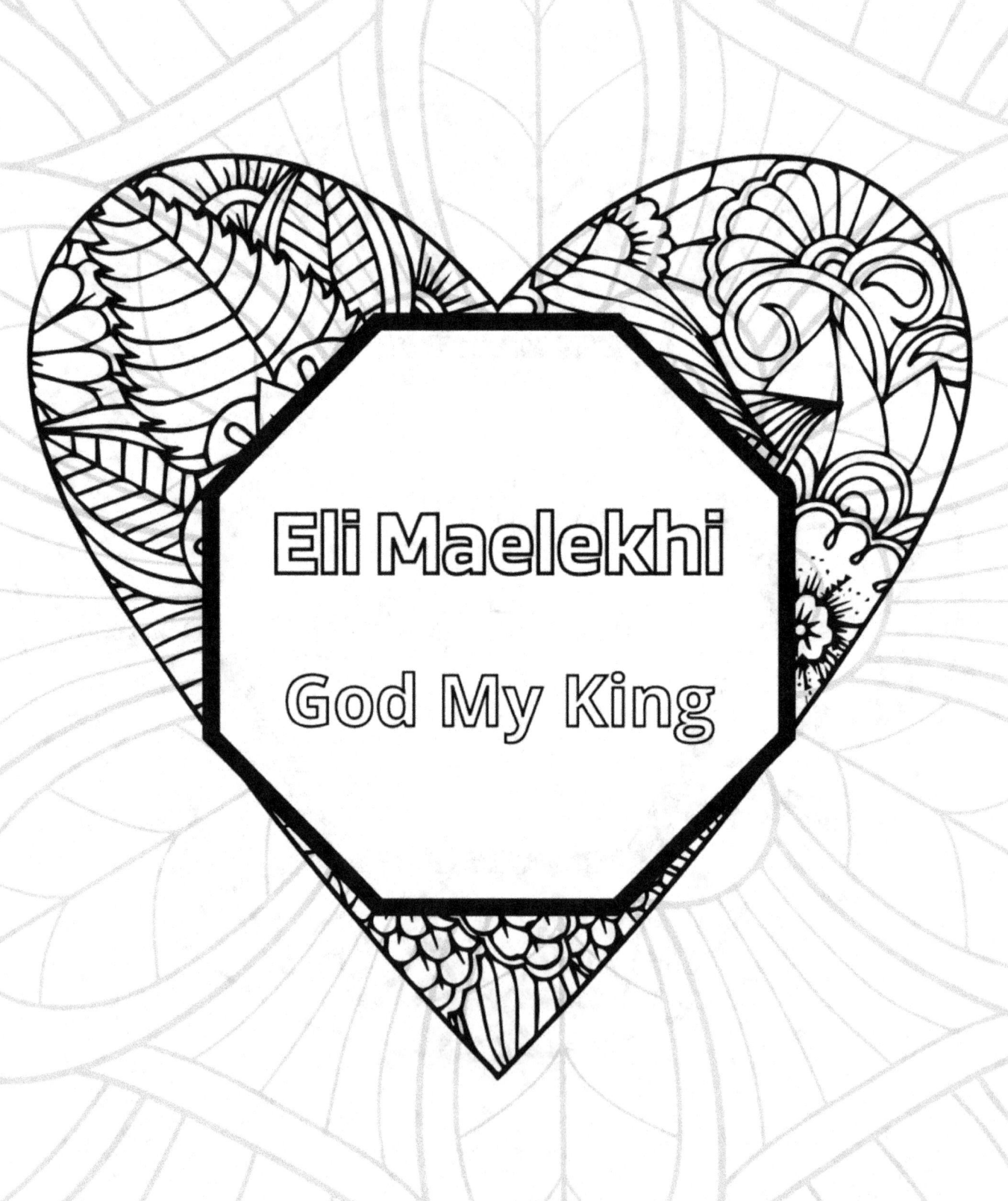

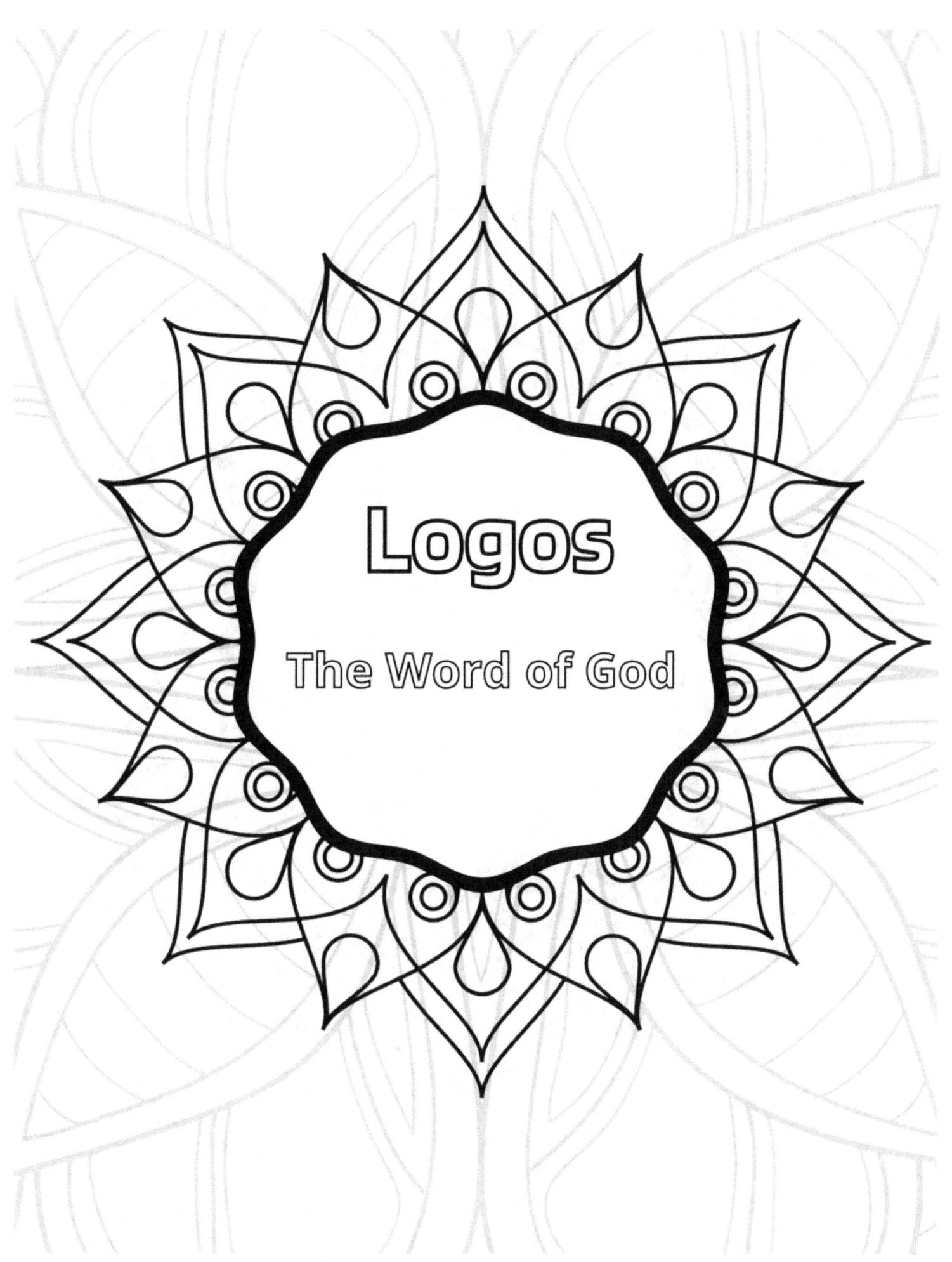

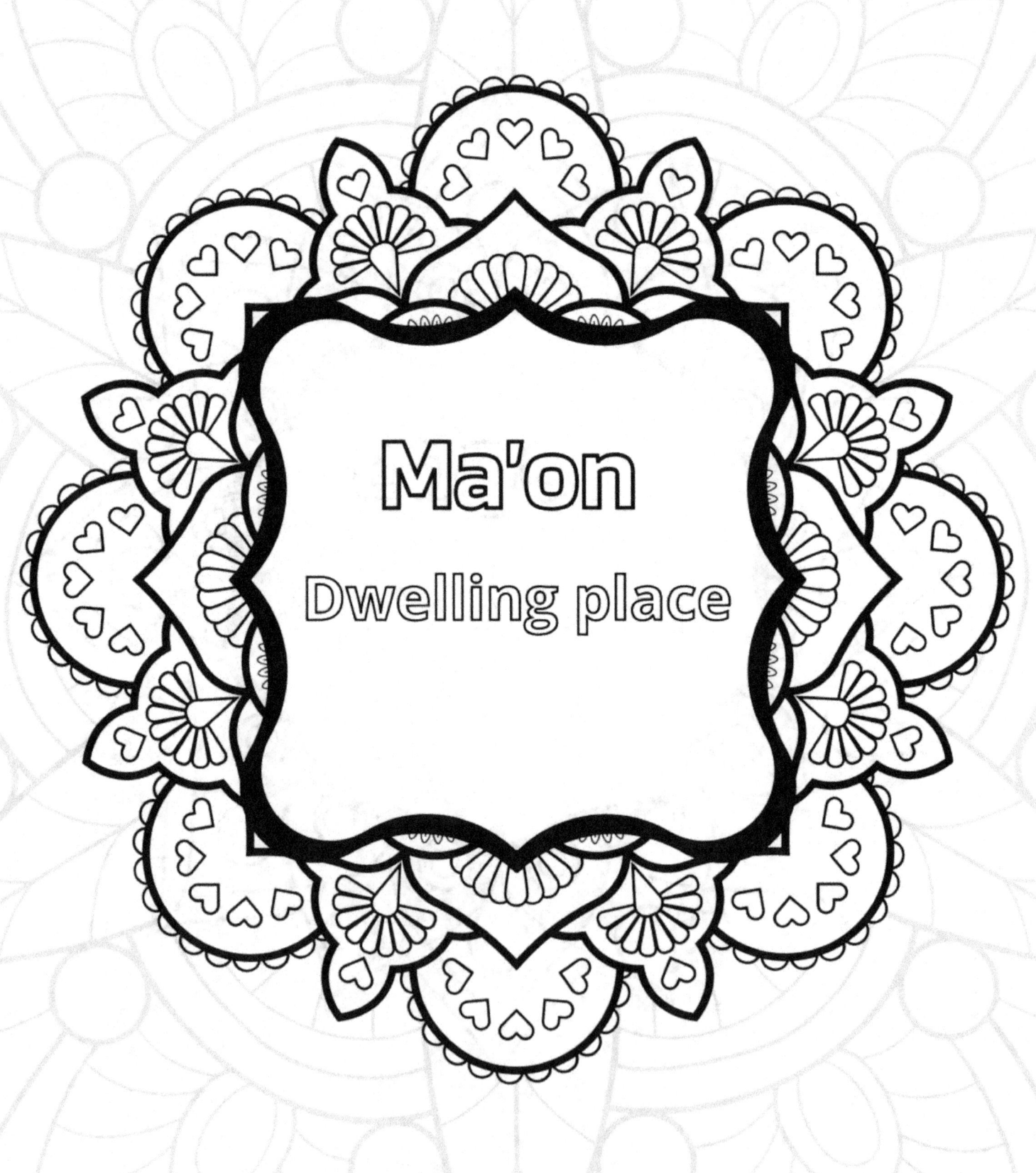

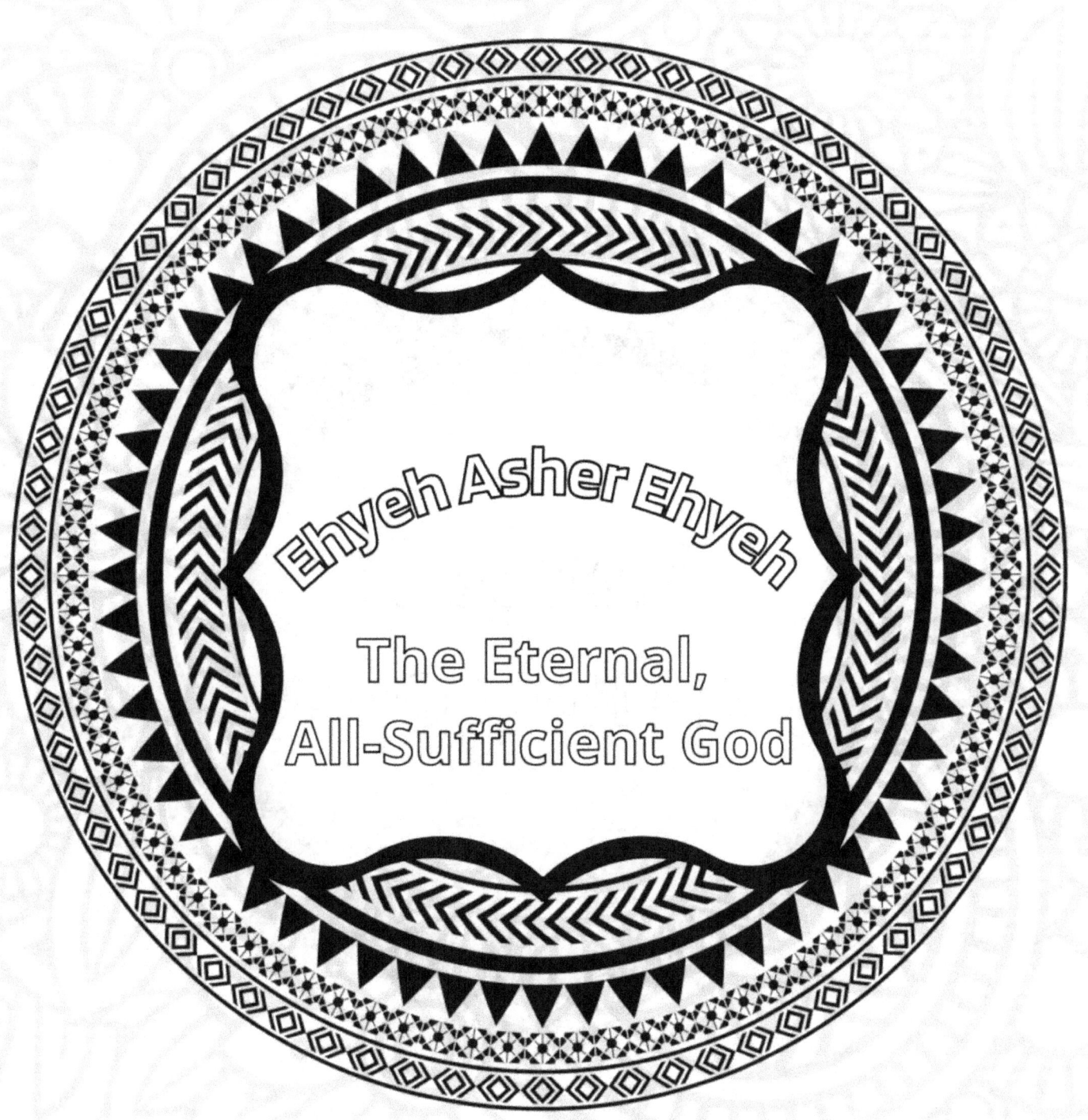

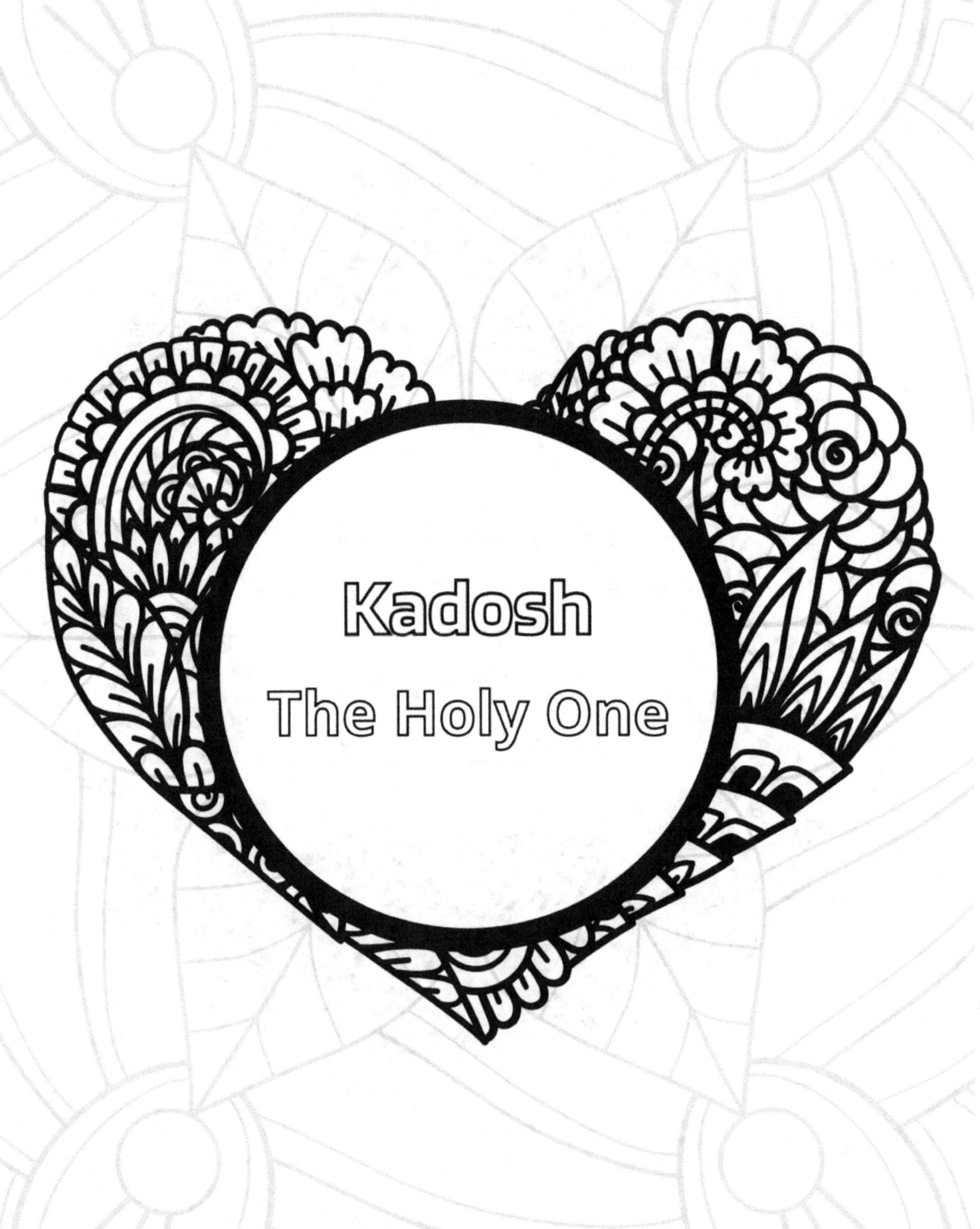

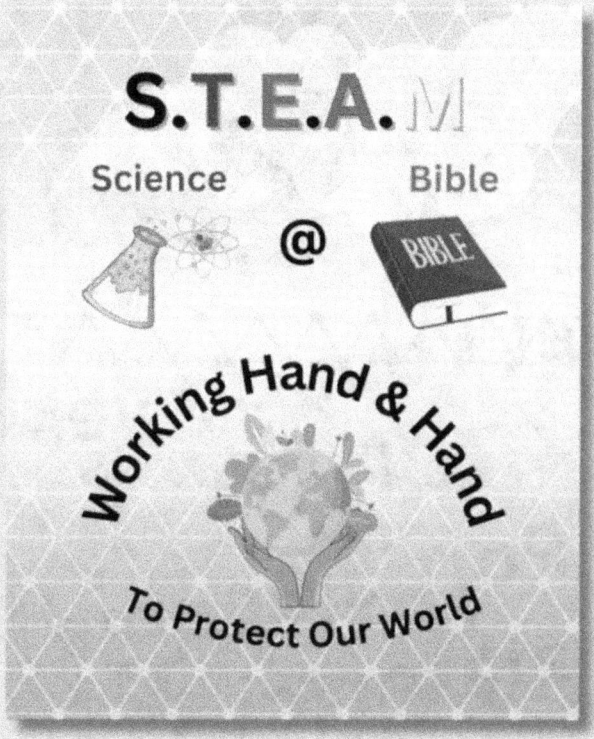
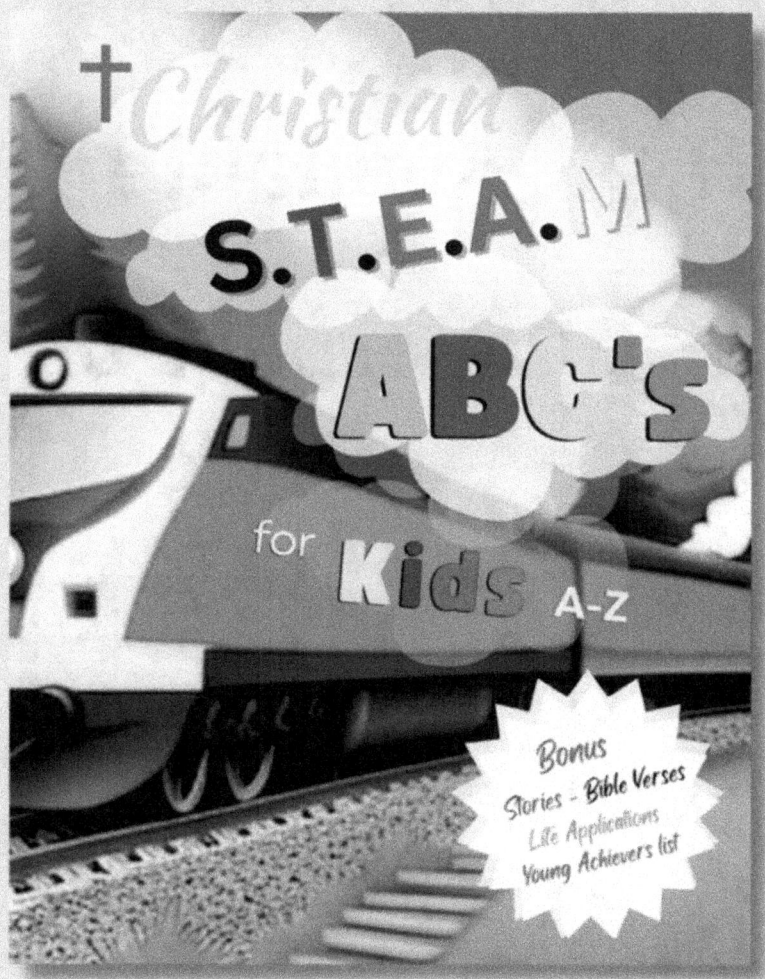
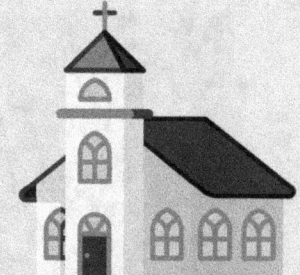

Get Your Copies TODAY!
by Portia George
Amazon.com

Church

Paperback or eBook

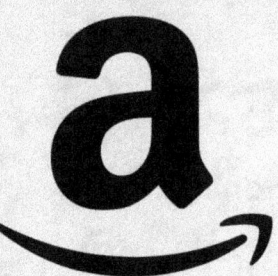

Get Your Copies TODAY!
by Portia George
Amazon.com

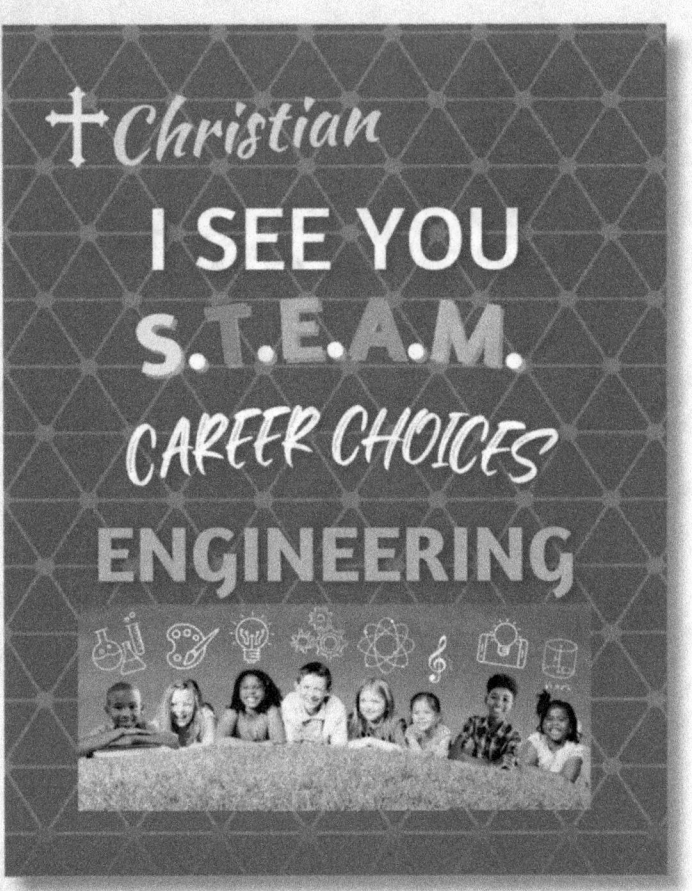

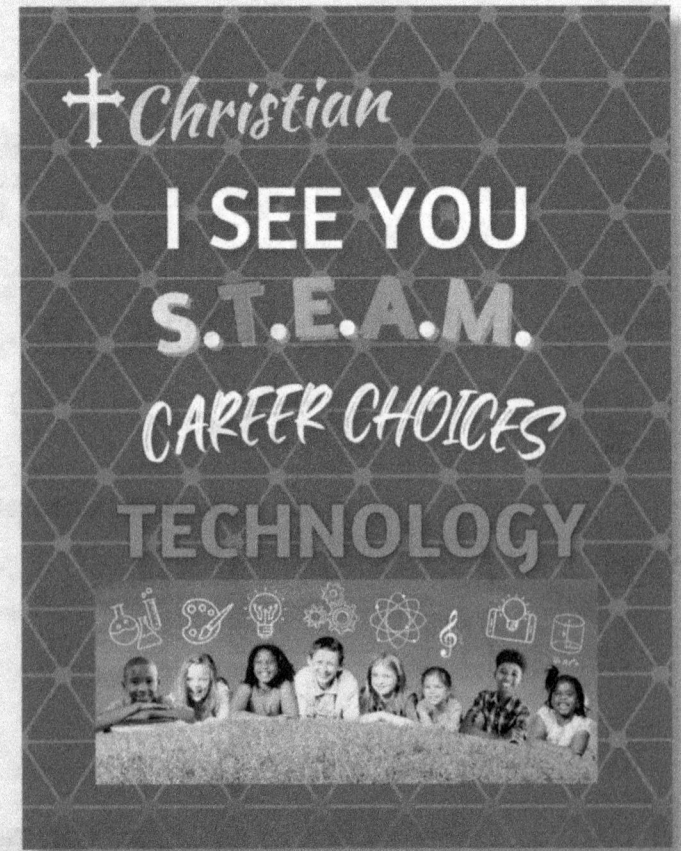

Available

Paperback or eBook

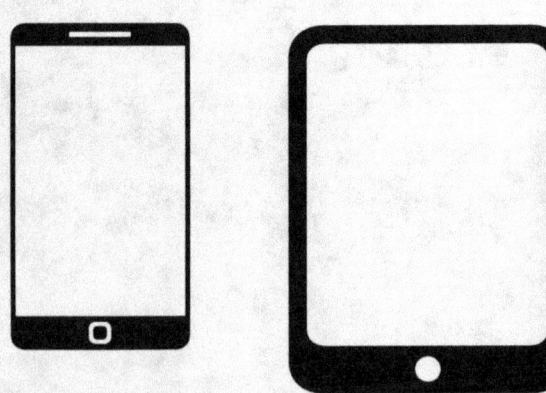

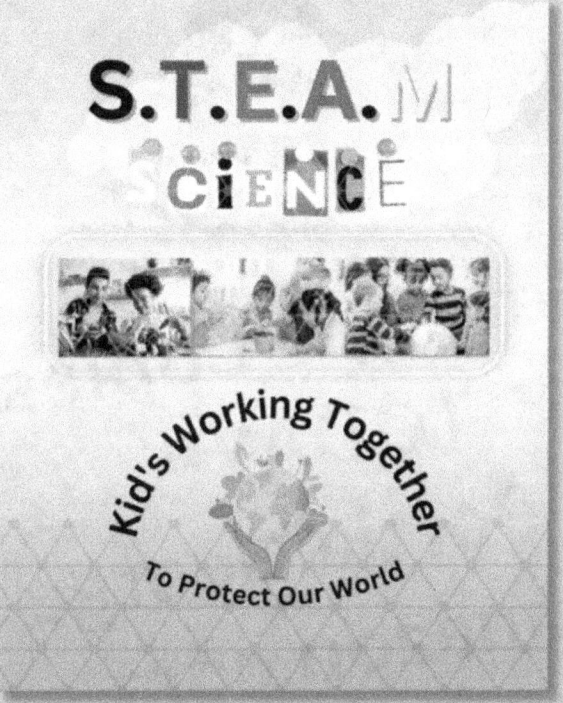

a
Get Your Copies TODAY!
by Portia George
Amazon.com

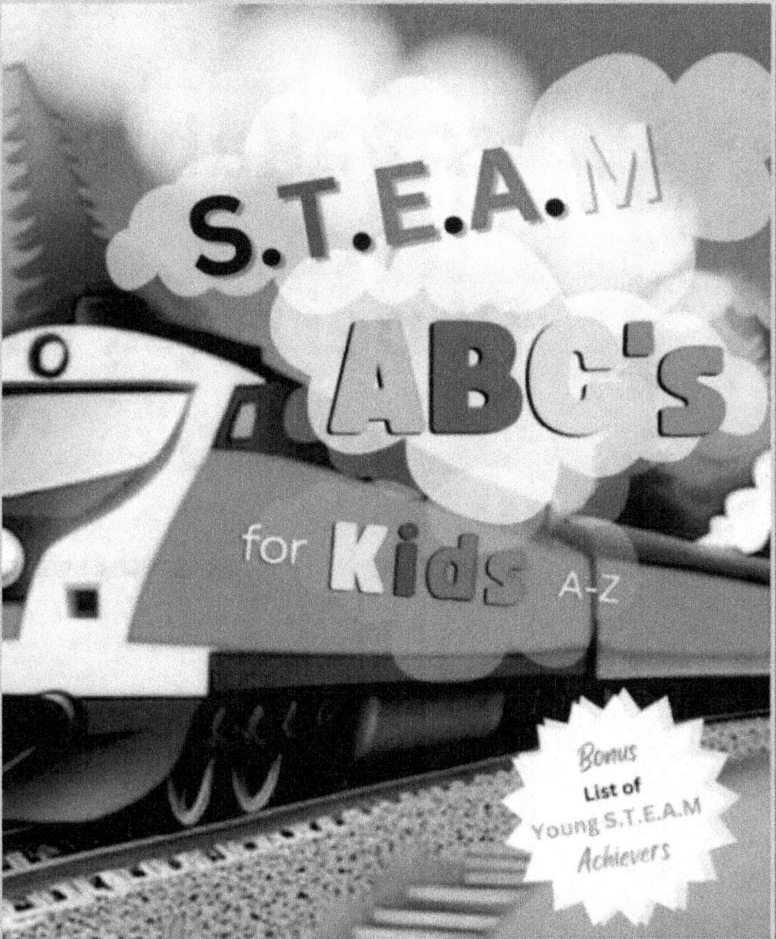

School

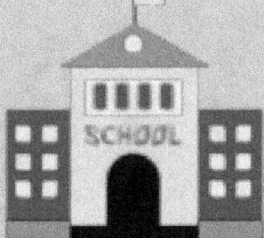

Paperback or eBook

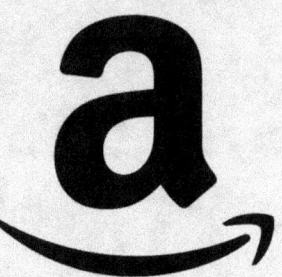

Get Your Copies TODAY!
by Portia George
Amazon.com

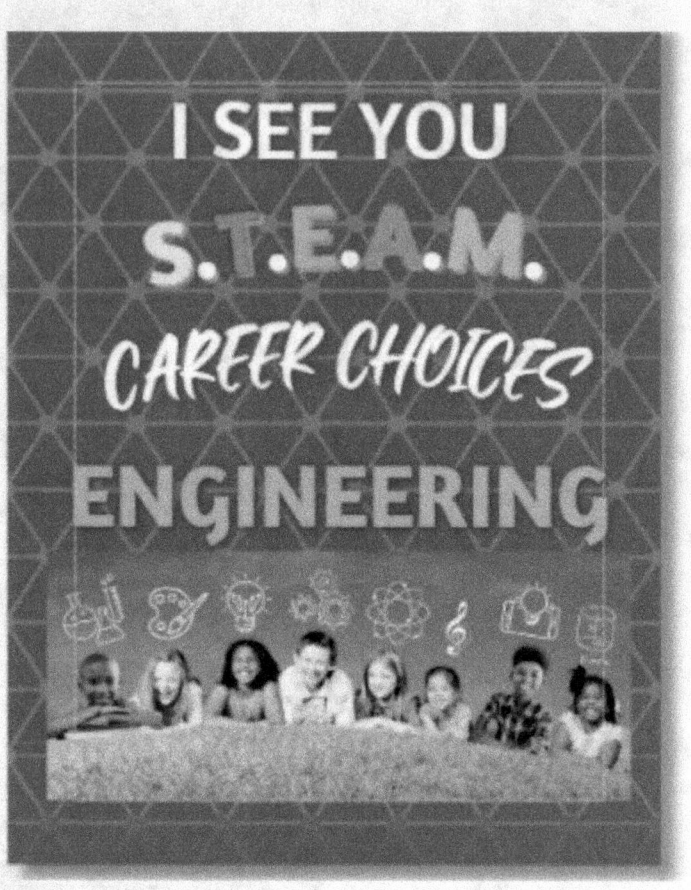

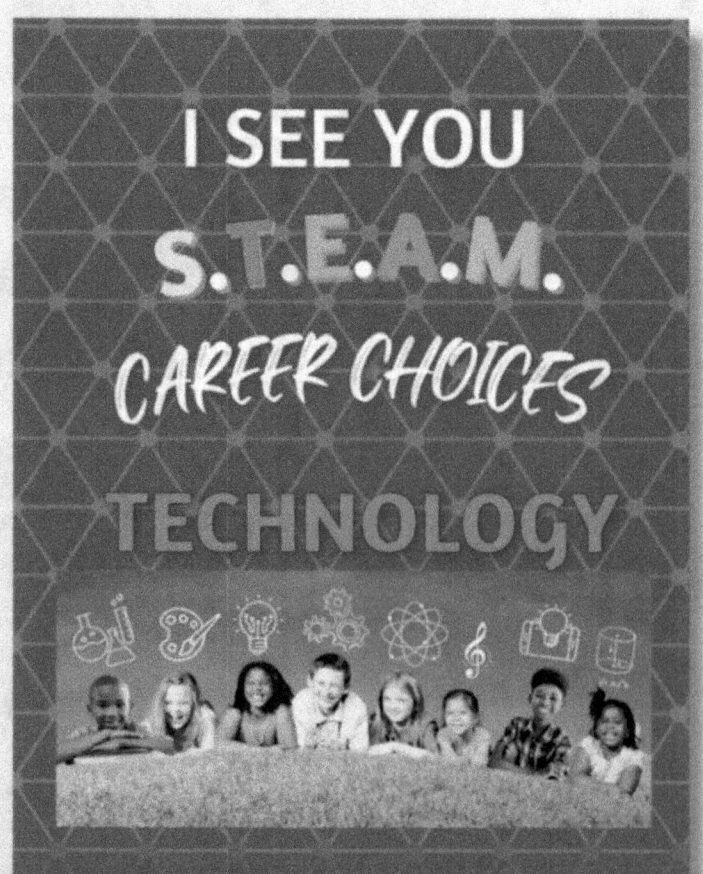

Available

Paperback or eBook

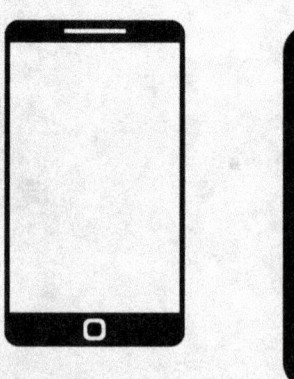